FAITH

THE
FAITHLESS

JODY HOUSER | JOE EISMA | KATE NIEMCZYK | MARGUERITE SAUVAGE

CONTENTS

Collection Cover Art: Elsa Charretier
with Tamra Bonvillain

Assistant Editor: Lauren Hitzhusen
Editor: Danny Khazem
Editor-in-Chief: Warren Simons

VALIANT®

Faith®: The Faithless. Published by Valiant Entertainment LLC. Office of Publication: 350 Seventh Avenue, New York, NY 10001. Printed in the U.S.A. First Printing. ISBN: 9781682152195.

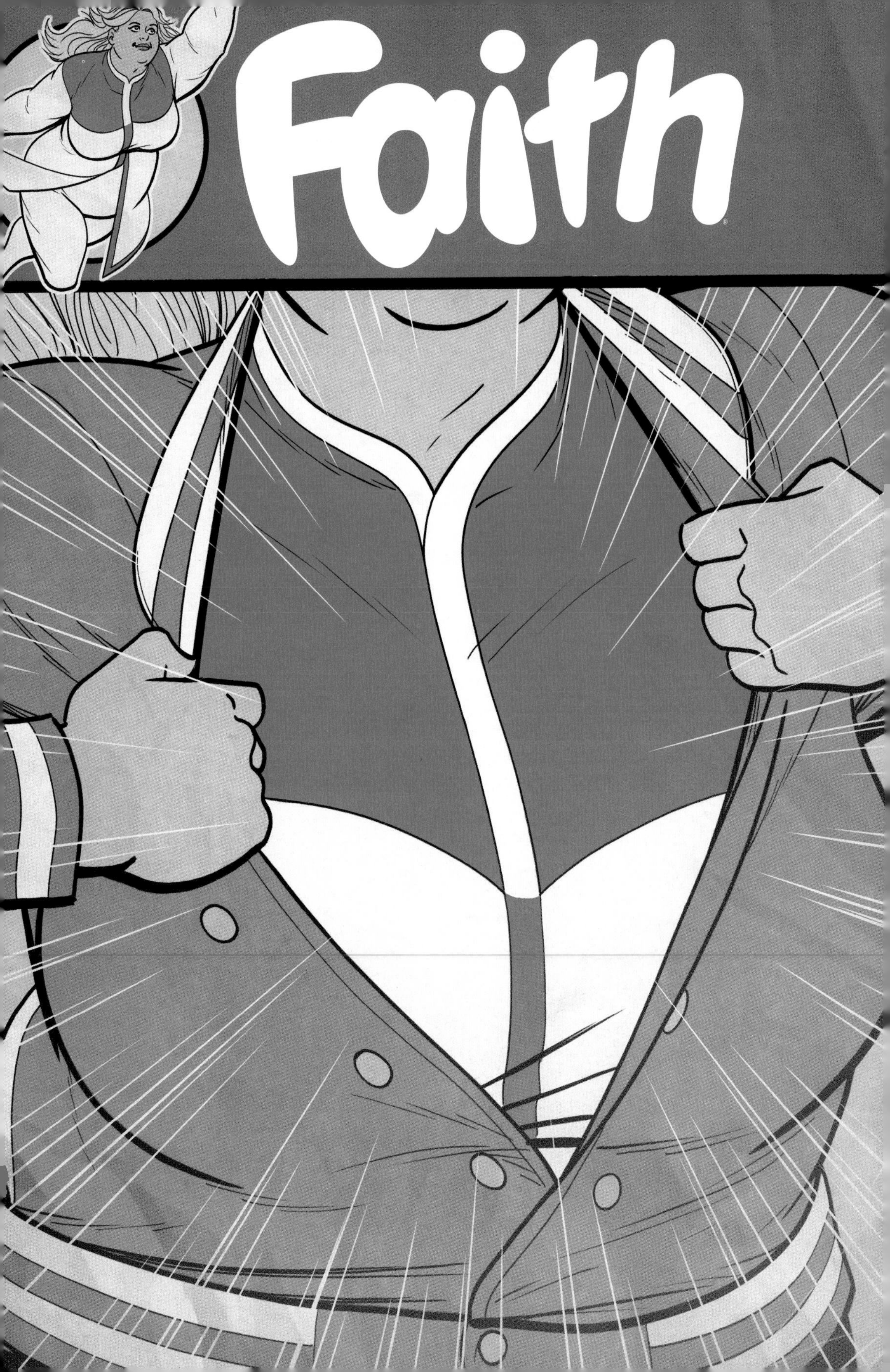
Faith

When a car accident left her orphaned, Faith Herbert was raised by her loving grandmother and found comfort in comic books, science fiction movies, and other fantastic tales of superheroes. In her teens she would discover her fantasies were reality when it was revealed she was a psiot -- a human being born with the potential for incredible abilities. When the powers were activated, she discovered she had the ability to fly and a companion field that allowed her to carry objects with her mind. Faith then joined a group of fellow psiots called the Renegades. She's since left her Renegade family behind to take on the world's challenges on her own. She may have a lot to learn about the superhero game, but if there's one thing she's always had, it's...

Faith.

■ The story so far...

Faith Herbert--in her down time from saving lives as the high-flying Zephyr--works a day job at an online magazine called ZipLine under the disguise of mild-mannered Summer Smith!

All of her closest coworkers--Jay and Paige--are aware of her double life, even including her boss Mimi!

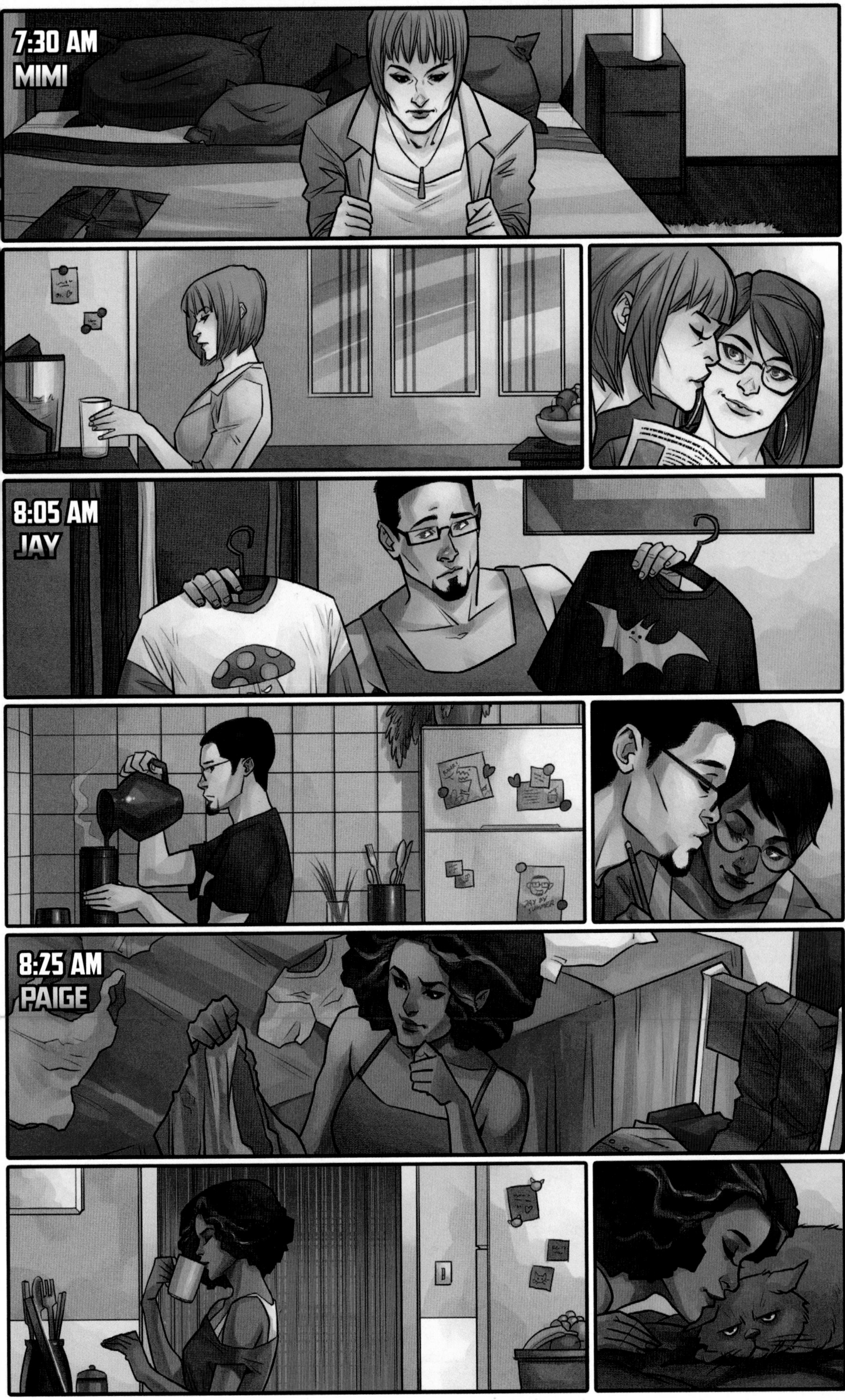
7:30 AM
MIMI
8:05 AM
JAY
8:25 AM
PAIGE

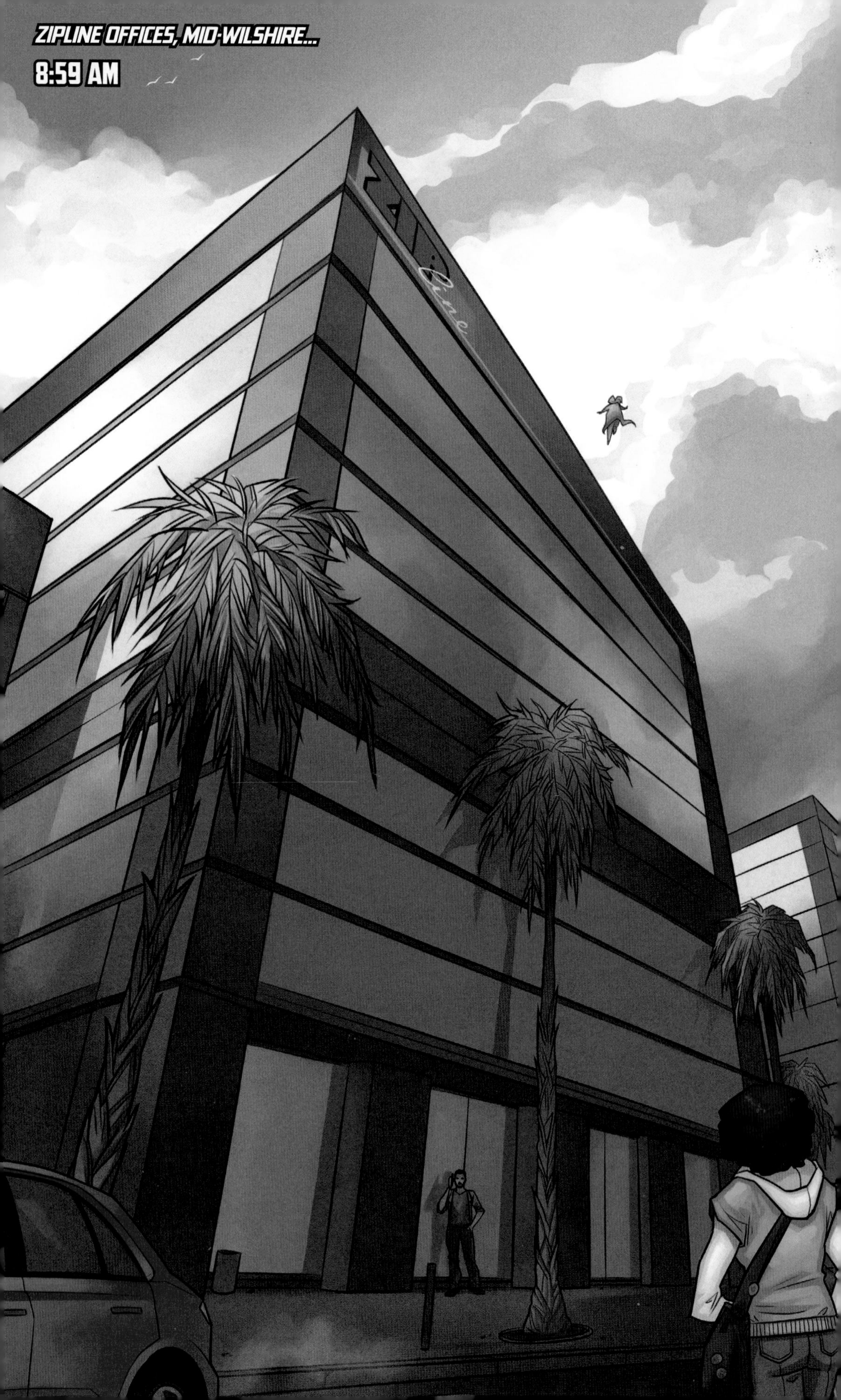
ZIPLINE OFFICES, MID-WILSHIRE...
8:59 AM

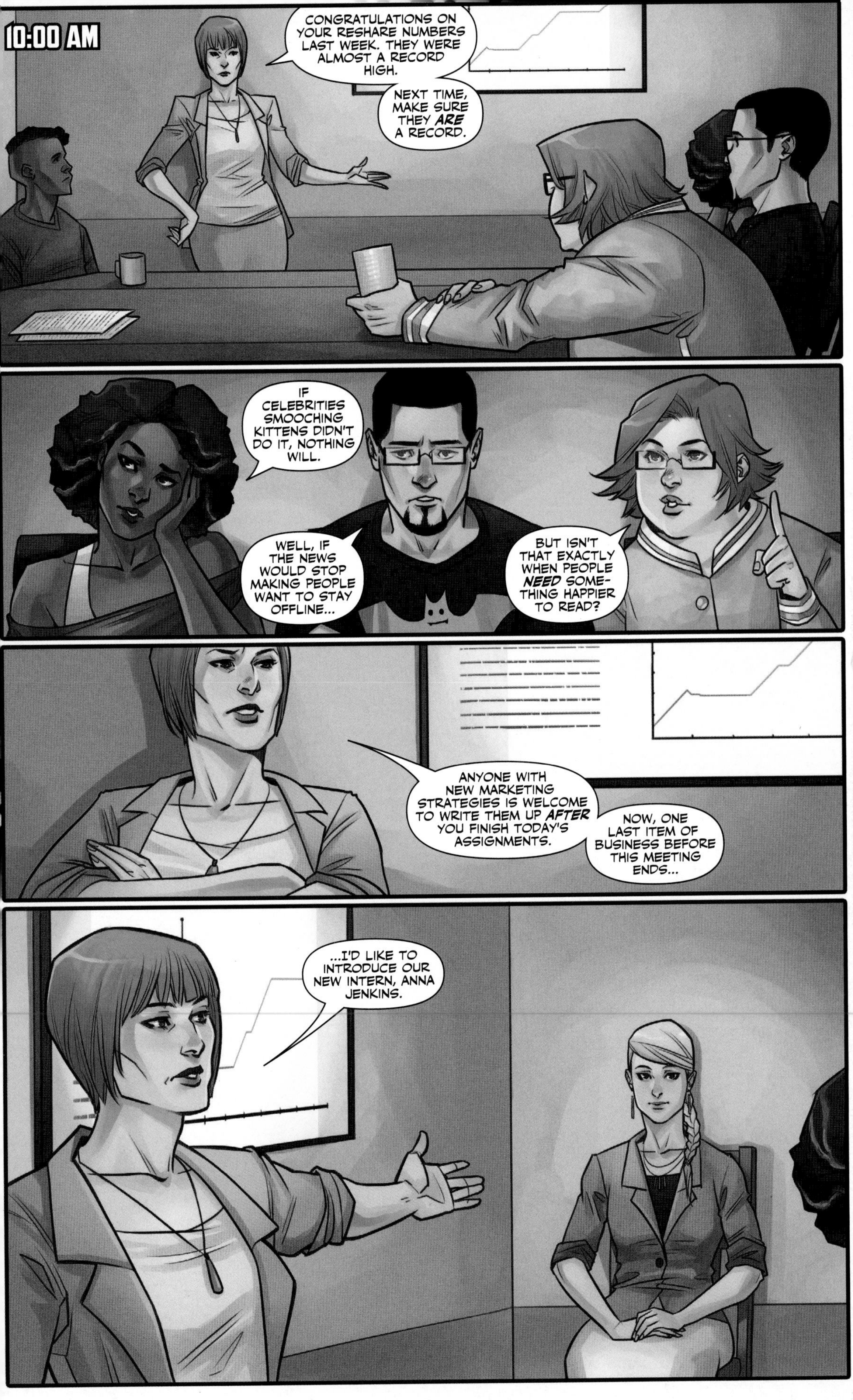
10:00 AM
CONGRATULATIONS ON YOUR RESHARE NUMBERS LAST WEEK. THEY WERE ALMOST A RECORD HIGH.
NEXT TIME, MAKE SURE THEY *ARE* A RECORD.
IF CELEBRITIES SMOOCHING KITTENS DIDN'T DO IT, NOTHING WILL.
WELL, IF THE NEWS WOULD STOP MAKING PEOPLE WANT TO STAY OFFLINE...
BUT ISN'T THAT EXACTLY WHEN PEOPLE *NEED* SOME-THING HAPPIER TO READ?
ANYONE WITH NEW MARKETING STRATEGIES IS WELCOME TO WRITE THEM UP *AFTER* YOU FINISH TODAY'S ASSIGNMENTS.
NOW, ONE LAST ITEM OF BUSINESS BEFORE THIS MEETING ENDS...
...I'D LIKE TO INTRODUCE OUR NEW INTERN, ANNA JENKINS.

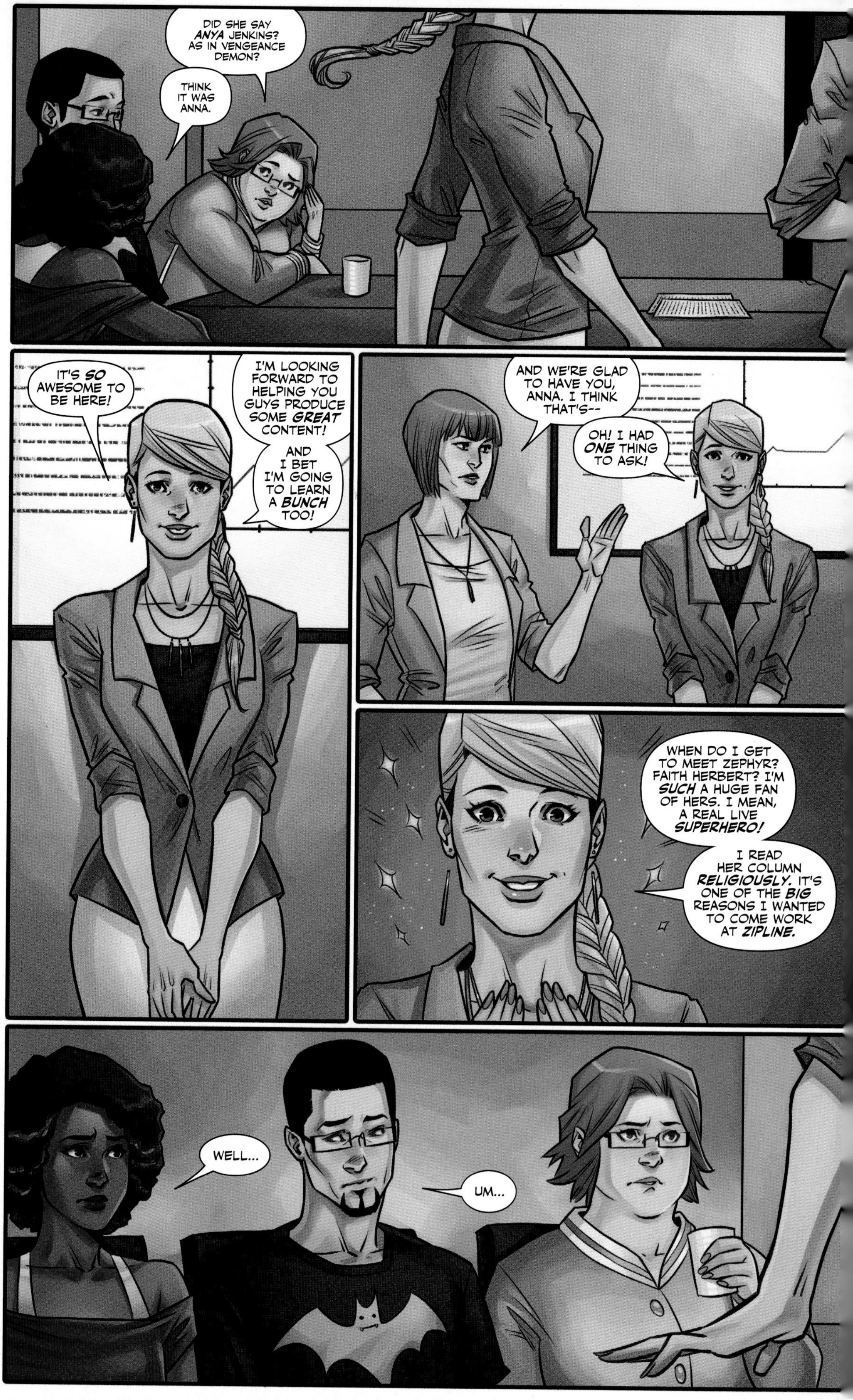
DID SHE SAY ANYA JENKINS? AS IN VENGEANCE DEMON?
THINK IT WAS ANNA.
IT'S SO AWESOME TO BE HERE!
I'M LOOKING FORWARD TO HELPING YOU GUYS PRODUCE SOME GREAT CONTENT!
AND I BET I'M GOING TO LEARN A BUNCH TOO!
AND WE'RE GLAD TO HAVE YOU, ANNA. I THINK THAT'S--
OH! I HAD ONE THING TO ASK!
WHEN DO I GET TO MEET ZEPHYR? FAITH HERBERT? I'M SUCH A HUGE FAN OF HERS. I MEAN, A REAL LIVE SUPERHERO!
I READ HER COLUMN RELIGIOUSLY. IT'S ONE OF THE BIG REASONS I WANTED TO COME WORK AT ZIPLINE.
WELL...
UM...

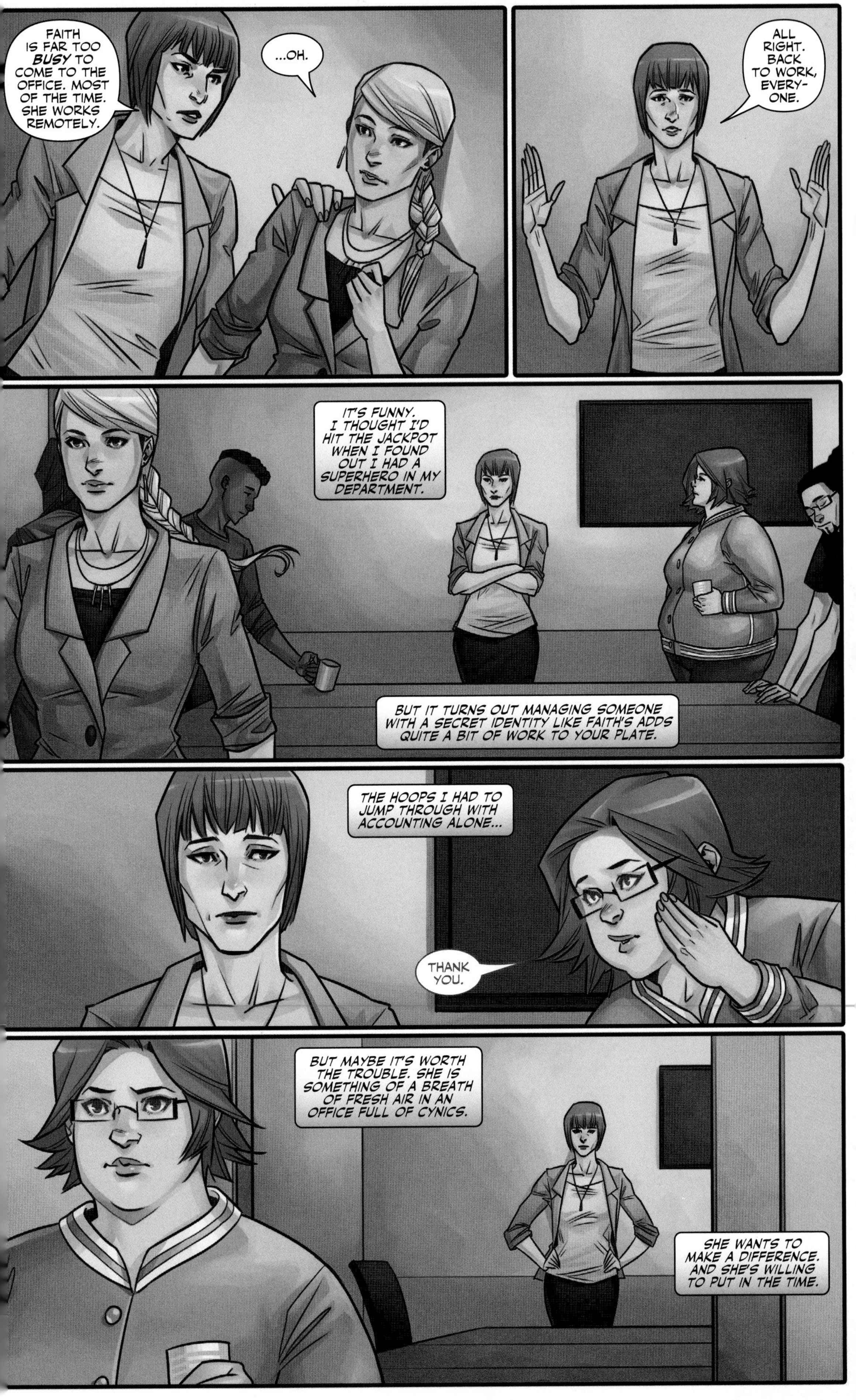

FAITH IS FAR TOO BUSY TO COME TO THE OFFICE. MOST OF THE TIME. SHE WORKS REMOTELY.
...OH.
ALL RIGHT. BACK TO WORK, EVERY-ONE.
IT'S FUNNY. I THOUGHT I'D HIT THE JACKPOT WHEN I FOUND OUT I HAD A SUPERHERO IN MY DEPARTMENT.
BUT IT TURNS OUT MANAGING SOMEONE WITH A SECRET IDENTITY LIKE FAITH'S ADDS QUITE A BIT OF WORK TO YOUR PLATE.
THE HOOPS I HAD TO JUMP THROUGH WITH ACCOUNTING ALONE...
THANK YOU.
BUT MAYBE IT'S WORTH THE TROUBLE. SHE IS SOMETHING OF A BREATH OF FRESH AIR IN AN OFFICE FULL OF CYNICS.
SHE WANTS TO MAKE A DIFFERENCE. AND SHE'S WILLING TO PUT IN THE TIME.

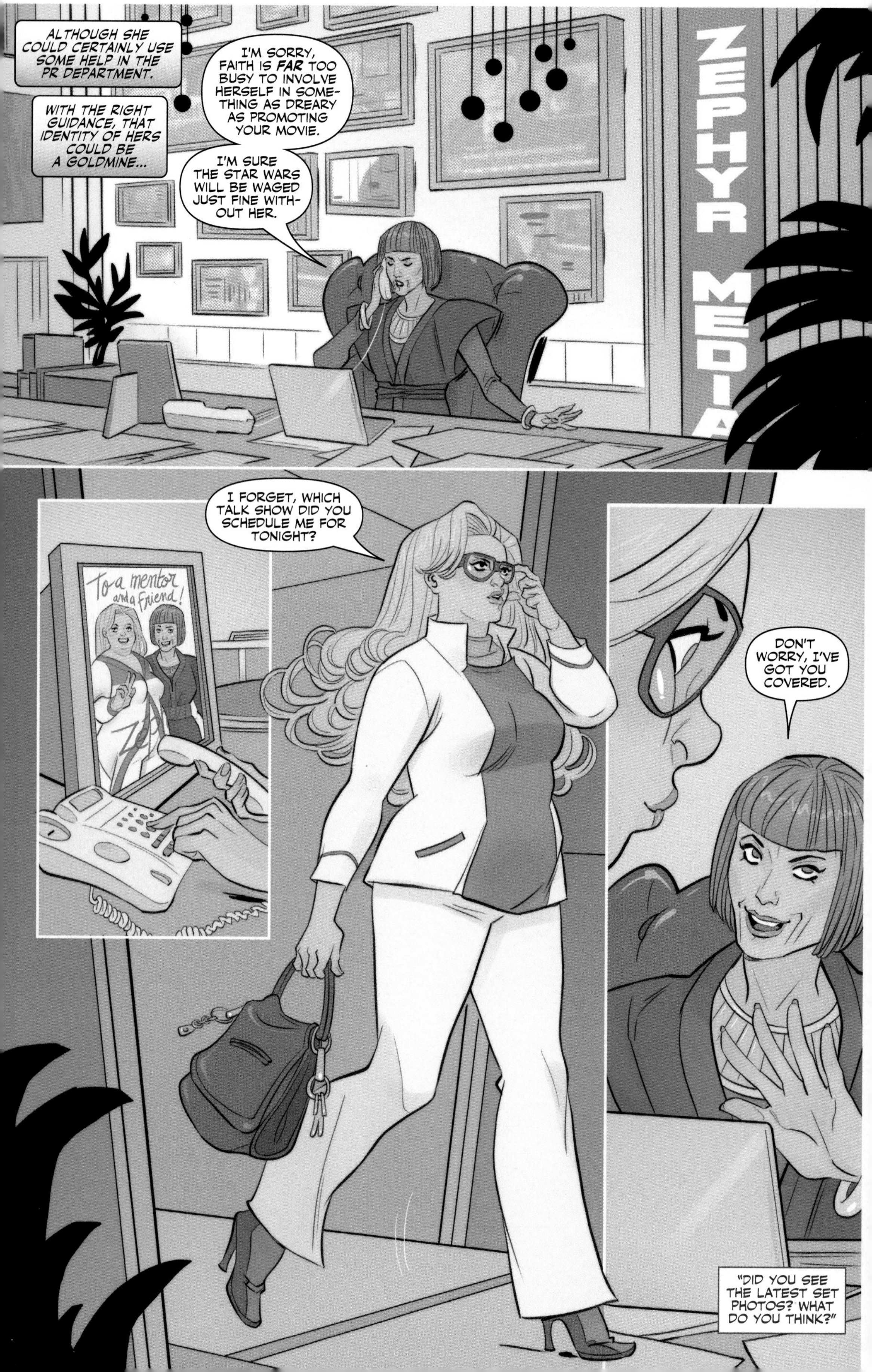

ALTHOUGH SHE COULD CERTAINLY USE SOME HELP IN THE PR DEPARTMENT.
WITH THE RIGHT GUIDANCE, THAT IDENTITY OF HERS COULD BE A GOLDMINE...
I'M SORRY, FAITH IS FAR TOO BUSY TO INVOLVE HERSELF IN SOMETHING AS DREARY AS PROMOTING YOUR MOVIE.
I'M SURE THE STAR WARS WILL BE WAGED JUST FINE WITHOUT HER.
ZEPHYR MEDIA
To a mentor and a friend!
I FORGET, WHICH TALK SHOW DID YOU SCHEDULE ME FOR TONIGHT?
DON'T WORRY, I'VE GOT YOU COVERED.
"DID YOU SEE THE LATEST SET PHOTOS? WHAT DO YOU THINK?"

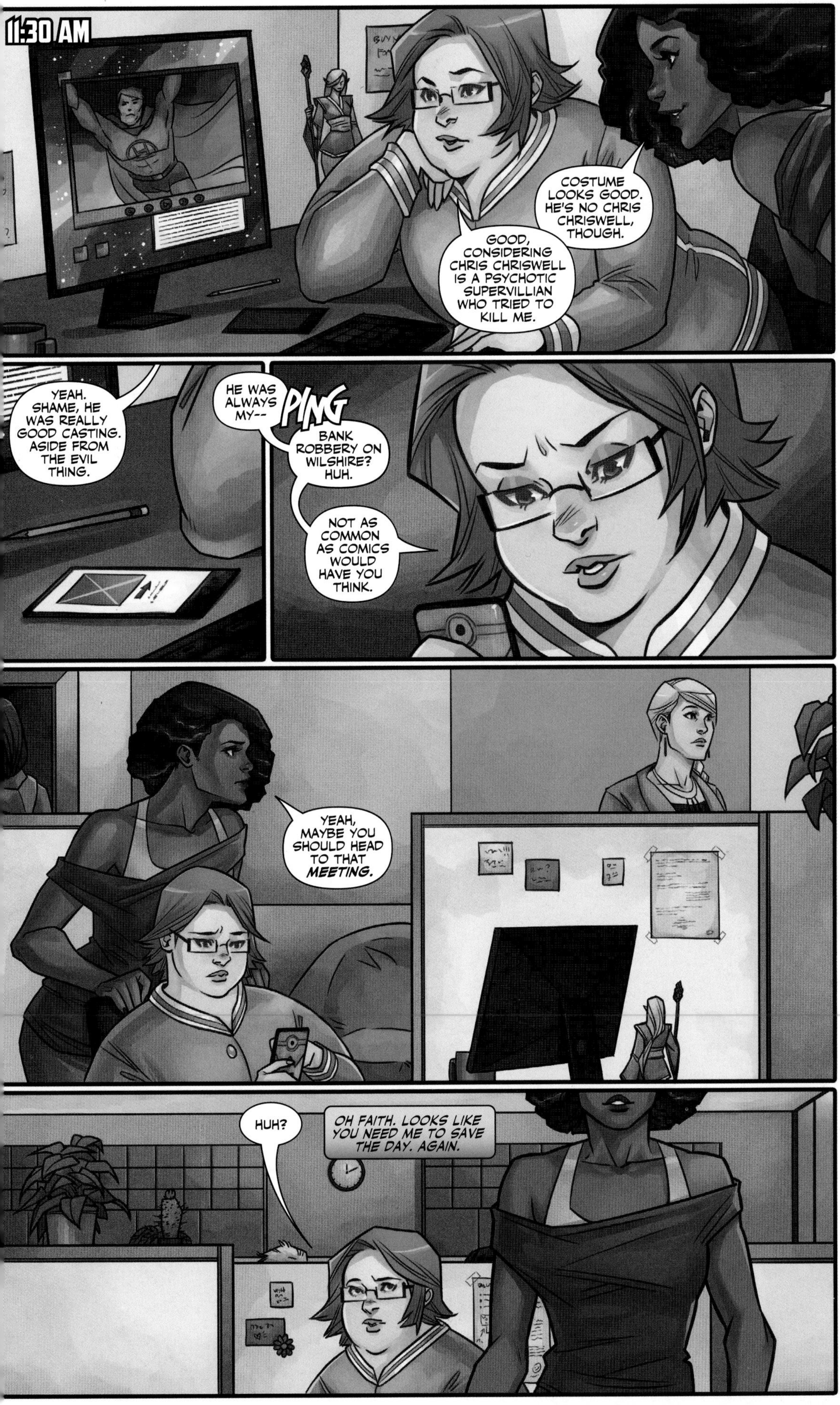
11:30 AM
COSTUME LOOKS GOOD. HE'S NO CHRIS CHRISWELL, THOUGH.
GOOD, CONSIDERING CHRIS CHRISWELL IS A PSYCHOTIC SUPERVILLIAN WHO TRIED TO KILL ME.
YEAH. SHAME, HE WAS REALLY GOOD CASTING. ASIDE FROM THE EVIL THING.
HE WAS ALWAYS MY--
PING
BANK ROBBERY ON WILSHIRE? HUH.
NOT AS COMMON AS COMICS WOULD HAVE YOU THINK.
YEAH, MAYBE YOU SHOULD HEAD TO THAT *MEETING*.
HUH?
OH FAITH. LOOKS LIKE YOU NEED ME TO SAVE THE DAY. AGAIN.

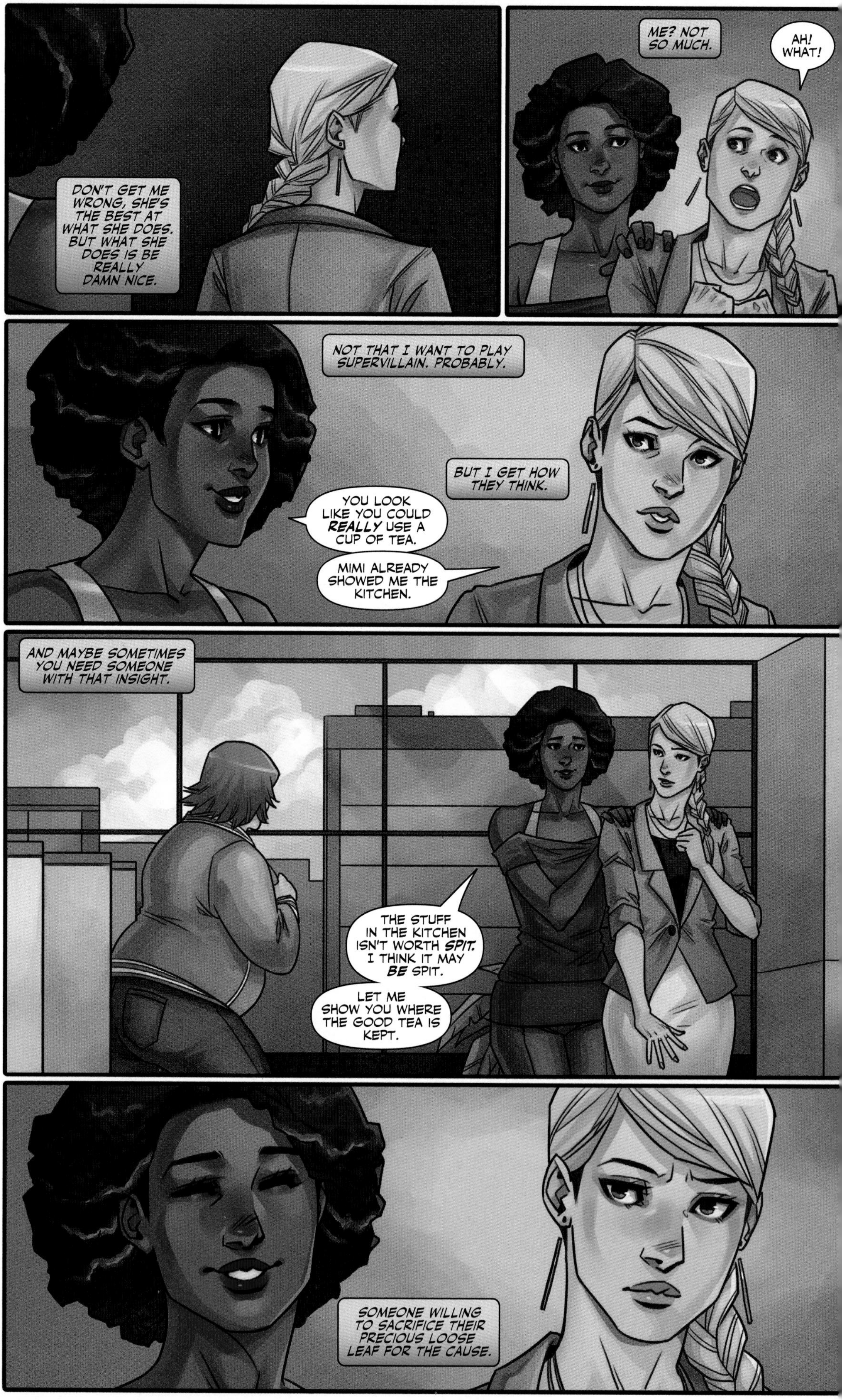
DON'T GET ME WRONG, SHE'S THE BEST AT WHAT SHE DOES. BUT WHAT SHE DOES IS BE REALLY DAMN NICE.
ME? NOT SO MUCH.
AH! WHAT!
NOT THAT I WANT TO PLAY SUPERVILLAIN. PROBABLY.
BUT I GET HOW THEY THINK.
YOU LOOK LIKE YOU COULD *REALLY* USE A CUP OF TEA.
MIMI ALREADY SHOWED ME THE KITCHEN.
AND MAYBE SOMETIMES YOU NEED SOMEONE WITH THAT INSIGHT.
THE STUFF IN THE KITCHEN ISN'T WORTH *SPIT.* I THINK IT MAY *BE* SPIT.
LET ME SHOW YOU WHERE THE GOOD TEA IS KEPT.
SOMEONE WILLING TO SACRIFICE THEIR PRECIOUS LOOSE LEAF FOR THE CAUSE.

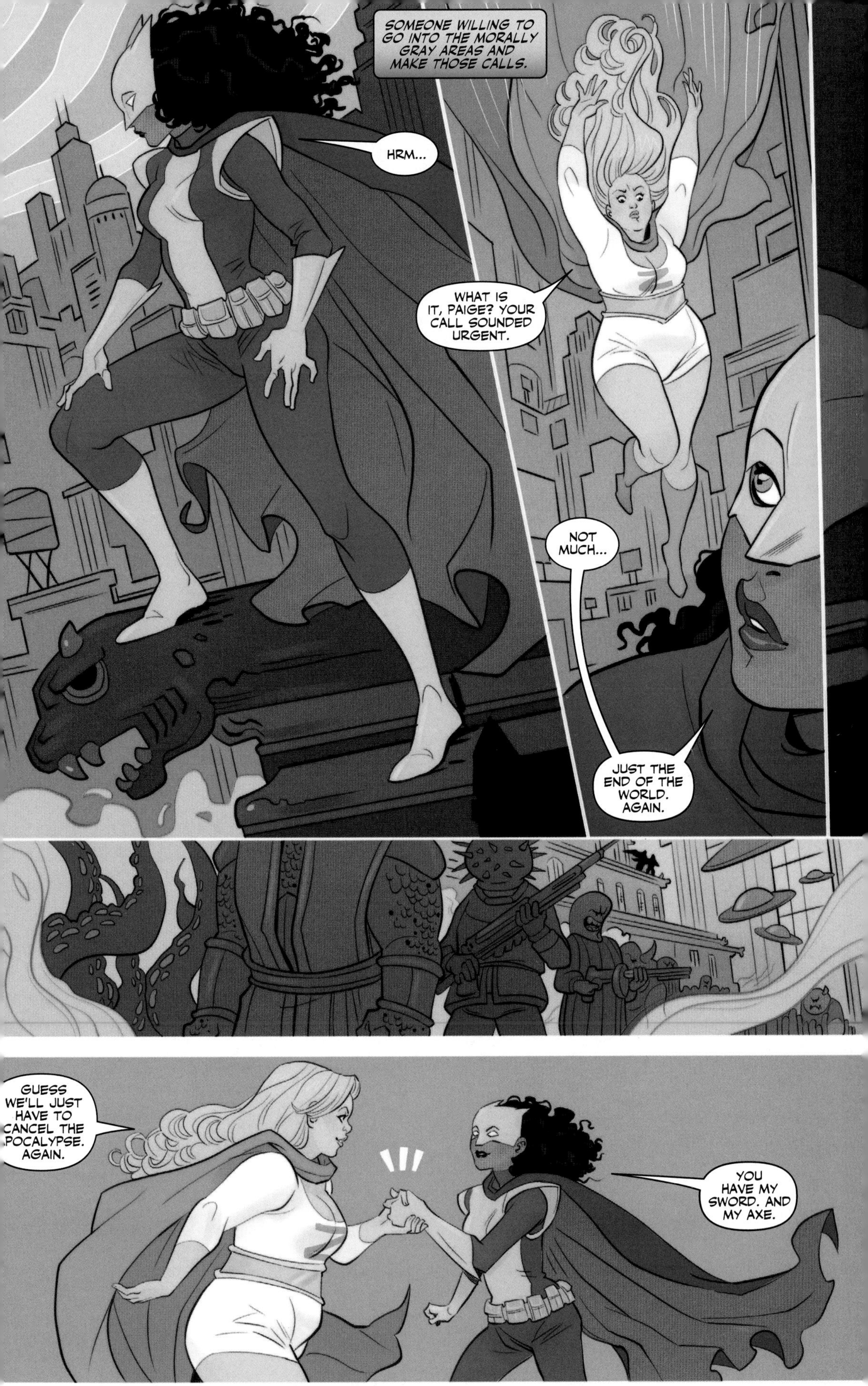
SOMEONE WILLING TO GO INTO THE MORALLY GRAY AREAS AND MAKE THOSE CALLS.
HRM...
WHAT IS IT, PAIGE? YOUR CALL SOUNDED URGENT.
NOT MUCH...
JUST THE END OF THE WORLD. AGAIN.
GUESS WE'LL JUST HAVE TO CANCEL THE POCALYPSE. AGAIN.
YOU HAVE MY SWORD. AND MY AXE.

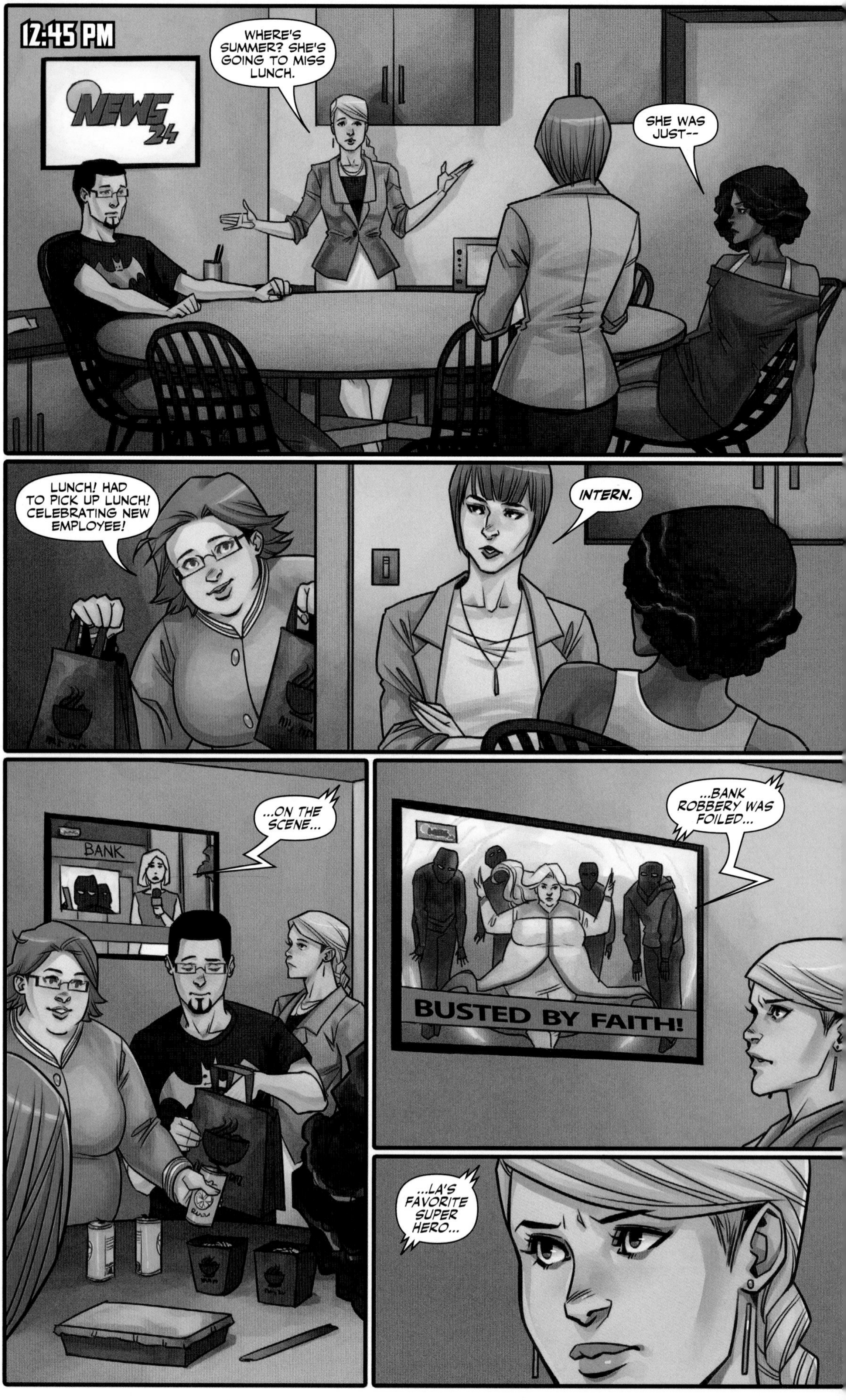
12:45 PM
NEWS 24
WHERE'S SUMMER? SHE'S GOING TO MISS LUNCH.
SHE WAS JUST--
LUNCH! HAD TO PICK UP LUNCH! CELEBRATING NEW EMPLOYEE!
INTERN.
BANK
...ON THE SCENE...
...BANK ROBBERY WAS FOILED...
BUSTED BY FAITH!
...LA'S FAVORITE SUPER HERO...

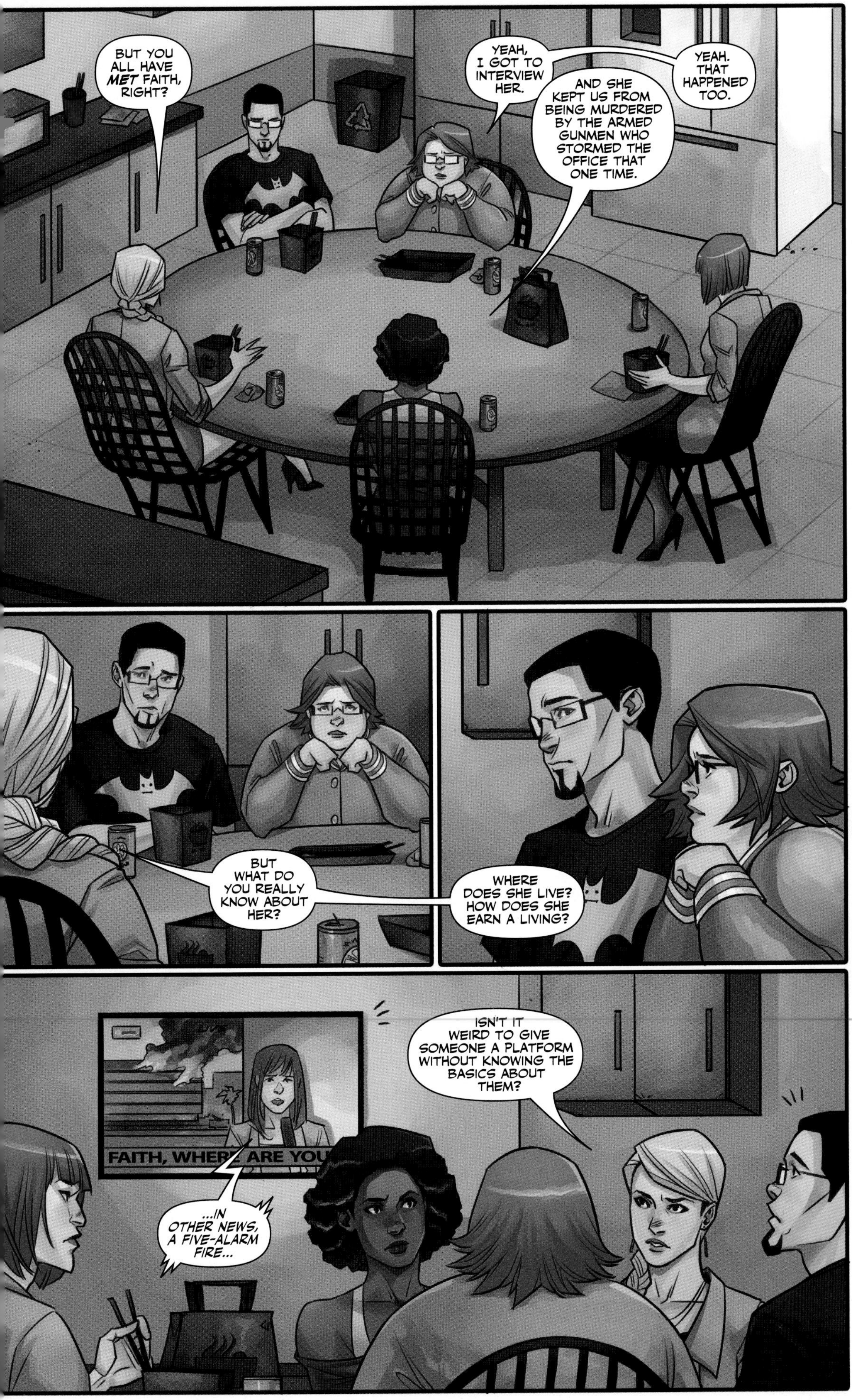
BUT YOU ALL HAVE *MET* FAITH, RIGHT?
YEAH, I GOT TO INTERVIEW HER.
AND SHE KEPT US FROM BEING MURDERED BY THE ARMED GUNMEN WHO STORMED THE OFFICE THAT ONE TIME.
YEAH. THAT HAPPENED TOO.
BUT WHAT DO YOU REALLY KNOW ABOUT HER?
WHERE DOES SHE LIVE? HOW DOES SHE EARN A LIVING?
ISN'T IT WEIRD TO GIVE SOMEONE A PLATFORM WITHOUT KNOWING THE BASICS ABOUT THEM?
FAITH, WHERE ARE YOU
...IN OTHER NEWS, A FIVE-ALARM FIRE...

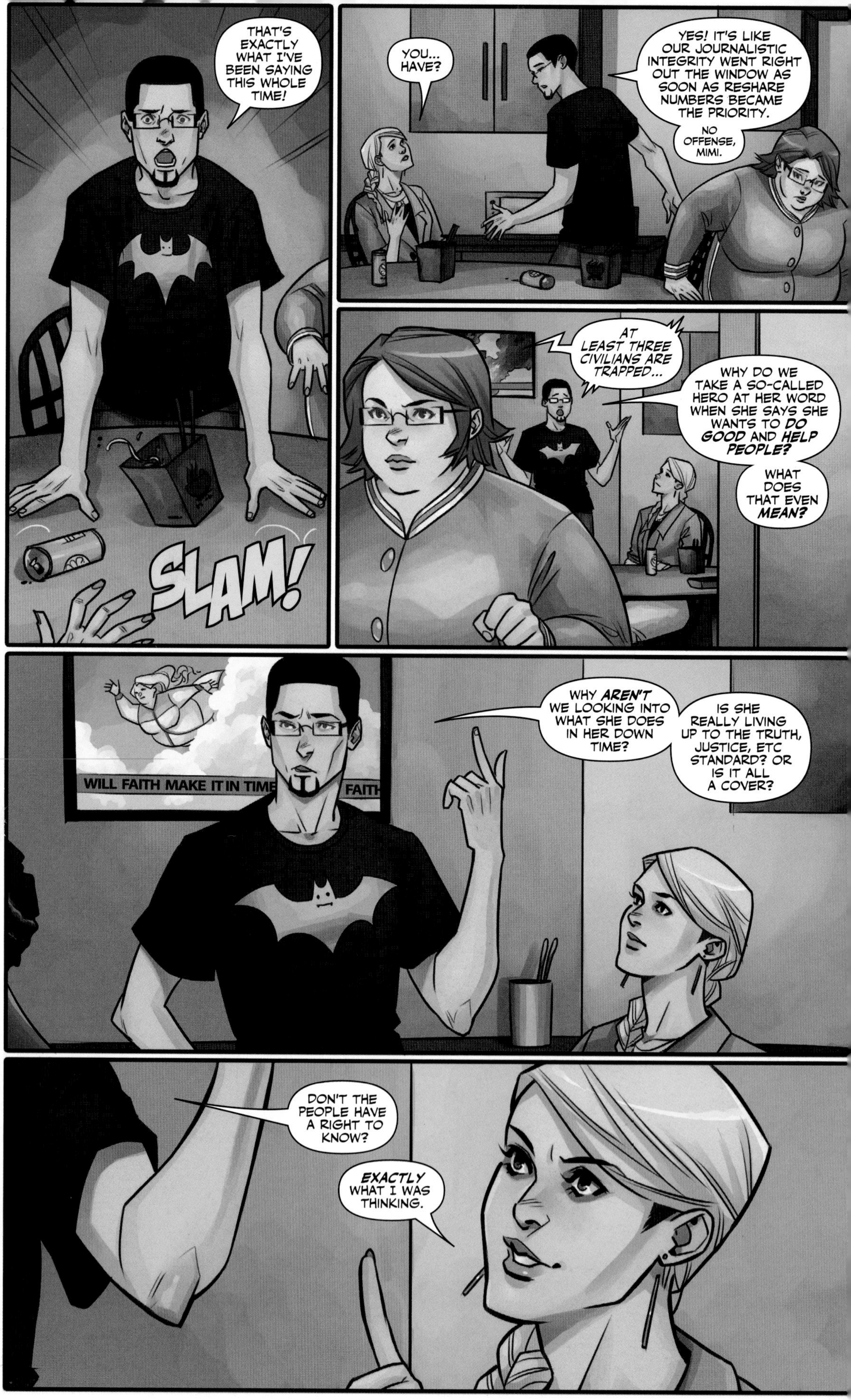
THAT'S EXACTLY WHAT I'VE BEEN SAYING THIS WHOLE TIME!
SLAM!
YOU... HAVE?
YES! IT'S LIKE OUR JOURNALISTIC INTEGRITY WENT RIGHT OUT THE WINDOW AS SOON AS RESHARE NUMBERS BECAME THE PRIORITY.
NO OFFENSE, MIMI.
AT LEAST THREE CIVILIANS ARE TRAPPED...
WHY DO WE TAKE A SO-CALLED HERO AT HER WORD WHEN SHE SAYS SHE WANTS TO DO GOOD AND HELP PEOPLE?
WHAT DOES THAT EVEN MEAN?
WILL FAITH MAKE IT IN TIME
FAITH
WHY AREN'T WE LOOKING INTO WHAT SHE DOES IN HER DOWN TIME?
IS SHE REALLY LIVING UP TO THE TRUTH, JUSTICE, ETC STANDARD? OR IS IT ALL A COVER?
DON'T THE PEOPLE HAVE A RIGHT TO KNOW?
EXACTLY WHAT I WAS THINKING.

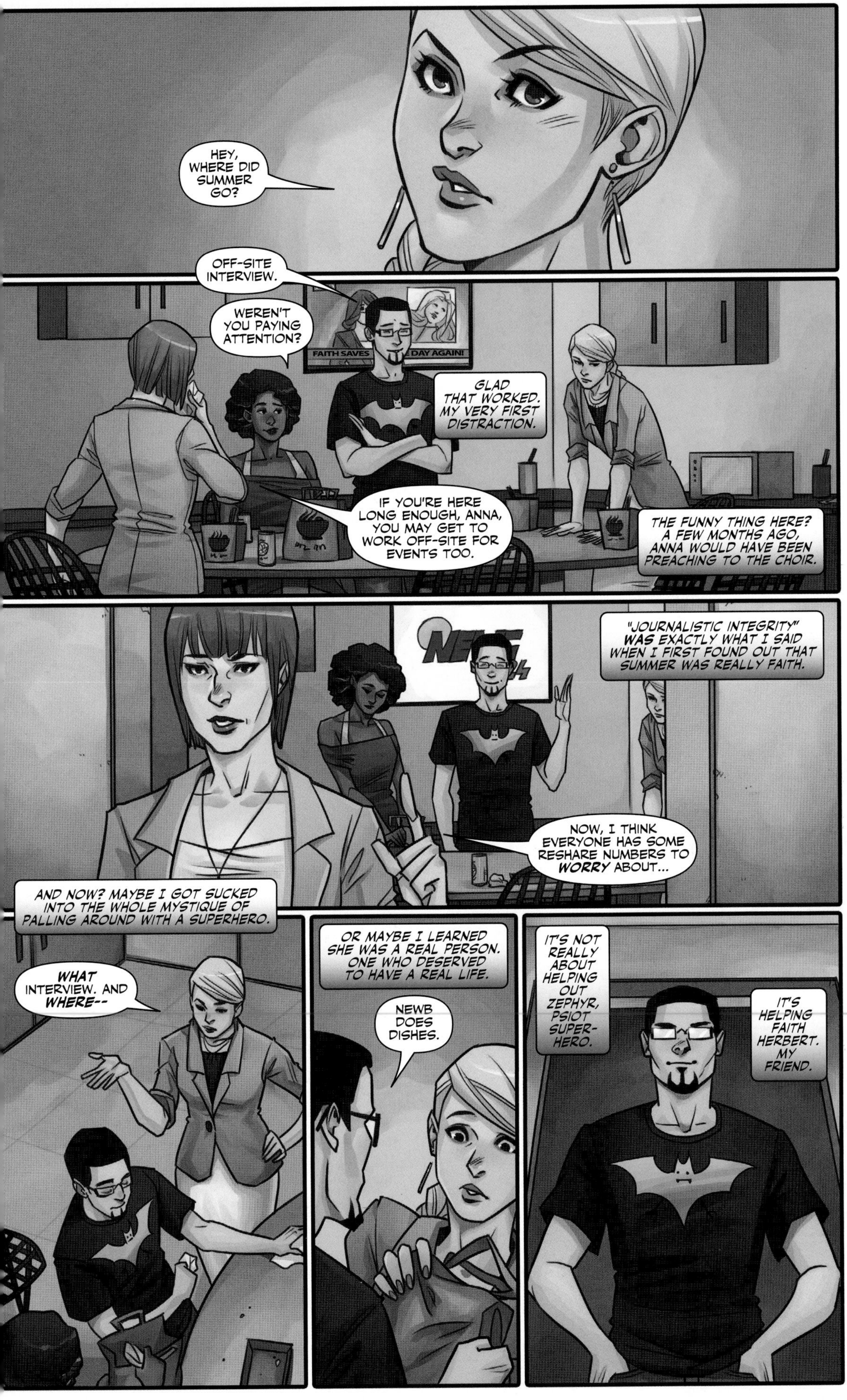

HEY, WHERE DID SUMMER GO?
OFF-SITE INTERVIEW.
WEREN'T YOU PAYING ATTENTION?
FAITH SAVES ... DAY AGAIN!
GLAD THAT WORKED. MY VERY FIRST DISTRACTION.
IF YOU'RE HERE LONG ENOUGH, ANNA, YOU MAY GET TO WORK OFF-SITE FOR EVENTS TOO.
THE FUNNY THING HERE? A FEW MONTHS AGO, ANNA WOULD HAVE BEEN PREACHING TO THE CHOIR.
"JOURNALISTIC INTEGRITY" WAS EXACTLY WHAT I SAID WHEN I FIRST FOUND OUT THAT SUMMER WAS REALLY FAITH.
NOW, I THINK EVERYONE HAS SOME RESHARE NUMBERS TO WORRY ABOUT...
AND NOW? MAYBE I GOT SUCKED INTO THE WHOLE MYSTIQUE OF PALLING AROUND WITH A SUPERHERO.
WHAT INTERVIEW. AND WHERE--
OR MAYBE I LEARNED SHE WAS A REAL PERSON. ONE WHO DESERVED TO HAVE A REAL LIFE.
NEWB DOES DISHES.
IT'S NOT REALLY ABOUT HELPING OUT ZEPHYR, PSIOT SUPER-HERO.
IT'S HELPING FAITH HERBERT. MY FRIEND.

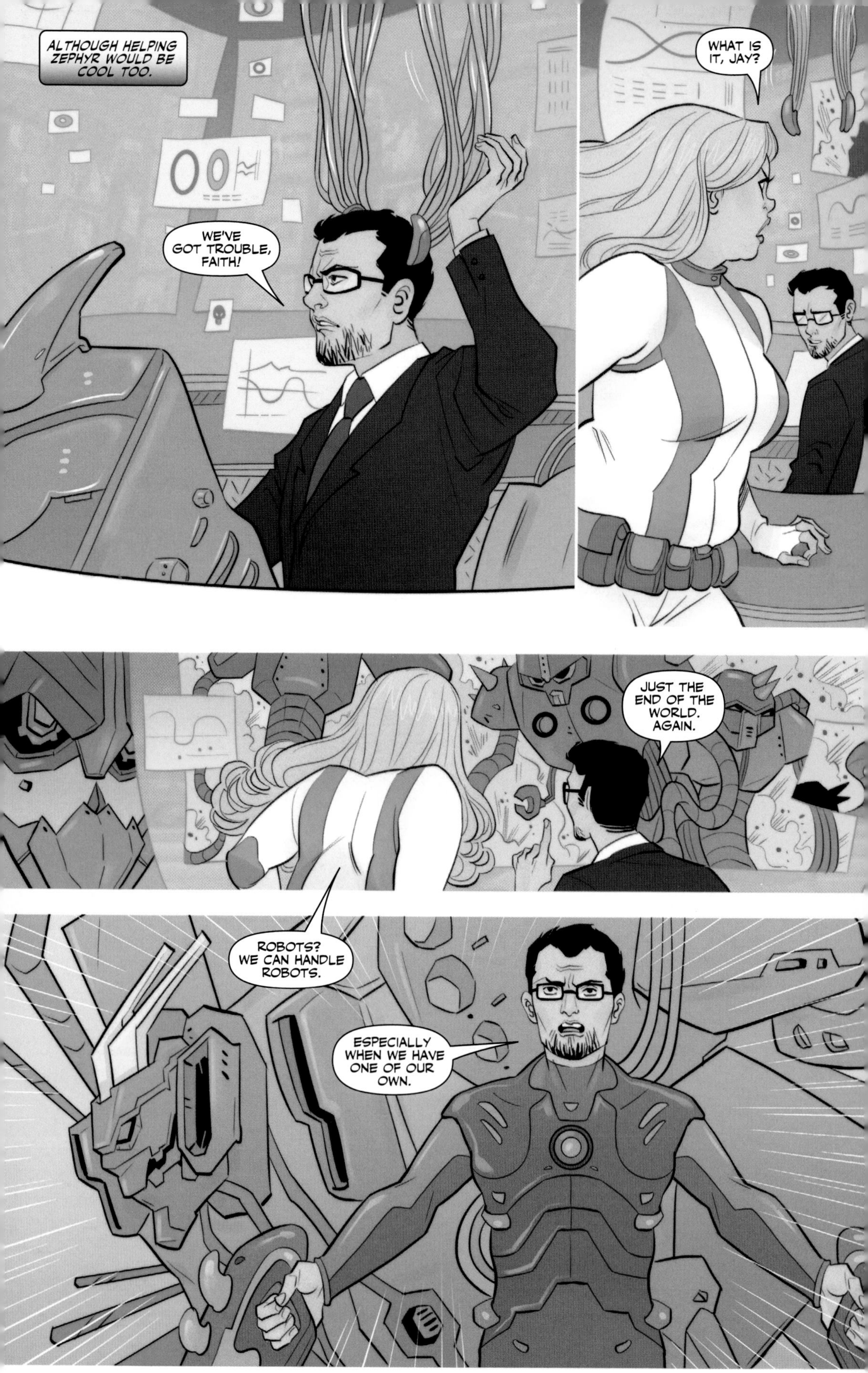
ALTHOUGH HELPING ZEPHYR WOULD BE COOL TOO.
WE'VE GOT TROUBLE, FAITH!
WHAT IS IT, JAY?
JUST THE END OF THE WORLD. AGAIN.
ROBOTS? WE CAN HANDLE ROBOTS.
ESPECIALLY WHEN WE HAVE ONE OF OUR OWN.

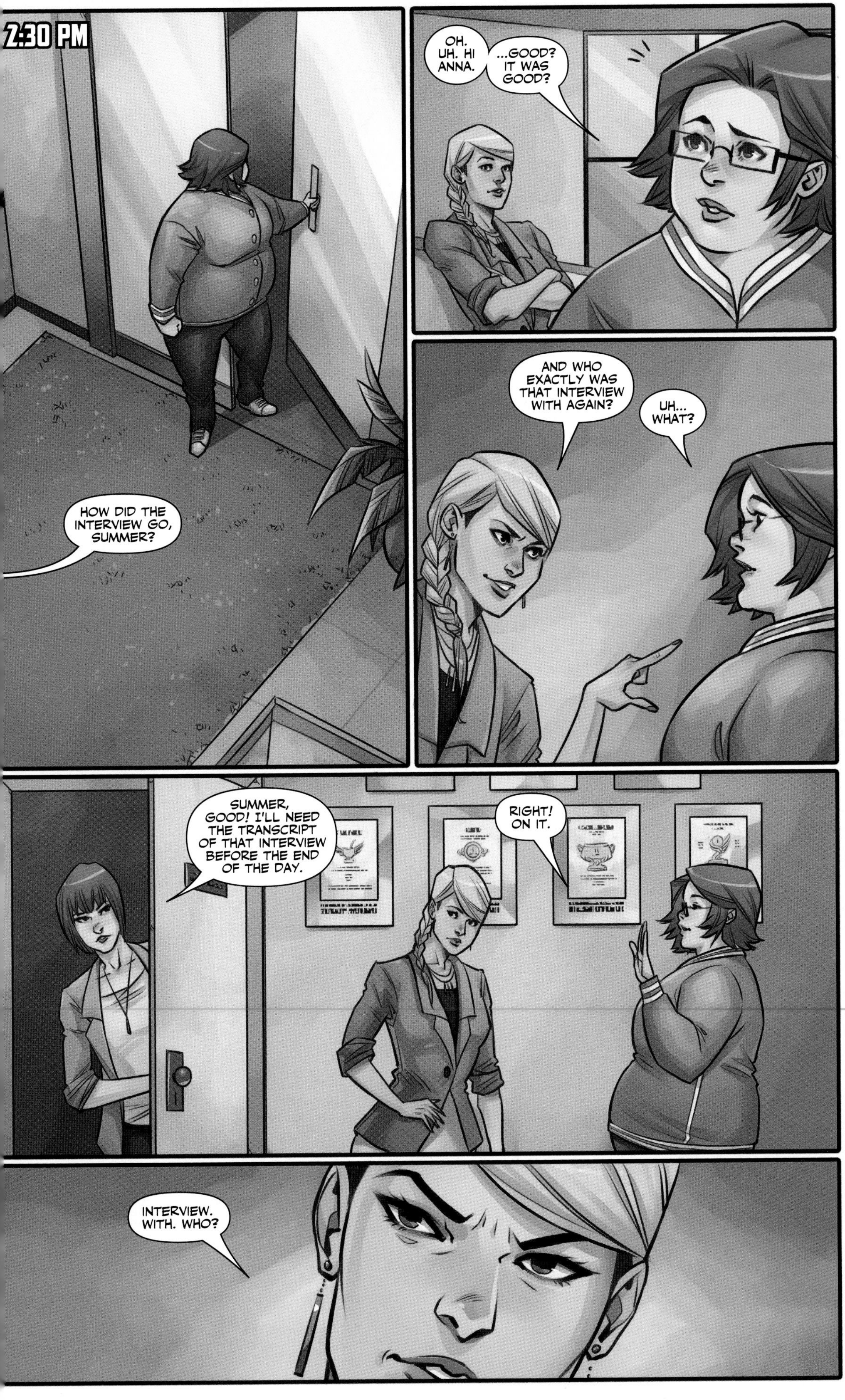
2:30 PM
HOW DID THE INTERVIEW GO, SUMMER?
OH. UH. HI ANNA.
...GOOD? IT WAS GOOD?
AND WHO EXACTLY WAS THAT INTERVIEW WITH AGAIN?
UH... WHAT?
SUMMER, GOOD! I'LL NEED THE TRANSCRIPT OF THAT INTERVIEW BEFORE THE END OF THE DAY.
RIGHT! ON IT.
INTERVIEW. WITH. WHO?

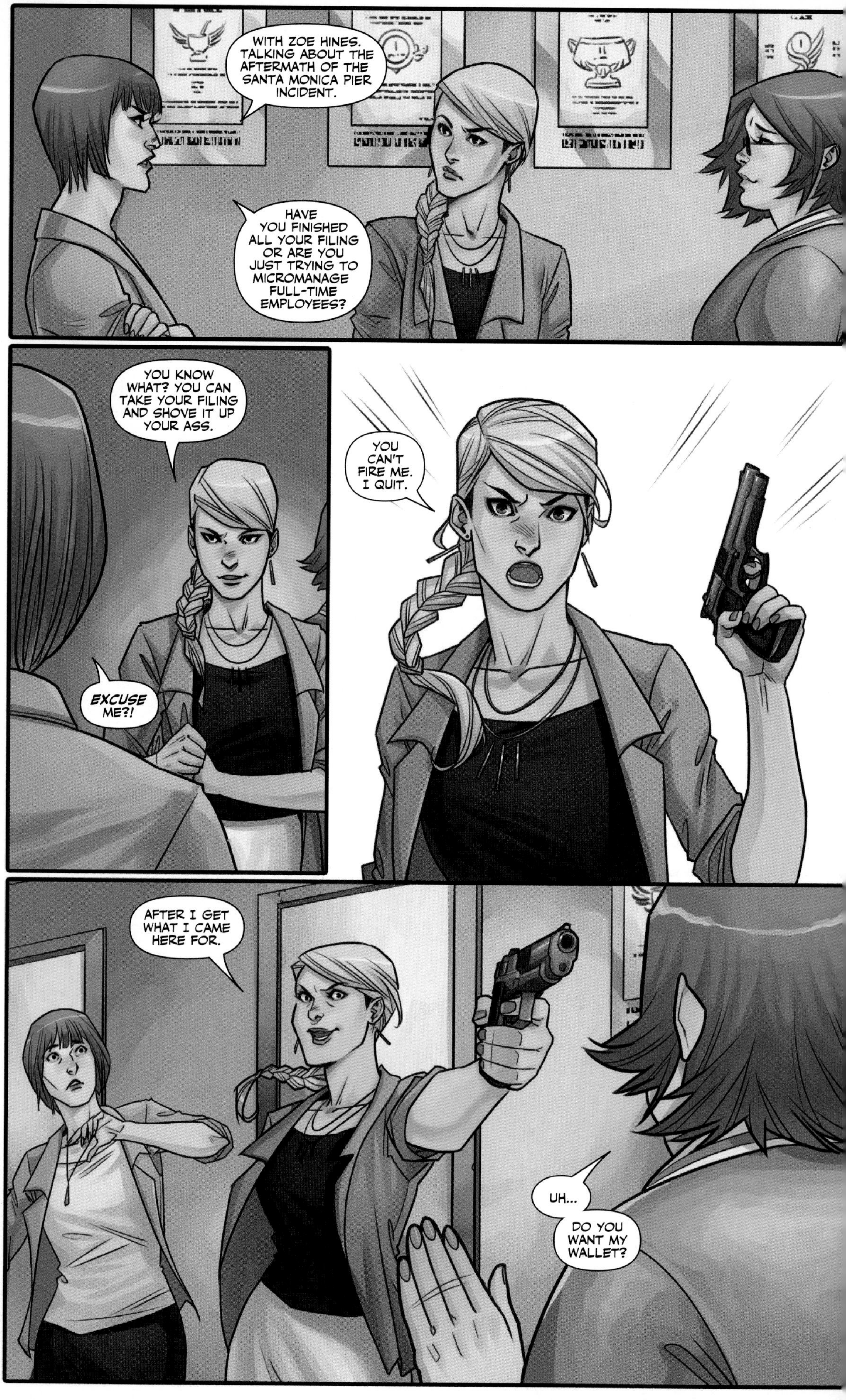
WITH ZOE HINES. TALKING ABOUT THE AFTERMATH OF THE SANTA MONICA PIER INCIDENT.
HAVE YOU FINISHED ALL YOUR FILING OR ARE YOU JUST TRYING TO MICROMANAGE FULL-TIME EMPLOYEES?
YOU KNOW WHAT? YOU CAN TAKE YOUR FILING AND SHOVE IT UP YOUR ASS.
EXCUSE ME?!
YOU CAN'T FIRE ME. I QUIT.
AFTER I GET WHAT I CAME HERE FOR.
UH...
DO YOU WANT MY WALLET?

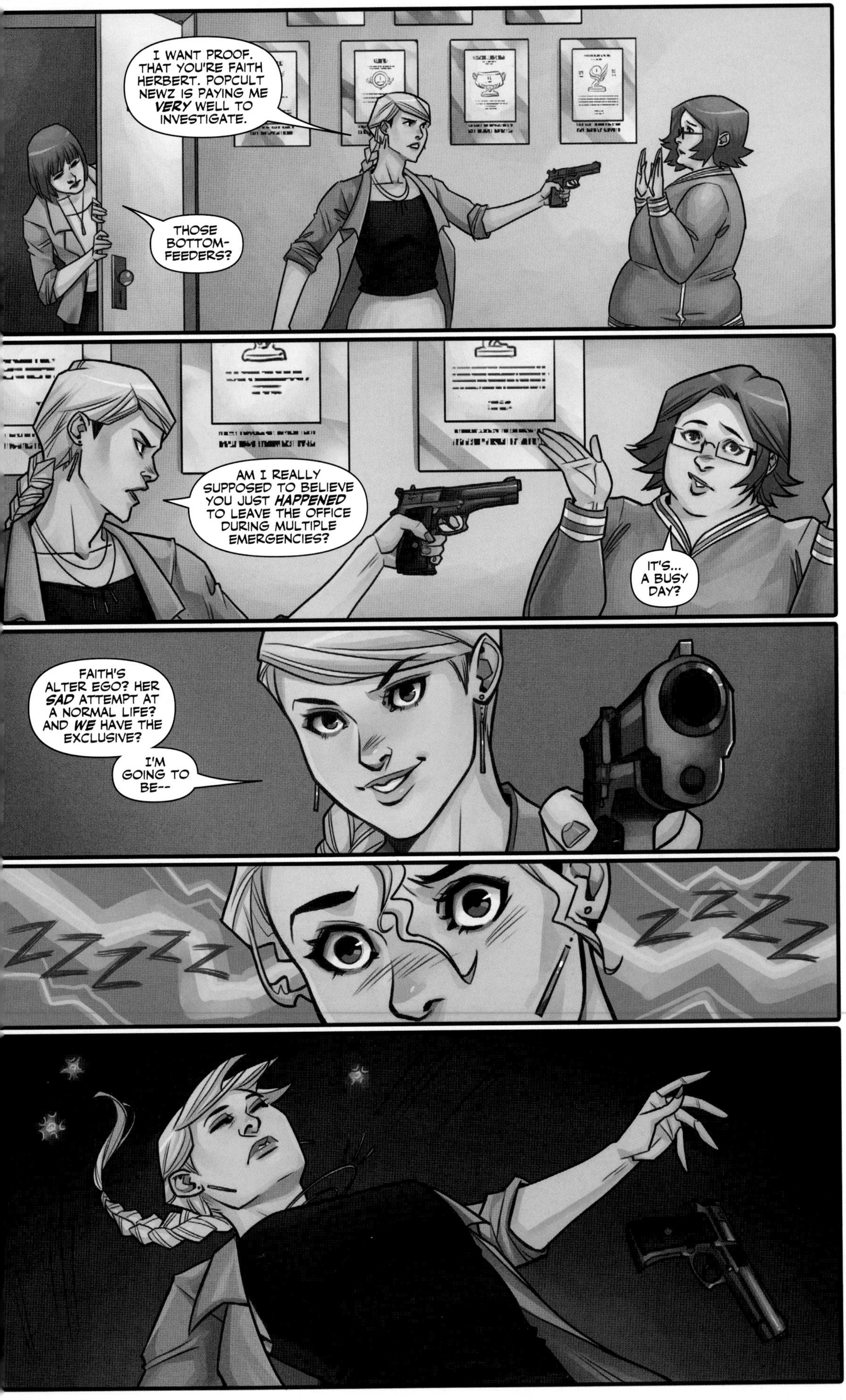
I WANT PROOF. THAT YOU'RE FAITH HERBERT. POPCULT NEWZ IS PAYING ME *VERY* WELL TO INVESTIGATE.
THOSE BOTTOM-FEEDERS?
AM I REALLY SUPPOSED TO BELIEVE YOU JUST *HAPPENED* TO LEAVE THE OFFICE DURING MULTIPLE EMERGENCIES?
IT'S... A BUSY DAY?
FAITH'S ALTER EGO? HER *SAD* ATTEMPT AT A NORMAL LIFE? AND *WE* HAVE THE EXCLUSIVE?
I'M GOING TO BE--
ZZZZZZ
ZZZZZ

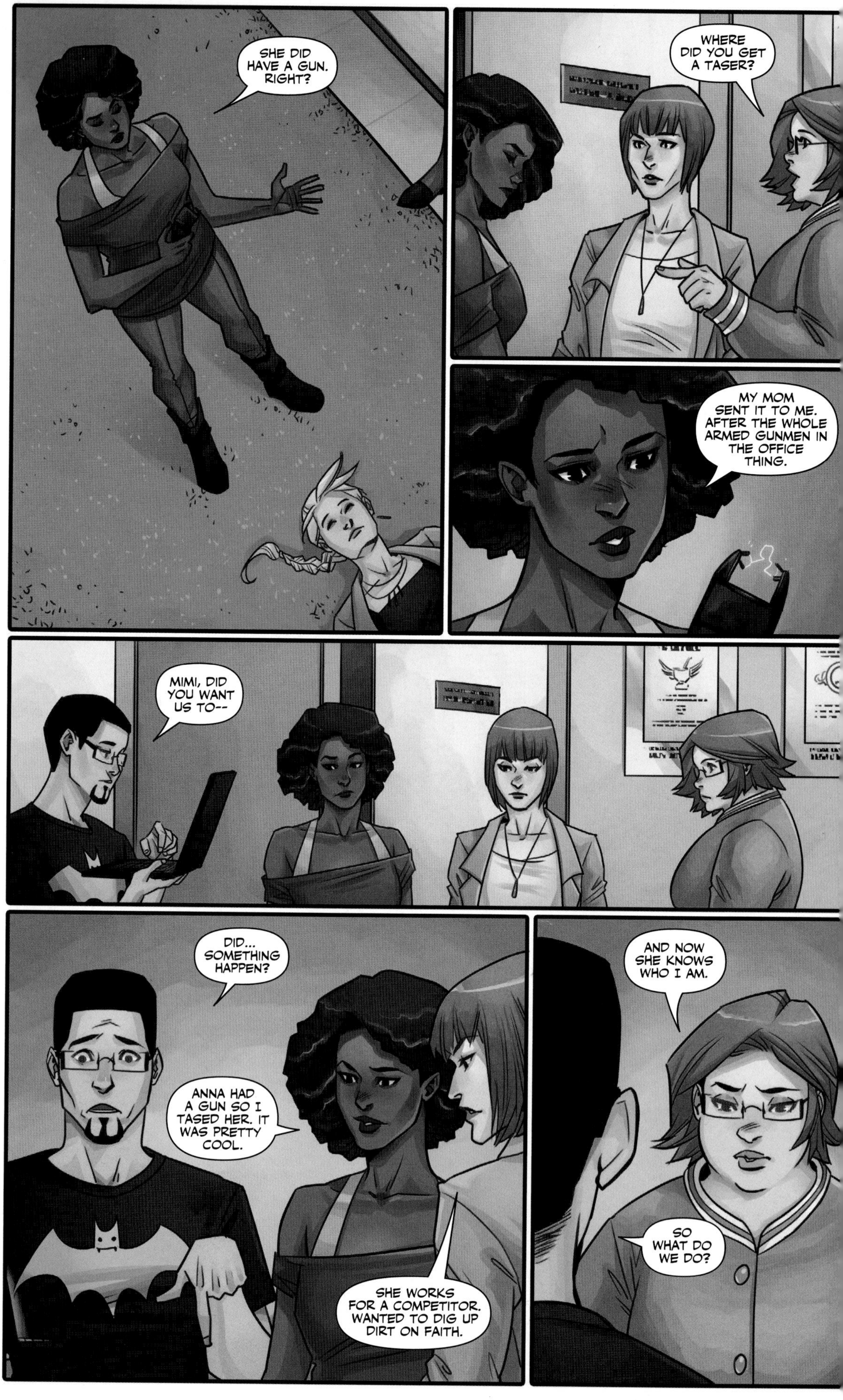

SHE DID HAVE A GUN. RIGHT?
WHERE DID YOU GET A TASER?
MY MOM SENT IT TO ME. AFTER THE WHOLE ARMED GUNMEN IN THE OFFICE THING.
MIMI, DID YOU WANT US TO--
DID... SOMETHING HAPPEN?
ANNA HAD A GUN SO I TASED HER. IT WAS PRETTY COOL.
SHE WORKS FOR A COMPETITOR. WANTED TO DIG UP DIRT ON FAITH.
AND NOW SHE KNOWS WHO I AM.
SO WHAT DO WE DO?

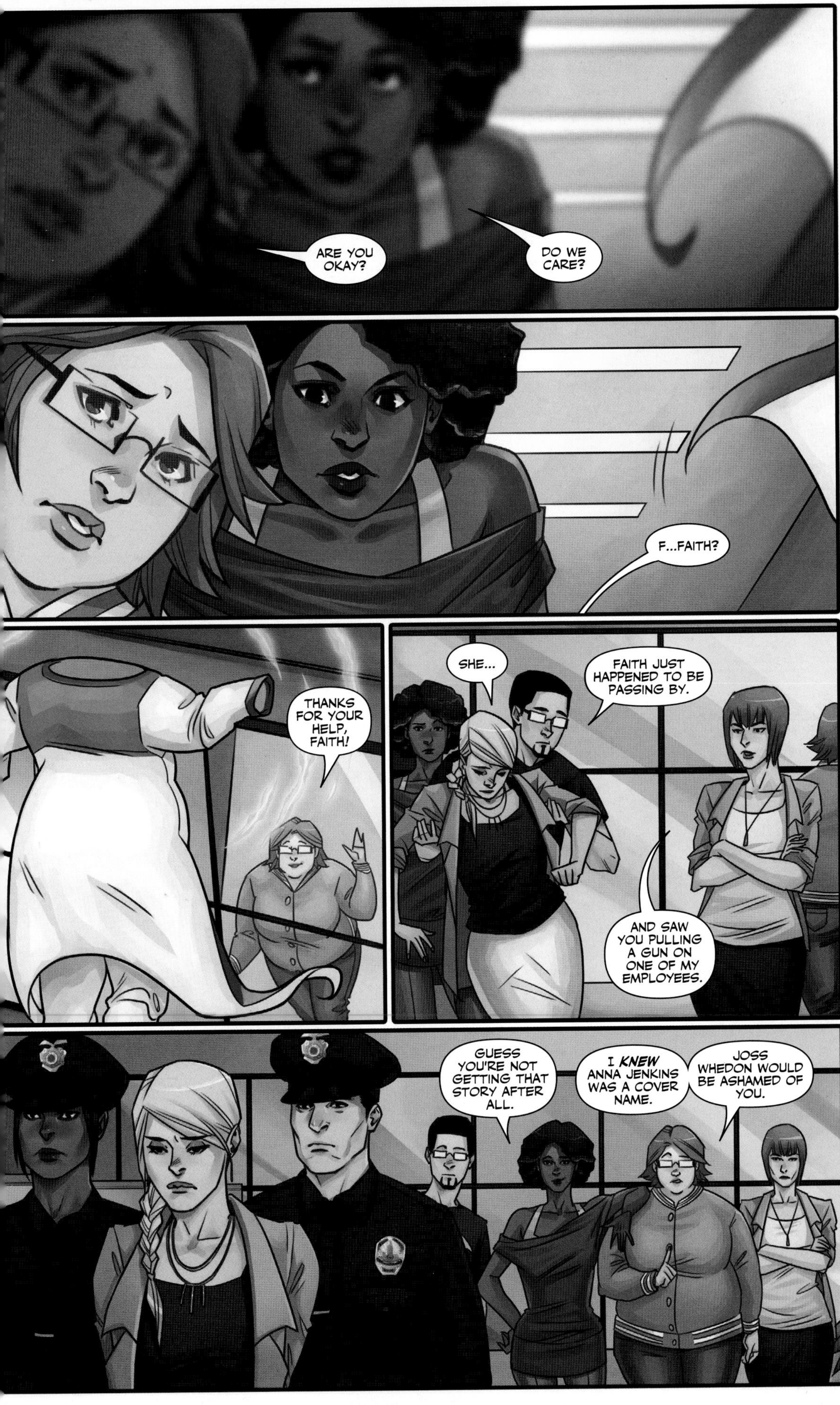
ARE YOU OKAY?
DO WE CARE?
F...FAITH?
THANKS FOR YOUR HELP, FAITH!
SHE...
FAITH JUST HAPPENED TO BE PASSING BY.
AND SAW YOU PULLING A GUN ON ONE OF MY EMPLOYEES.
GUESS YOU'RE NOT GETTING THAT STORY AFTER ALL.
I *KNEW* ANNA JENKINS WAS A COVER NAME.
JOSS WHEDON WOULD BE ASHAMED OF YOU.

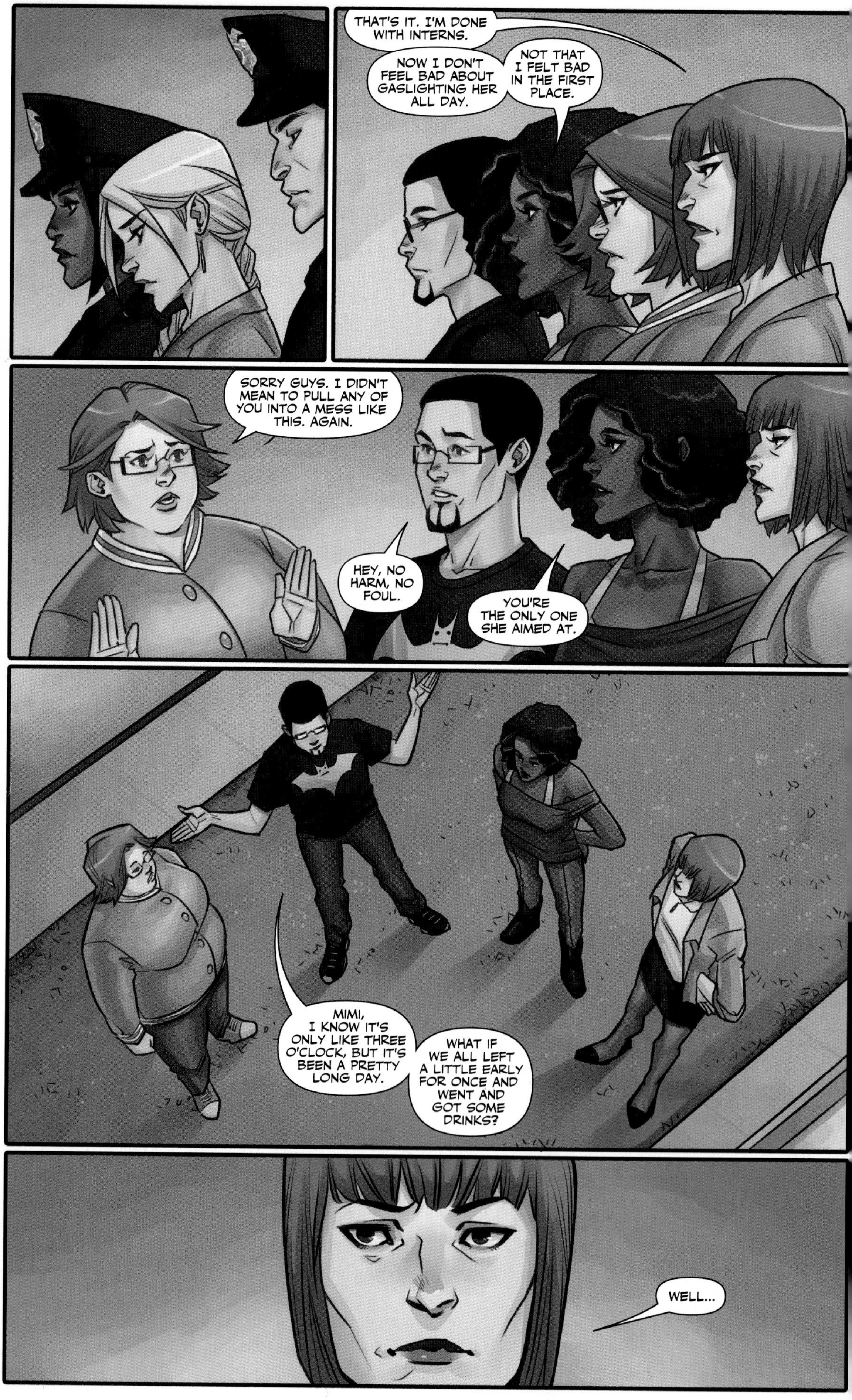
THAT'S IT. I'M DONE WITH INTERNS.
NOW I DON'T FEEL BAD ABOUT GASLIGHTING HER ALL DAY.
NOT THAT I FELT BAD IN THE FIRST PLACE.
SORRY GUYS. I DIDN'T MEAN TO PULL ANY OF YOU INTO A MESS LIKE THIS. AGAIN.
HEY, NO HARM, NO FOUL.
YOU'RE THE ONLY ONE SHE AIMED AT.
MIMI, I KNOW IT'S ONLY LIKE THREE O'CLOCK, BUT IT'S BEEN A PRETTY LONG DAY.
WHAT IF WE ALL LEFT A LITTLE EARLY FOR ONCE AND WENT AND GOT SOME DRINKS?
WELL...

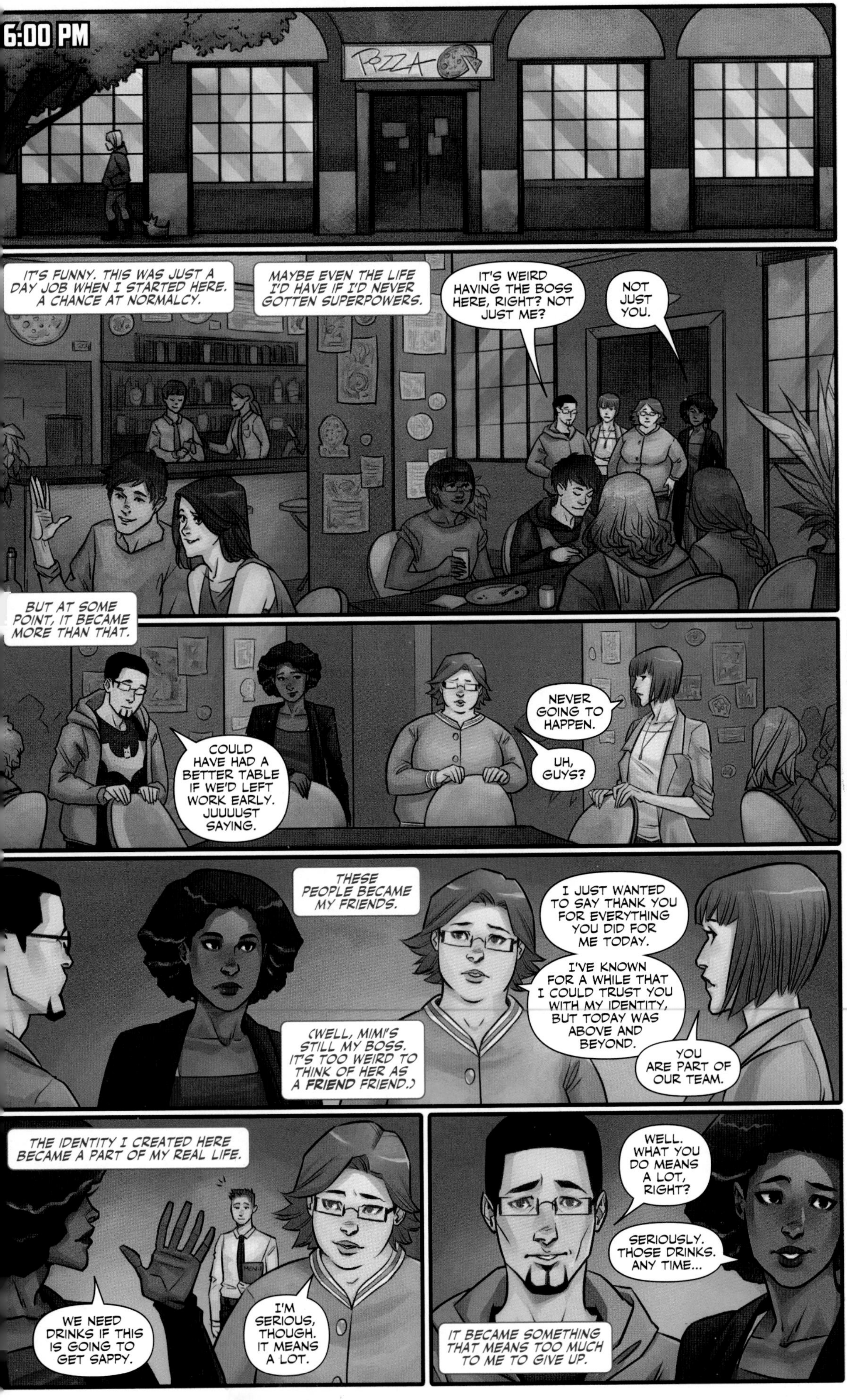
6:00 PM
PIZZA
IT'S FUNNY. THIS WAS JUST A DAY JOB WHEN I STARTED HERE. A CHANCE AT NORMALCY.
MAYBE EVEN THE LIFE I'D HAVE IF I'D NEVER GOTTEN SUPERPOWERS.
IT'S WEIRD HAVING THE BOSS HERE, RIGHT? NOT JUST ME?
NOT JUST YOU.
BUT AT SOME POINT, IT BECAME MORE THAN THAT.
COULD HAVE HAD A BETTER TABLE IF WE'D LEFT WORK EARLY. JUUUUST SAYING.
NEVER GOING TO HAPPEN.
UH, GUYS?
THESE PEOPLE BECAME MY FRIENDS.
(WELL, MIMI'S STILL MY BOSS. IT'S TOO WEIRD TO THINK OF HER AS A FRIEND FRIEND.)
I JUST WANTED TO SAY THANK YOU FOR EVERYTHING YOU DID FOR ME TODAY.
I'VE KNOWN FOR A WHILE THAT I COULD TRUST YOU WITH MY IDENTITY, BUT TODAY WAS ABOVE AND BEYOND.
YOU ARE PART OF OUR TEAM.
THE IDENTITY I CREATED HERE BECAME A PART OF MY REAL LIFE.
WE NEED DRINKS IF THIS IS GOING TO GET SAPPY.
I'M SERIOUS, THOUGH. IT MEANS A LOT.
WELL. WHAT YOU DO MEANS A LOT, RIGHT?
SERIOUSLY. THOSE DRINKS. ANY TIME...
IT BECAME SOMETHING THAT MEANS TOO MUCH TO ME TO GIVE UP.

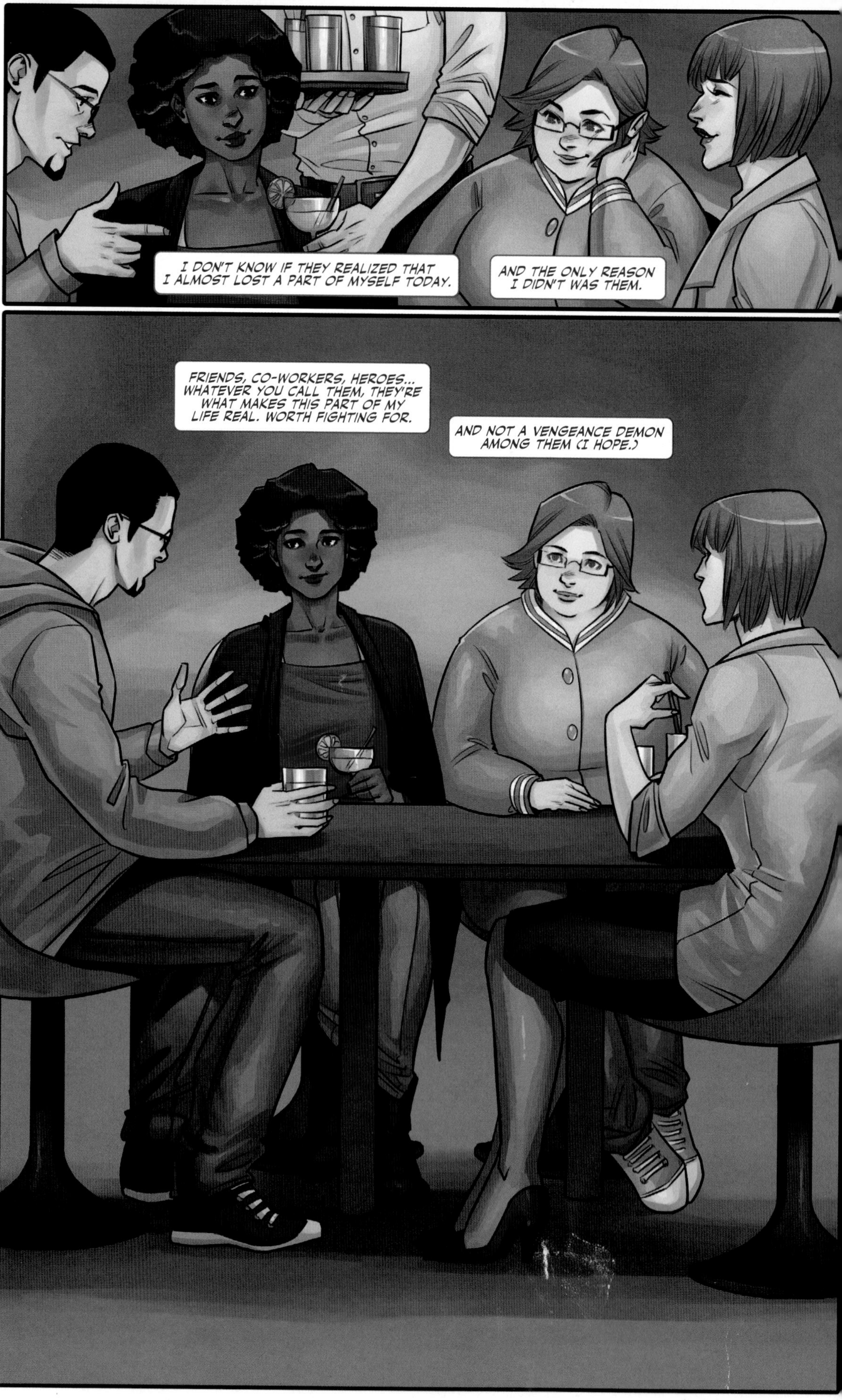
I DON'T KNOW IF THEY REALIZED THAT I ALMOST LOST A PART OF MYSELF TODAY.
AND THE ONLY REASON I DIDN'T WAS THEM.
FRIENDS, CO-WORKERS, HEROES... WHATEVER YOU CALL THEM, THEY'RE WHAT MAKES THIS PART OF MY LIFE REAL. WORTH FIGHTING FOR.
AND NOT A VENGEANCE DEMON AMONG THEM (I HOPE.)

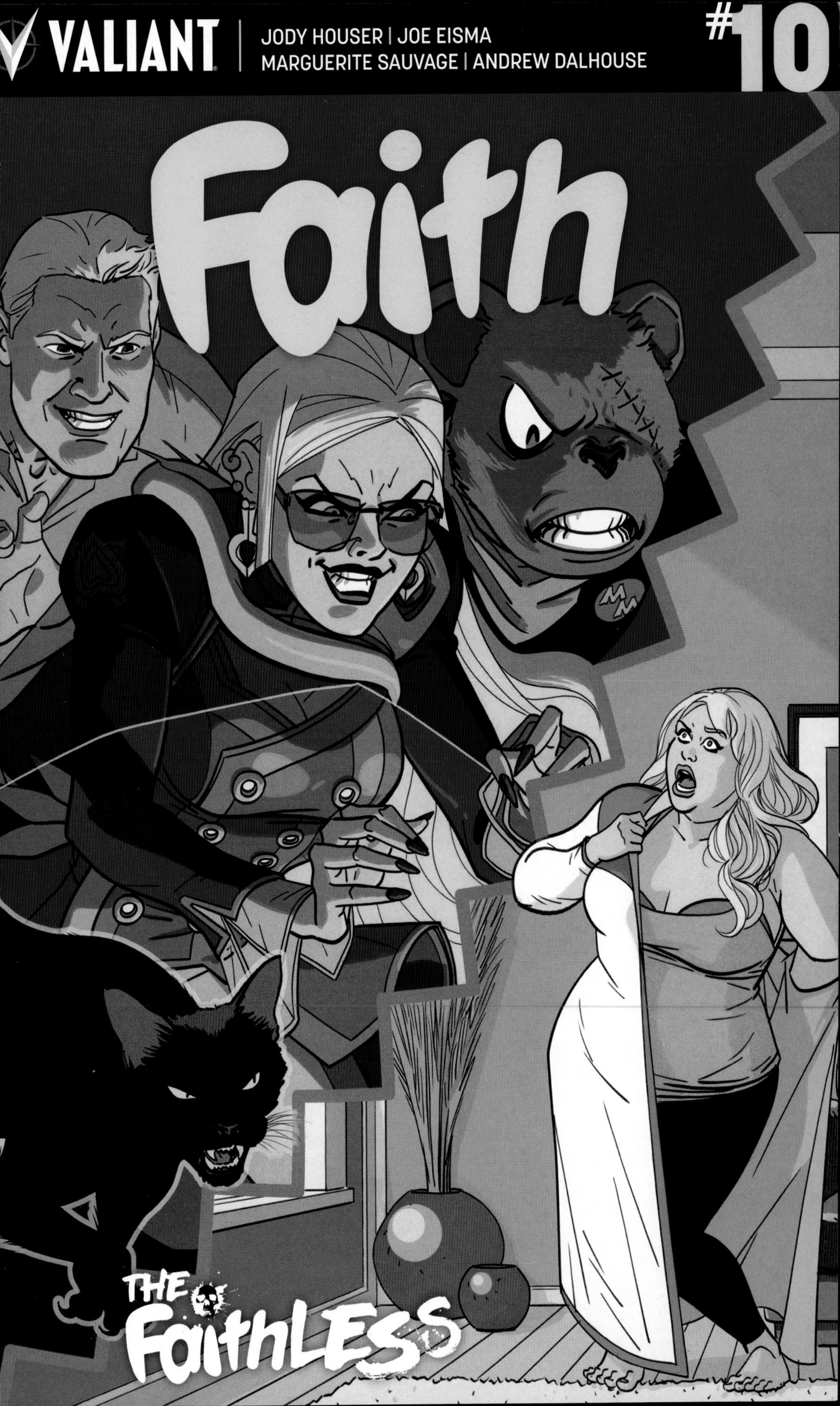
VALIANT
JODY HOUSER | JOE EISMA
MARGUERITE SAUVAGE | ANDREW DALHOUSE
#10
Faith
THE Faithless

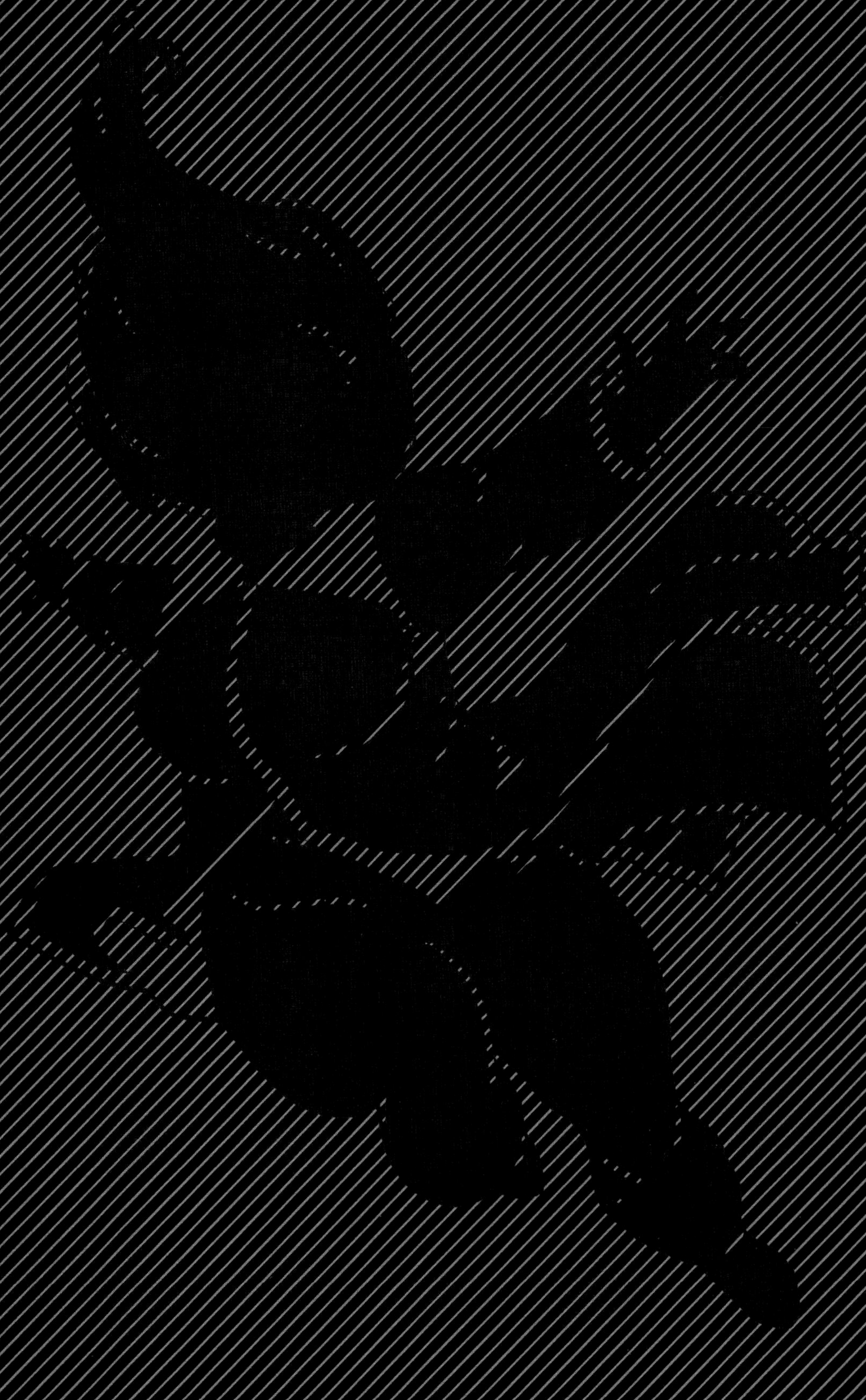

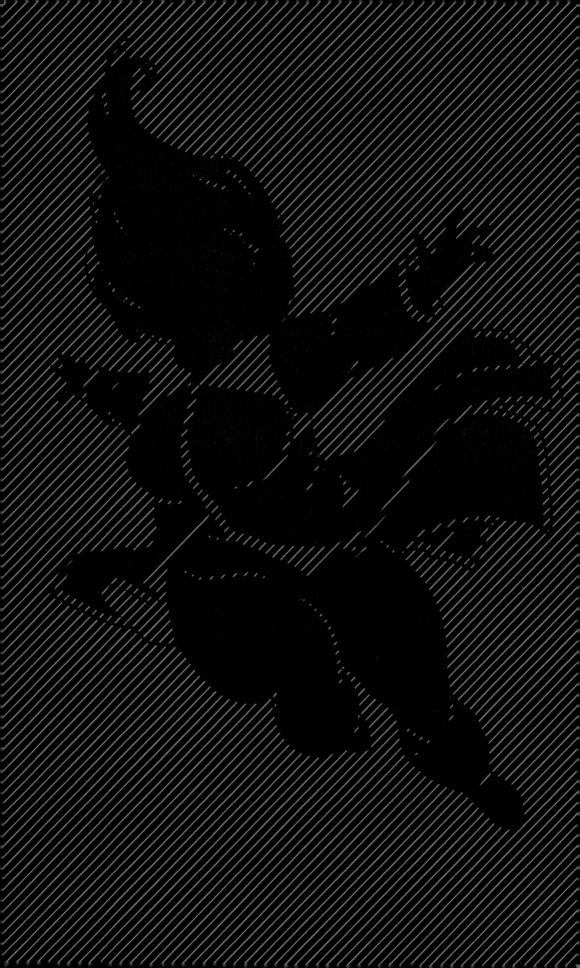

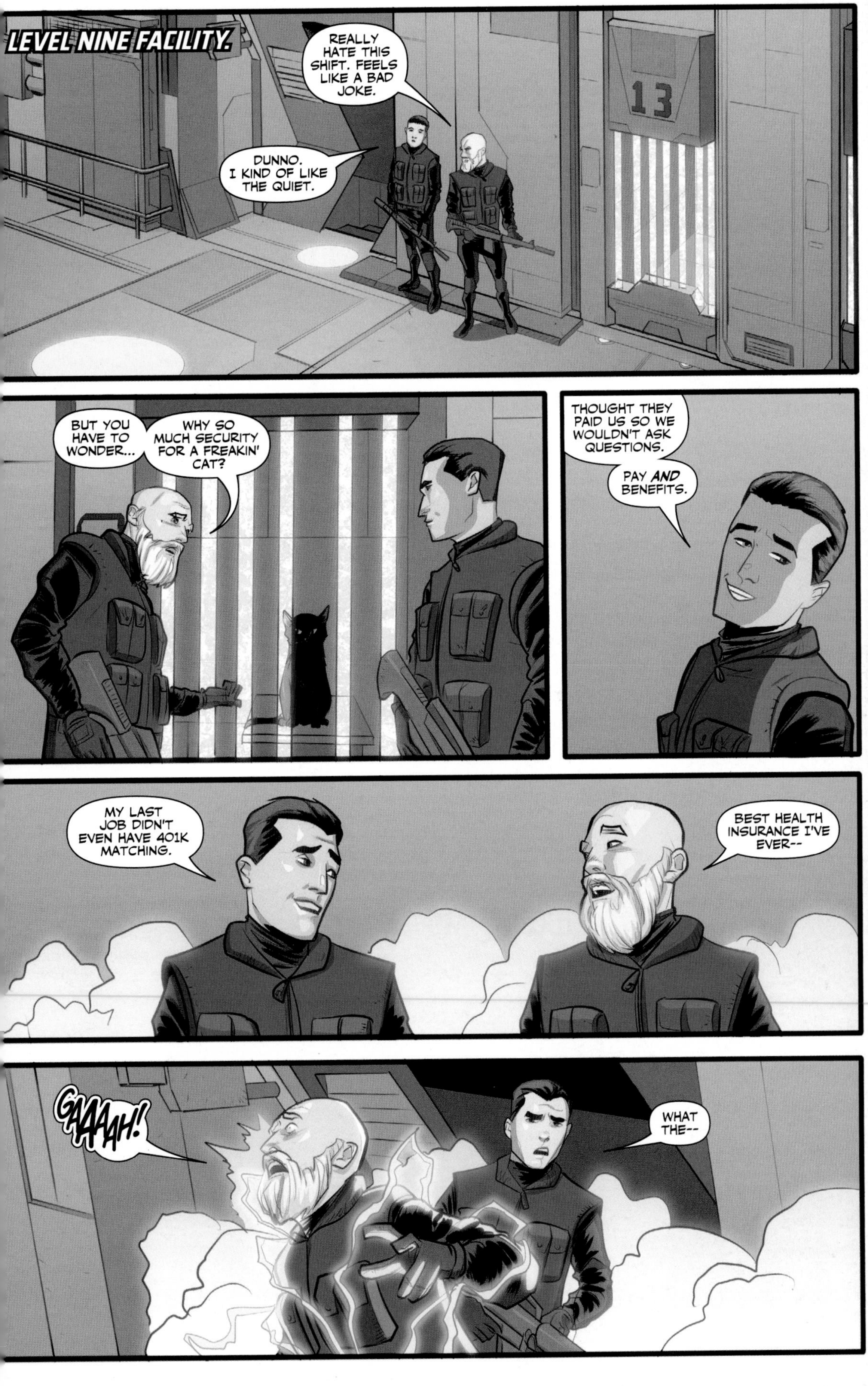

LEVEL NINE FACILITY.
REALLY HATE THIS SHIFT. FEELS LIKE A BAD JOKE.
DUNNO. I KIND OF LIKE THE QUIET.
13
BUT YOU HAVE TO WONDER...
WHY SO MUCH SECURITY FOR A FREAKIN' CAT?
THOUGHT THEY PAID US SO WE WOULDN'T ASK QUESTIONS.
PAY AND BENEFITS.
MY LAST JOB DIDN'T EVEN HAVE 401K MATCHING.
BEST HEALTH INSURANCE I'VE EVER--
GAAAAH!
WHAT THE--

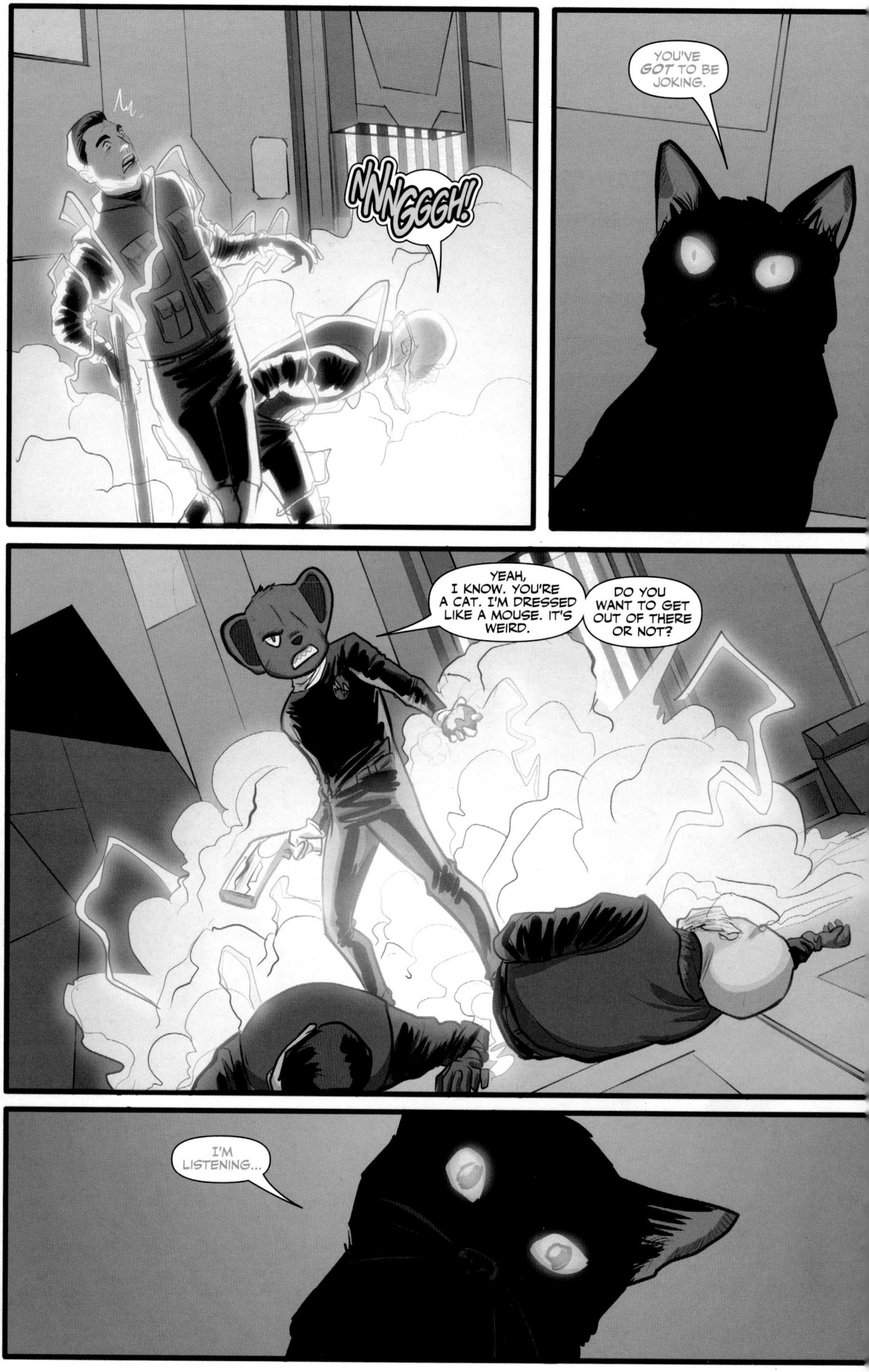
NNNGGGH!
YOU'VE GOT TO BE JOKING.
YEAH, I KNOW. YOU'RE A CAT. I'M DRESSED LIKE A MOUSE. IT'S WEIRD.
DO YOU WANT TO GET OUT OF THERE OR NOT?
I'M LISTENING...

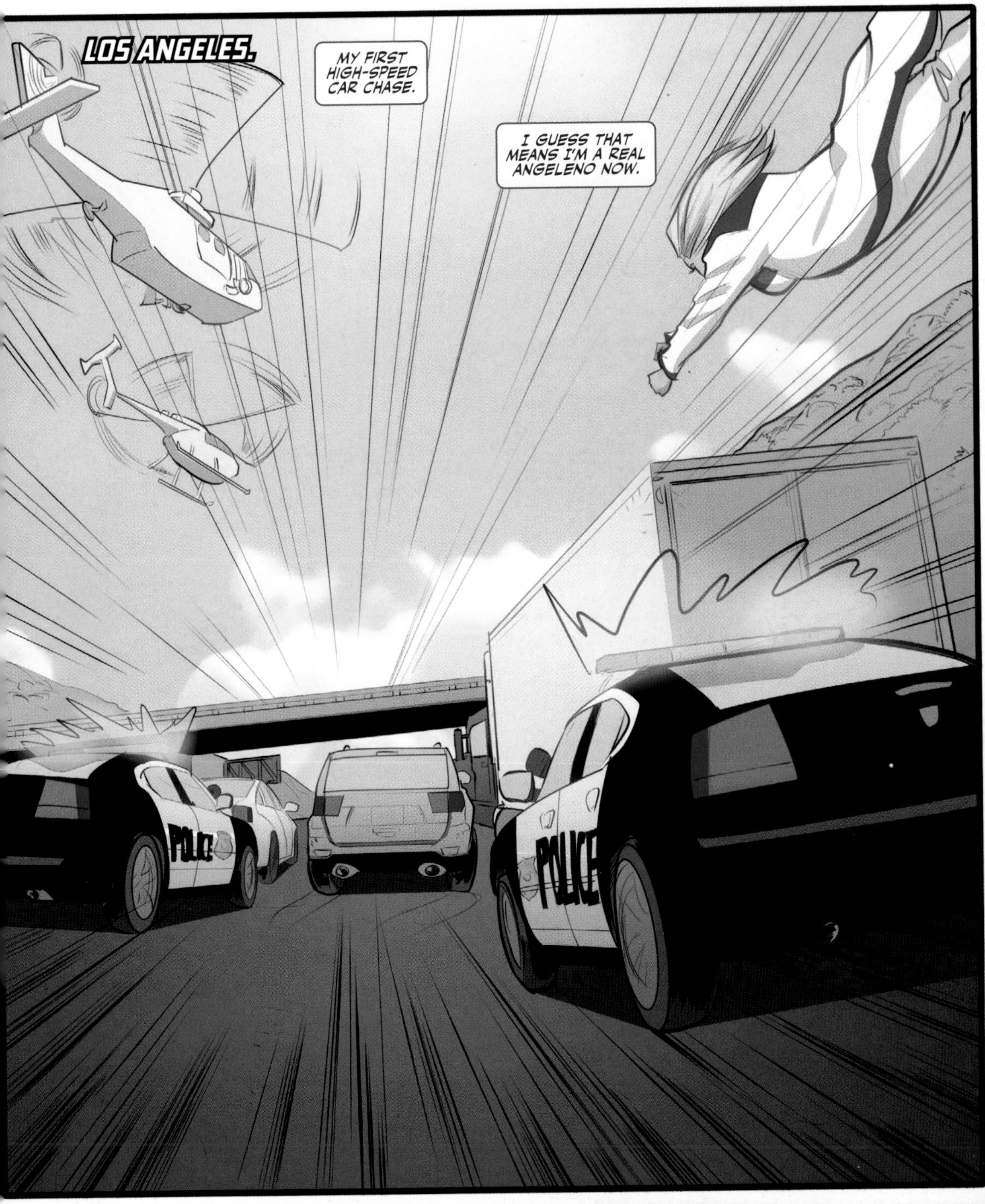
LOS ANGELES.
MY FIRST HIGH-SPEED CAR CHASE.
I GUESS THAT MEANS I'M A REAL ANGELENO NOW.
POLICE
POLICE

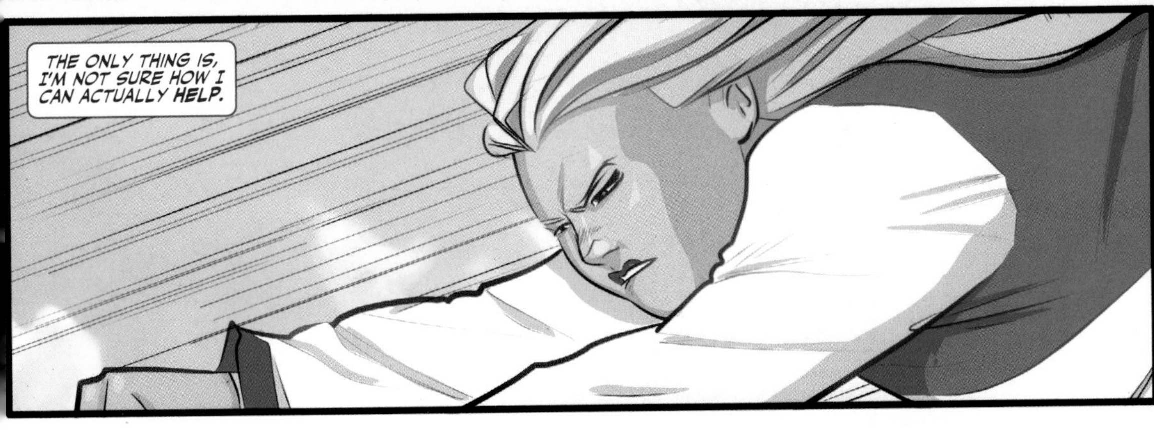
THE ONLY THING IS, I'M NOT SURE HOW I CAN ACTUALLY HELP.

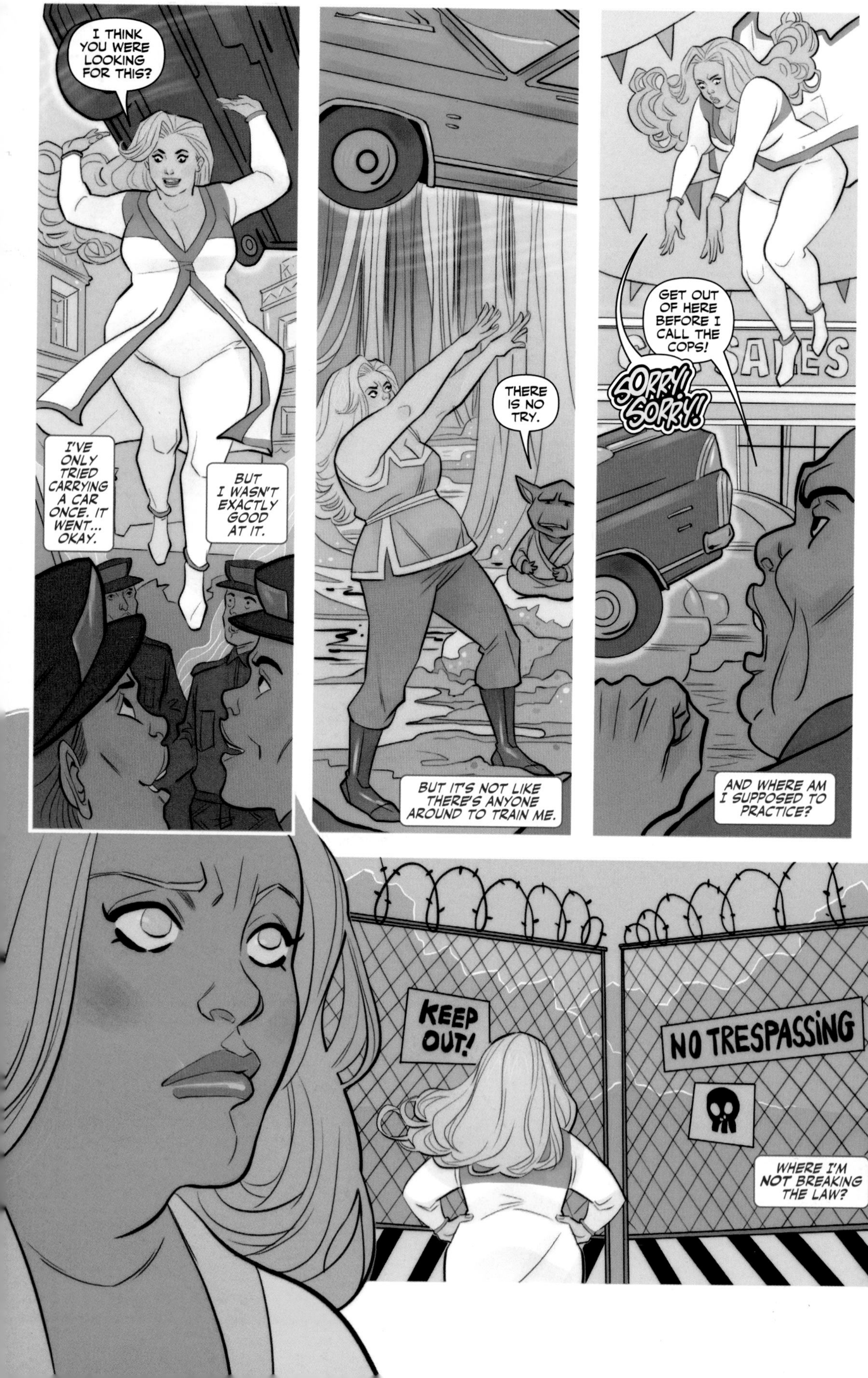
I THINK YOU WERE LOOKING FOR THIS?
I'VE ONLY TRIED CARRYING A CAR ONCE. IT WENT... OKAY.
BUT I WASN'T EXACTLY GOOD AT IT.
THERE IS NO TRY.
BUT IT'S NOT LIKE THERE'S ANYONE AROUND TO TRAIN ME.
GET OUT OF HERE BEFORE I CALL THE COPS!
SORRY! SORRY!
AND WHERE AM I SUPPOSED TO PRACTICE?
KEEP OUT!
NO TRESPASSING
WHERE I'M NOT BREAKING THE LAW?

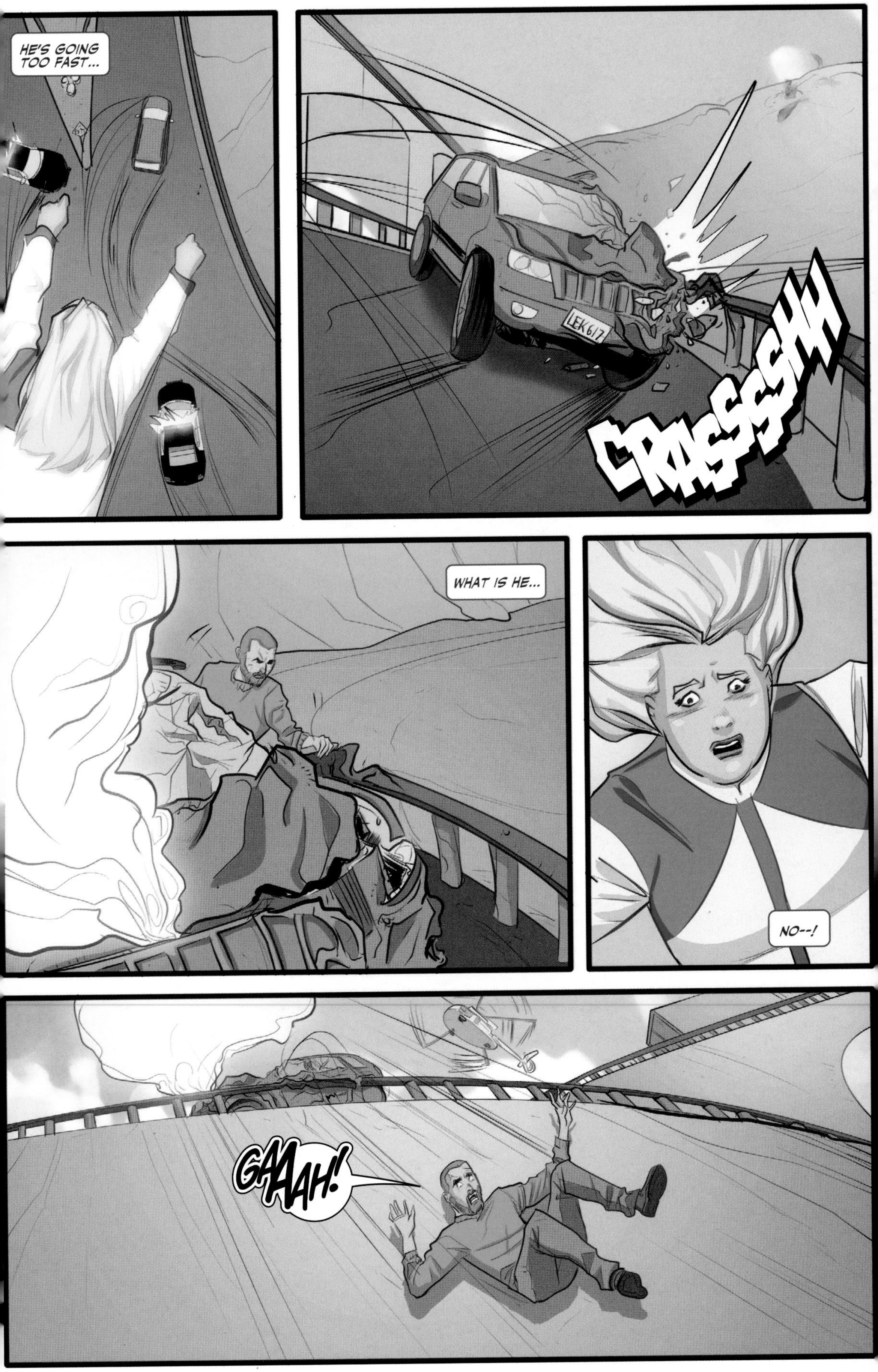
HE'S GOING TOO FAST...
LEK 617
CRASSSHH
WHAT IS HE...
NO--!
GAAAH!

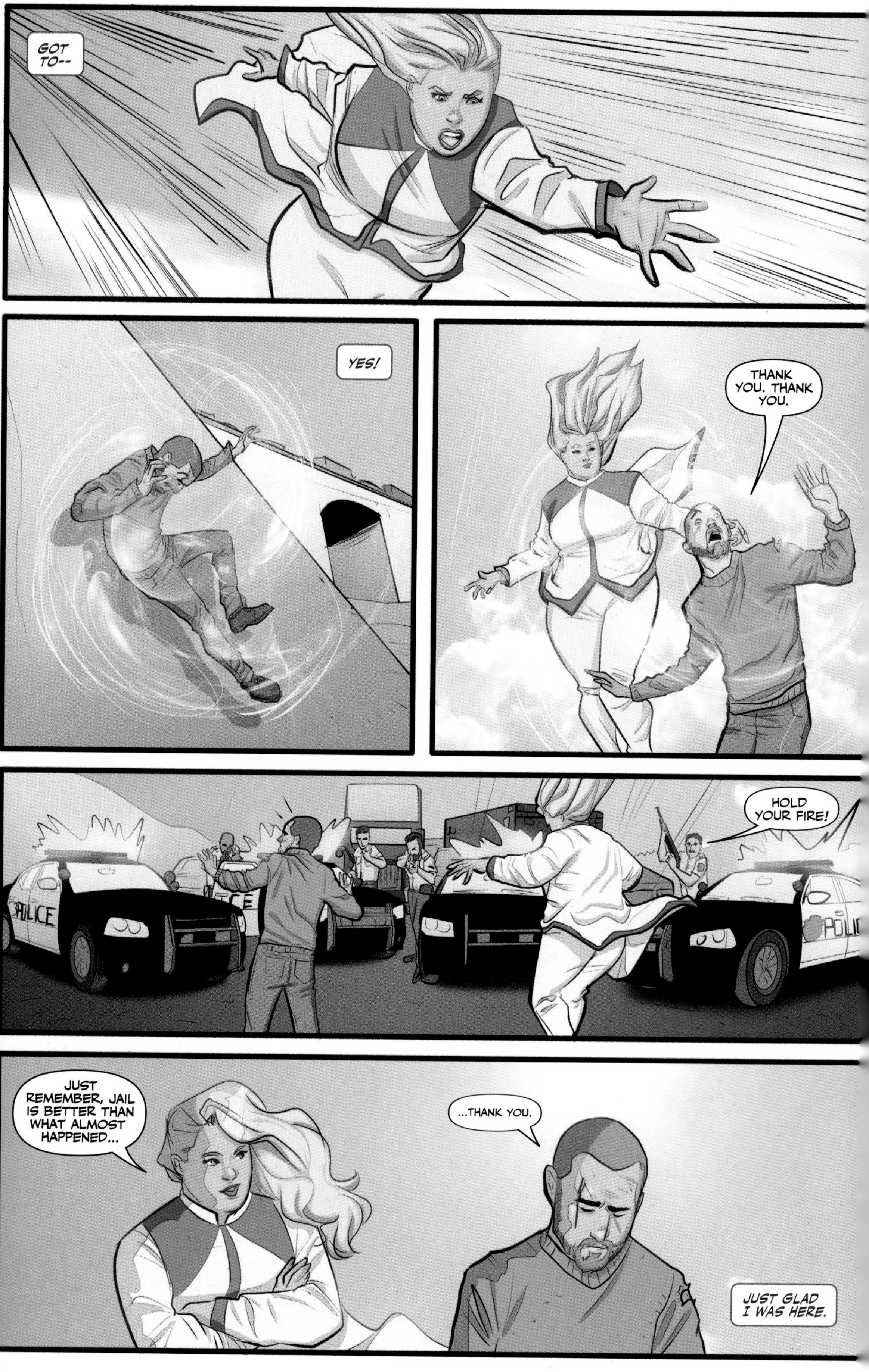
GOT TO--
YES!
THANK YOU. THANK YOU.
HOLD YOUR FIRE!
JUST REMEMBER, JAIL IS BETTER THAN WHAT ALMOST HAPPENED...
...THANK YOU.
JUST GLAD I WAS HERE.

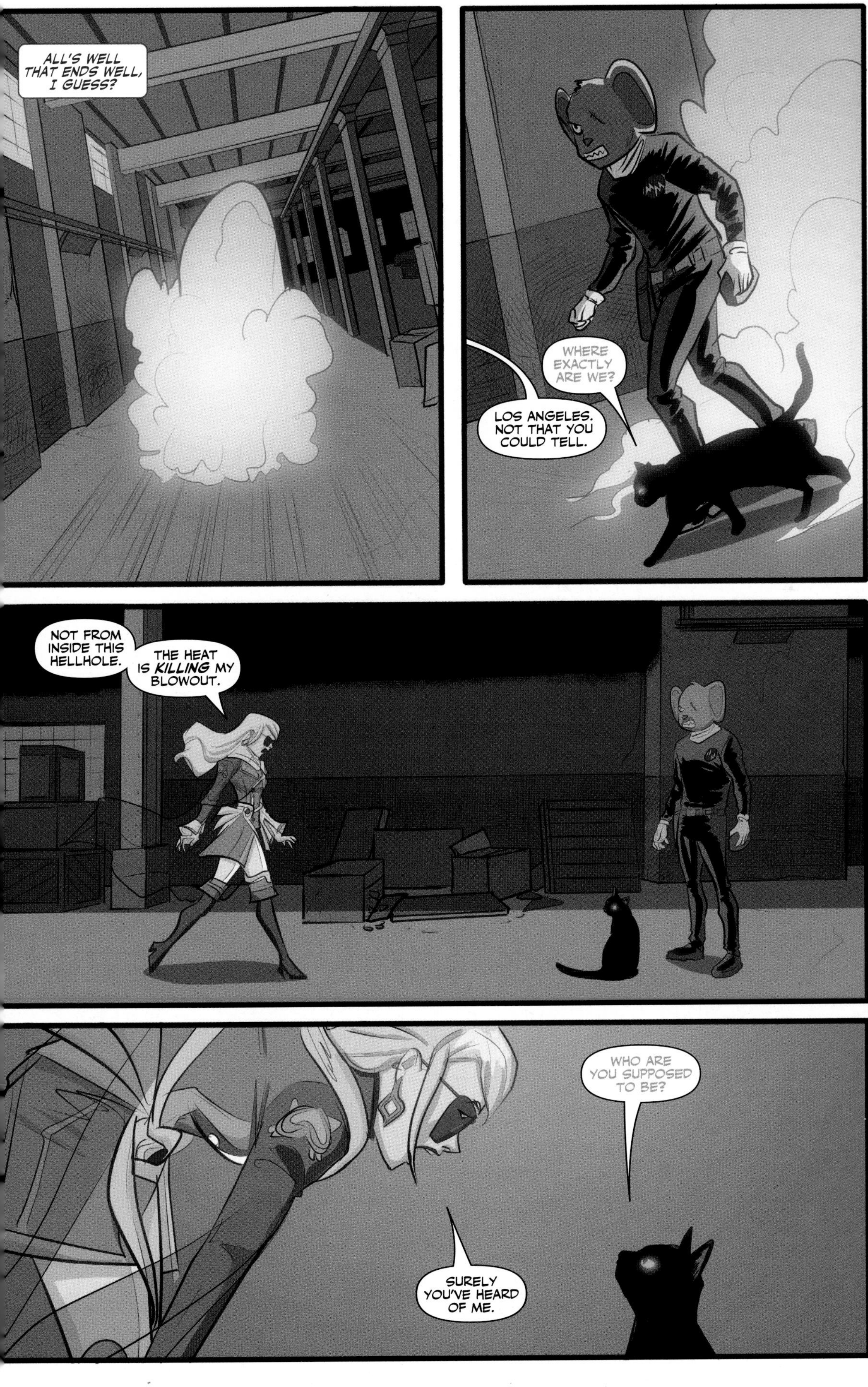
ALL'S WELL THAT ENDS WELL, I GUESS?
WHERE EXACTLY ARE WE?
LOS ANGELES. NOT THAT YOU COULD TELL.
NOT FROM INSIDE THIS HELLHOLE.
THE HEAT IS KILLING MY BLOWOUT.
WHO ARE YOU SUPPOSED TO BE?
SURELY YOU'VE HEARD OF ME.

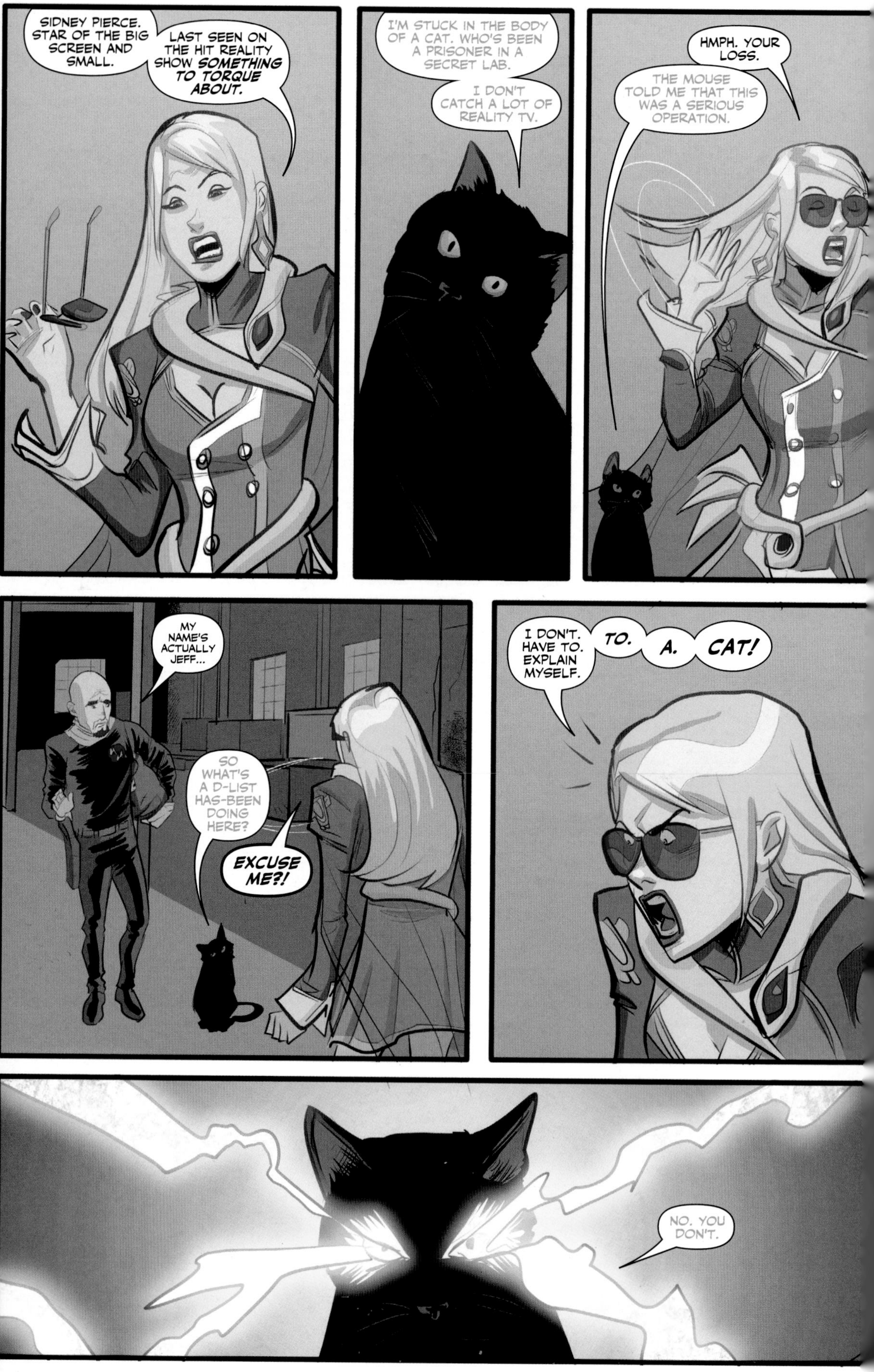
SIDNEY PIERCE. STAR OF THE BIG SCREEN AND SMALL.
LAST SEEN ON THE HIT REALITY SHOW *SOMETHING TO TORQUE ABOUT.*
I'M STUCK IN THE BODY OF A CAT. WHO'S BEEN A PRISONER IN A SECRET LAB.
I DON'T CATCH A LOT OF REALITY TV.
HMPH. YOUR LOSS.
THE MOUSE TOLD ME THAT THIS WAS A SERIOUS OPERATION.
MY NAME'S ACTUALLY JEFF...
SO WHAT'S A D-LIST HAS-BEEN DOING HERE?
EXCUSE ME?!
I DON'T. HAVE TO. EXPLAIN MYSELF.
TO.
A.
CAT!
NO. YOU DON'T.

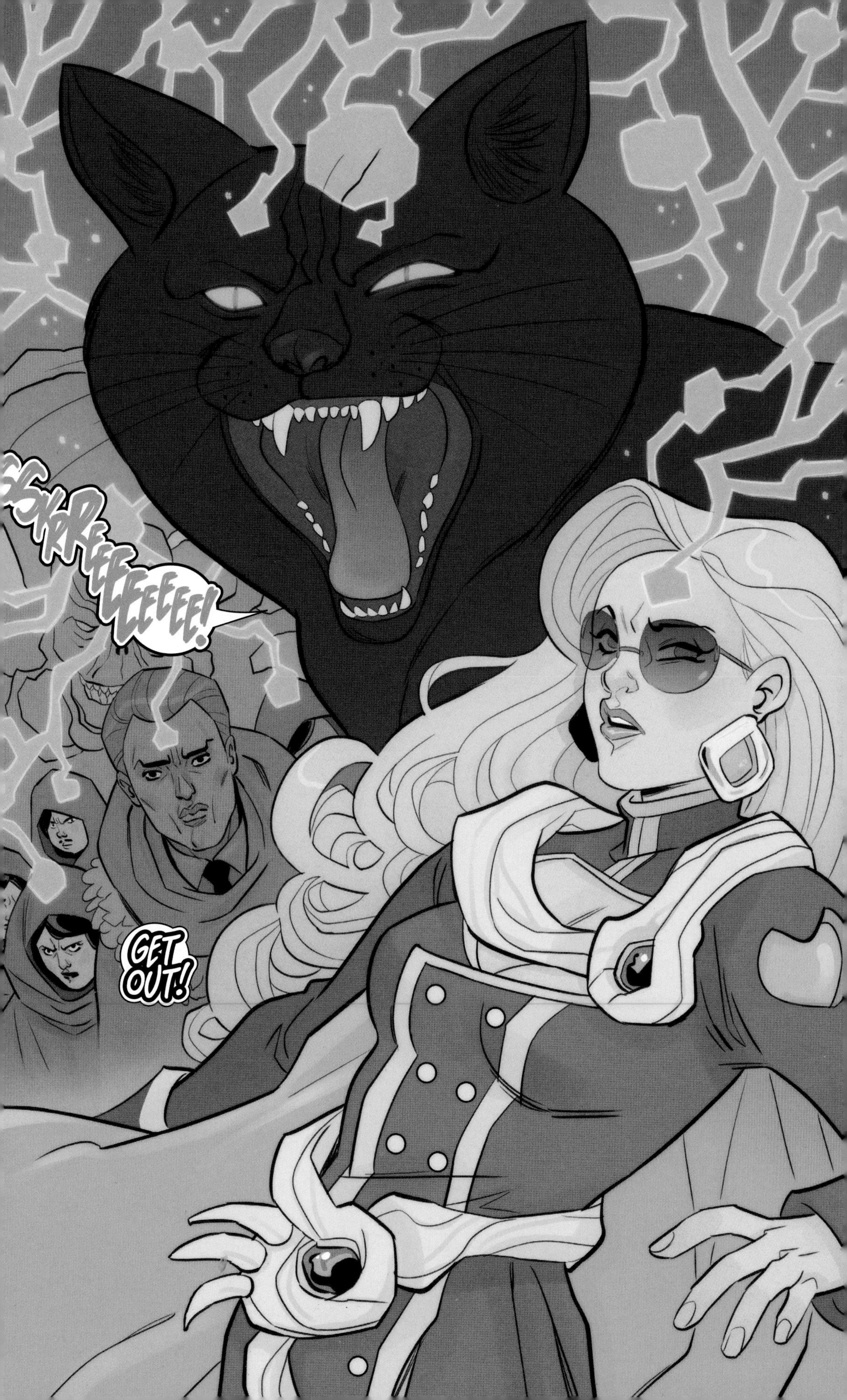
SKREEEEEEEEE!
GET OUT!

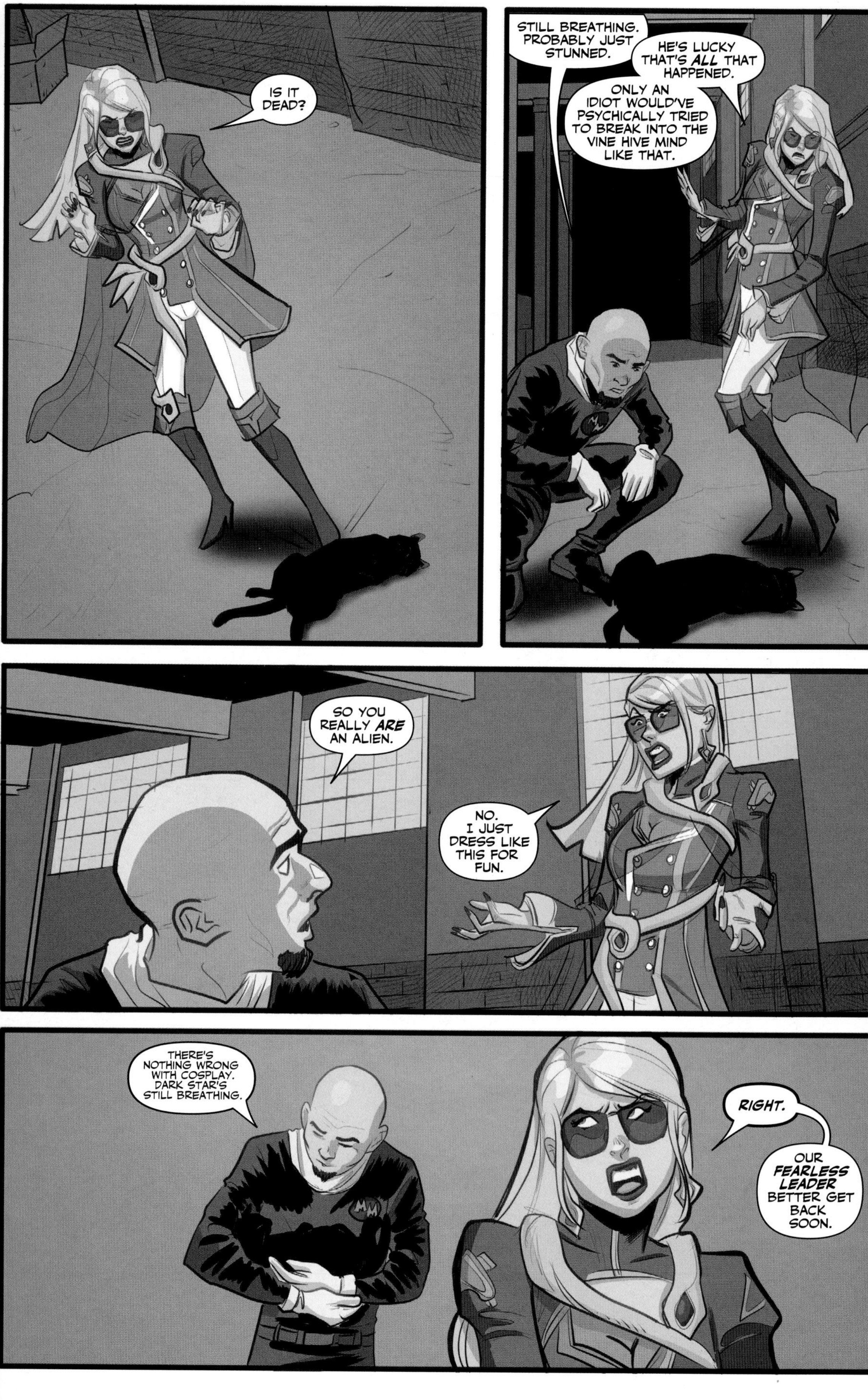
IS IT DEAD?
STILL BREATHING. PROBABLY JUST STUNNED.
HE'S LUCKY THAT'S ALL THAT HAPPENED.
ONLY AN IDIOT WOULD'VE PSYCHICALLY TRIED TO BREAK INTO THE VINE HIVE MIND LIKE THAT.
SO YOU REALLY ARE AN ALIEN.
NO. I JUST DRESS LIKE THIS FOR FUN.
THERE'S NOTHING WRONG WITH COSPLAY. DARK STAR'S STILL BREATHING.
RIGHT.
OUR FEARLESS LEADER BETTER GET BACK SOON.

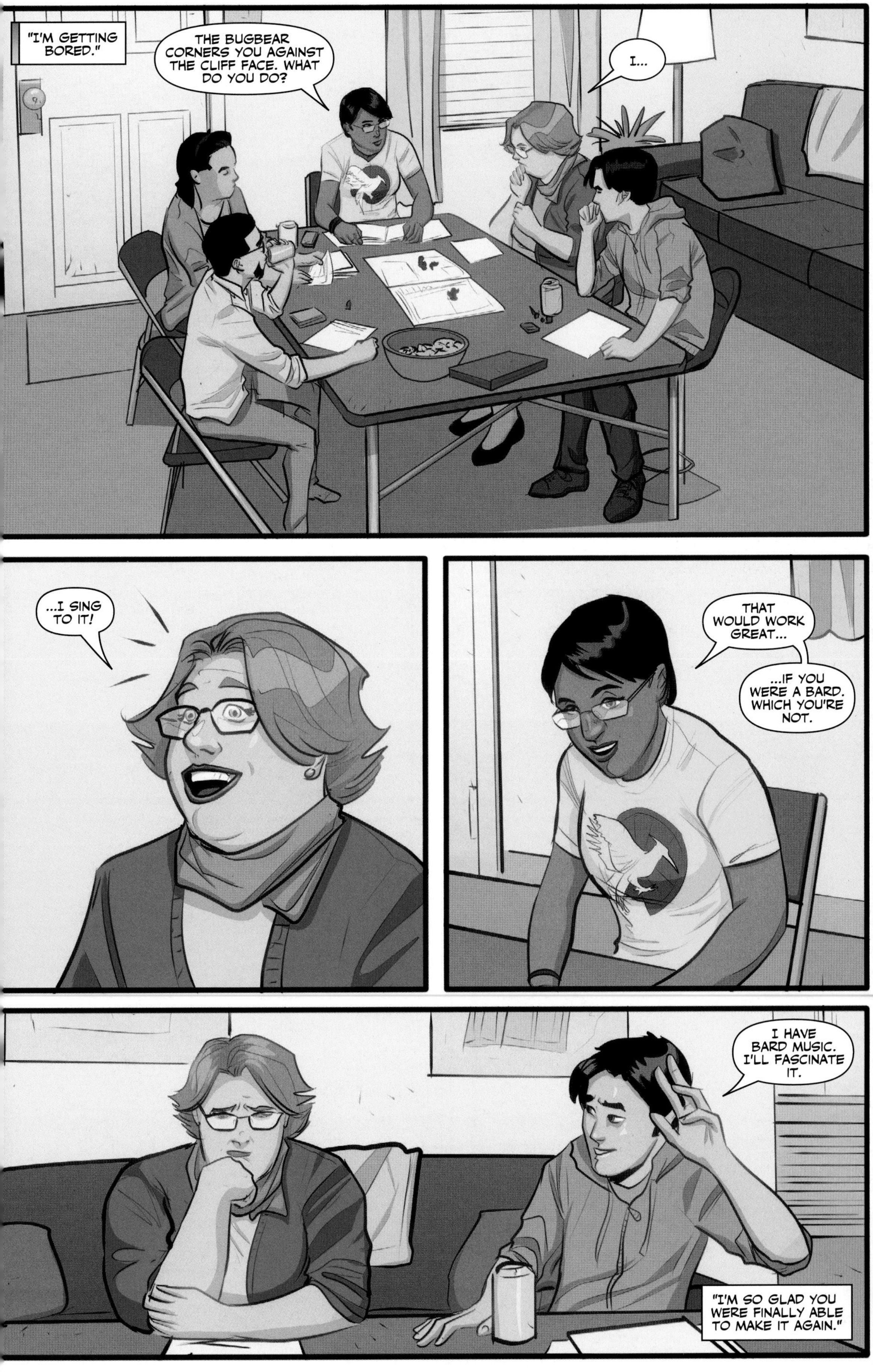
"I'M GETTING BORED."
THE BUGBEAR CORNERS YOU AGAINST THE CLIFF FACE. WHAT DO YOU DO?
I...
...I SING TO IT!
THAT WOULD WORK GREAT...
...IF YOU WERE A BARD. WHICH YOU'RE NOT.
I HAVE BARD MUSIC. I'LL FASCINATE IT.
"I'M SO GLAD YOU WERE FINALLY ABLE TO MAKE IT AGAIN."

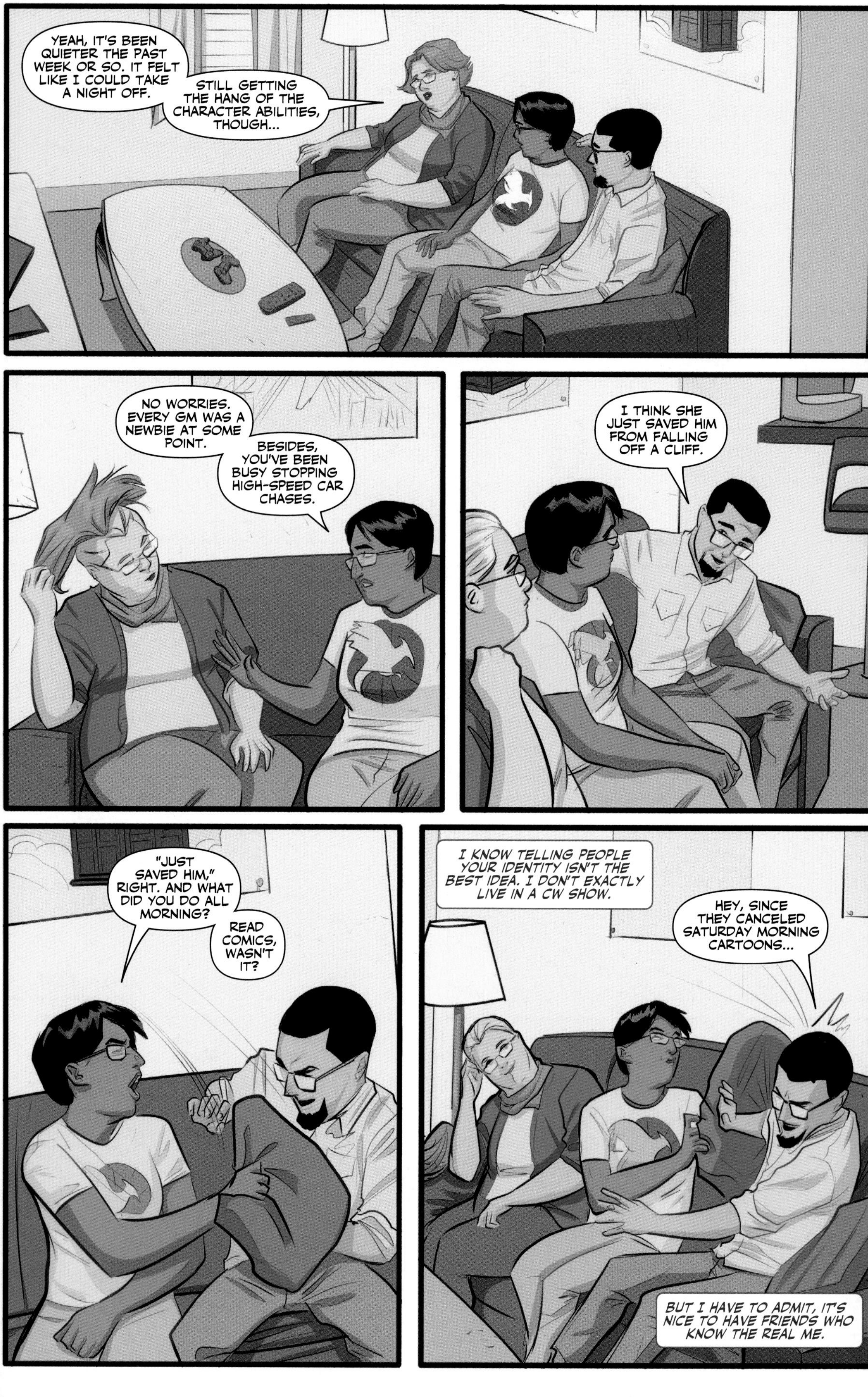
YEAH, IT'S BEEN QUIETER THE PAST WEEK OR SO. IT FELT LIKE I COULD TAKE A NIGHT OFF.
STILL GETTING THE HANG OF THE CHARACTER ABILITIES, THOUGH...
NO WORRIES. EVERY GM WAS A NEWBIE AT SOME POINT.
BESIDES, YOU'VE BEEN BUSY STOPPING HIGH-SPEED CAR CHASES.
I THINK SHE JUST SAVED HIM FROM FALLING OFF A CLIFF.
"JUST SAVED HIM," RIGHT. AND WHAT DID YOU DO ALL MORNING?
READ COMICS, WASN'T IT?
I KNOW TELLING PEOPLE YOUR IDENTITY ISN'T THE BEST IDEA. I DON'T EXACTLY LIVE IN A CW SHOW.
HEY, SINCE THEY CANCELED SATURDAY MORNING CARTOONS...
BUT I HAVE TO ADMIT, IT'S NICE TO HAVE FRIENDS WHO KNOW THE REAL ME.

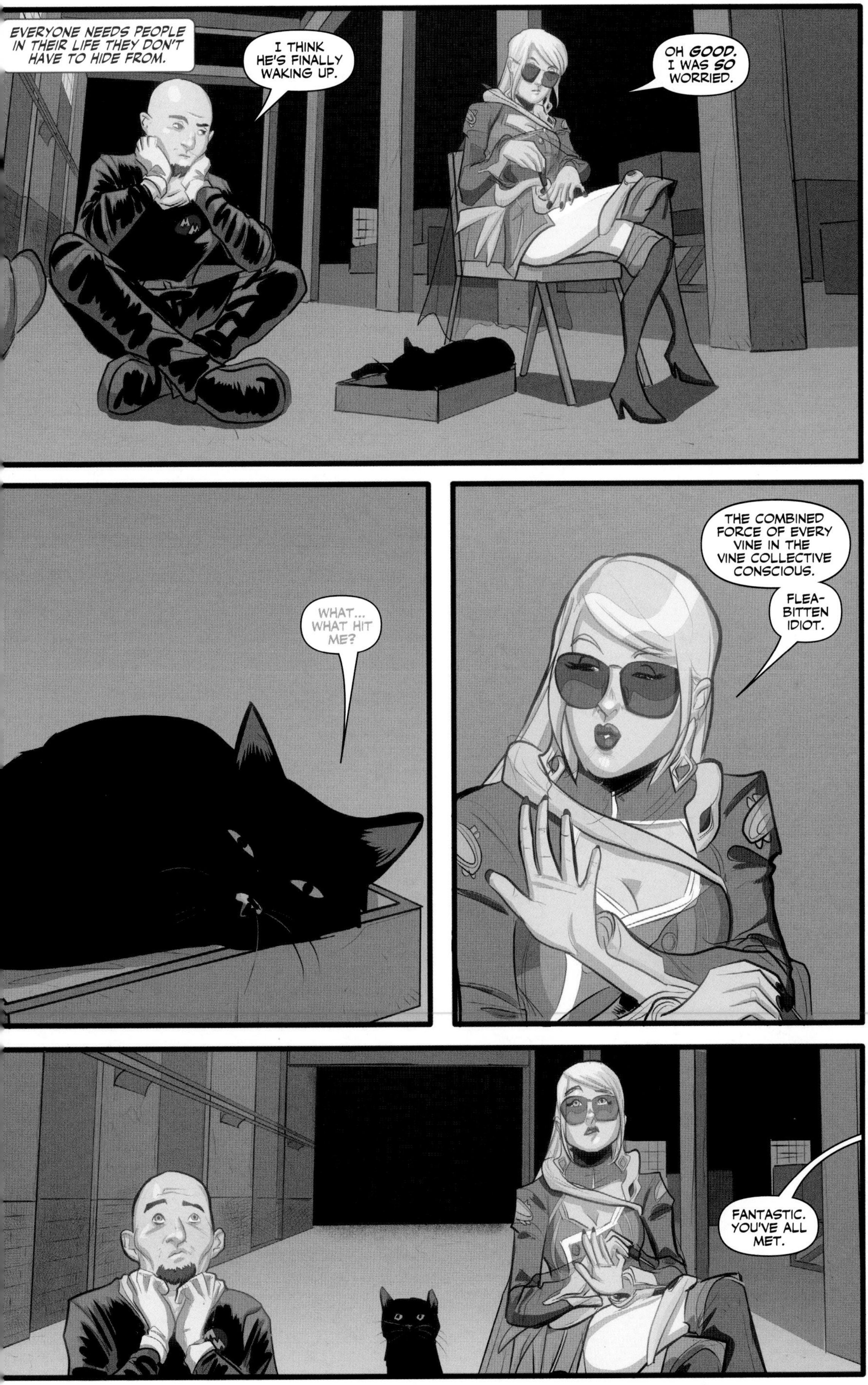
EVERYONE NEEDS PEOPLE IN THEIR LIFE THEY DON'T HAVE TO HIDE FROM.
I THINK HE'S FINALLY WAKING UP.
OH GOOD. I WAS SO WORRIED.
WHAT... WHAT HIT ME?
THE COMBINED FORCE OF EVERY VINE IN THE VINE COLLECTIVE CONSCIOUS.
FLEA-BITTEN IDIOT.
FANTASTIC. YOU'VE ALL MET.

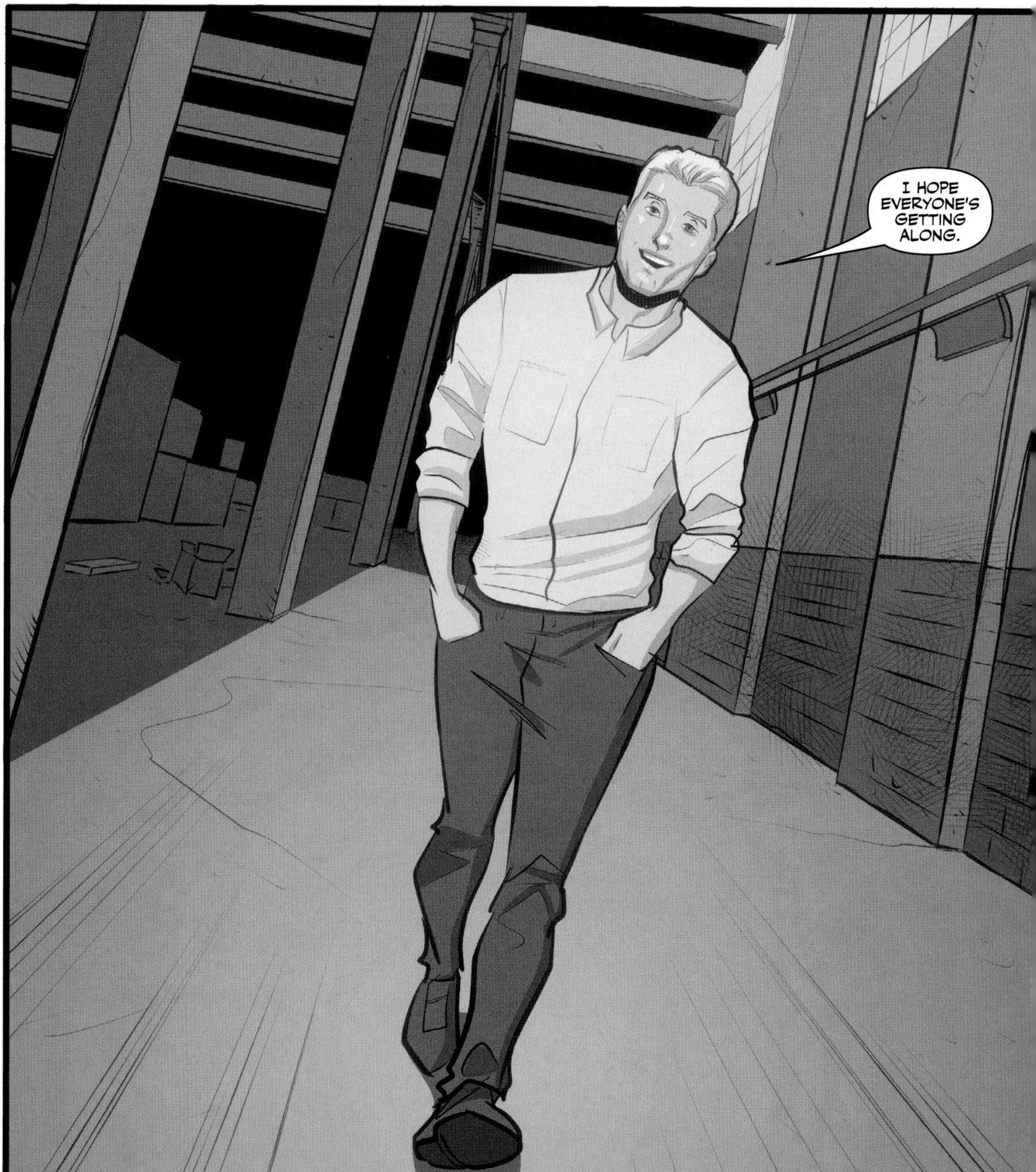
I HOPE EVERYONE'S GETTING ALONG.

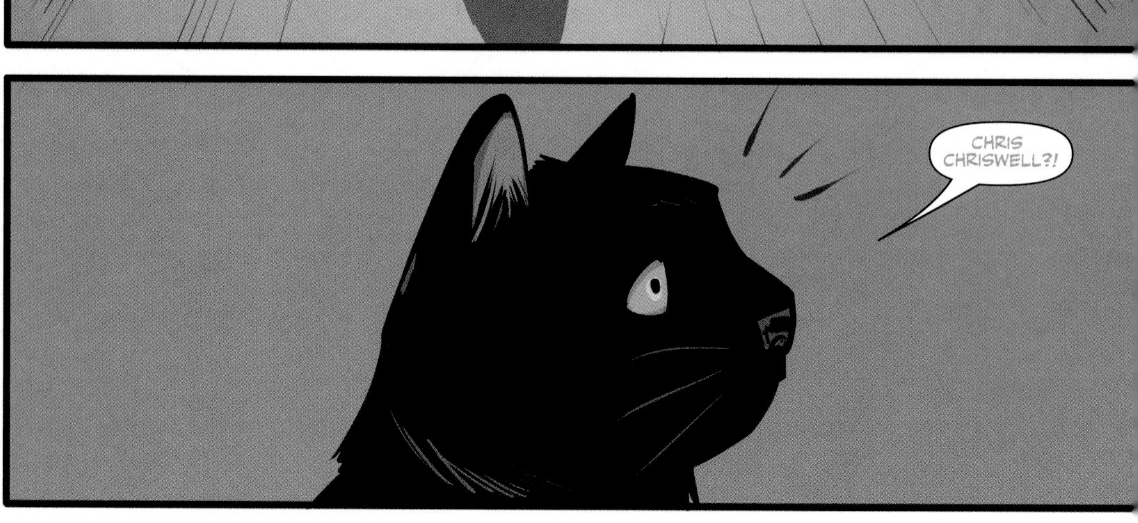
CHRIS CHRISWELL?!

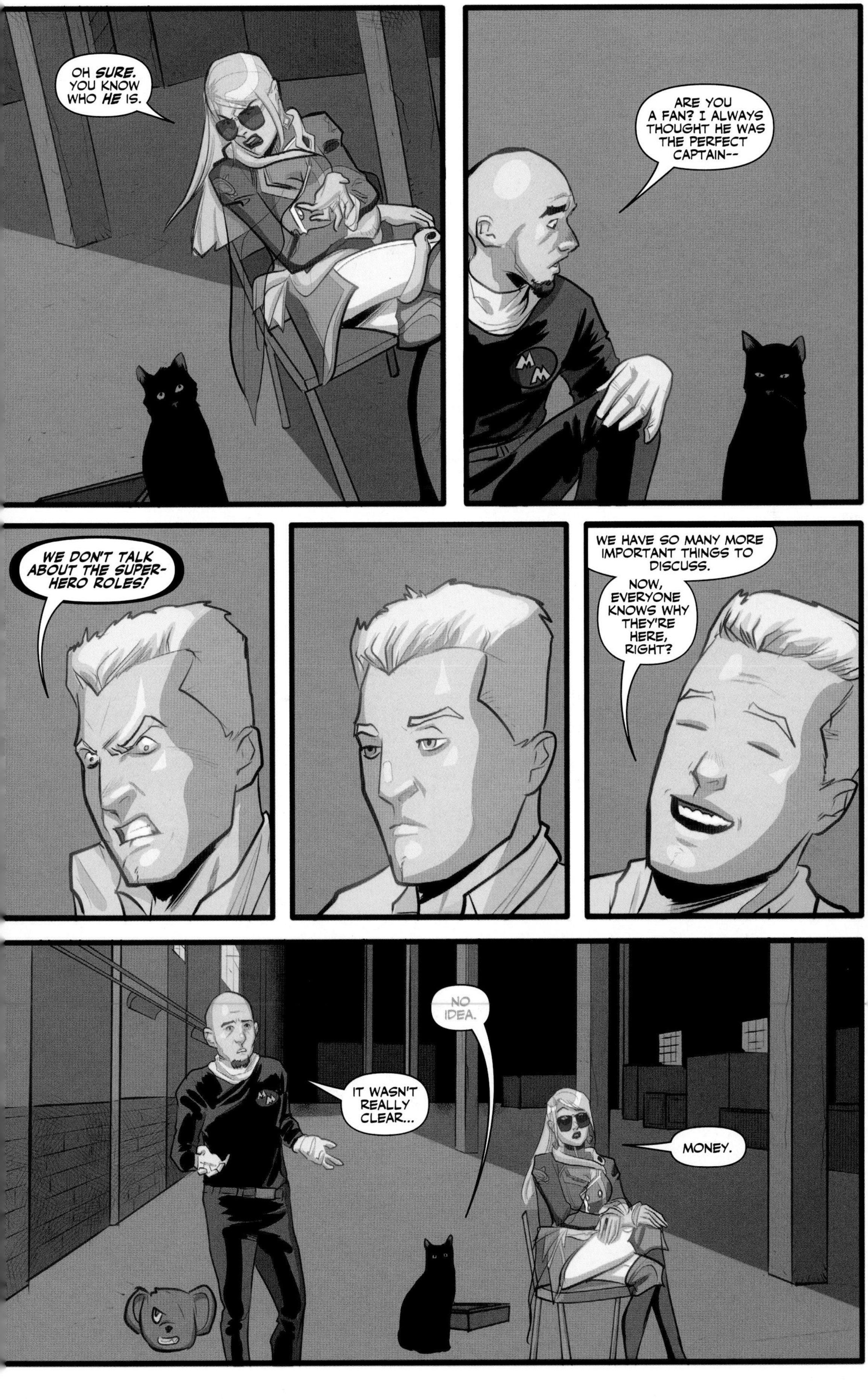
OH SURE. YOU KNOW WHO HE IS.
ARE YOU A FAN? I ALWAYS THOUGHT HE WAS THE PERFECT CAPTAIN--
WE DON'T TALK ABOUT THE SUPER-HERO ROLES!
WE HAVE SO MANY MORE IMPORTANT THINGS TO DISCUSS.
NOW, EVERYONE KNOWS WHY THEY'RE HERE, RIGHT?
NO IDEA.
IT WASN'T REALLY CLEAR...
MONEY.

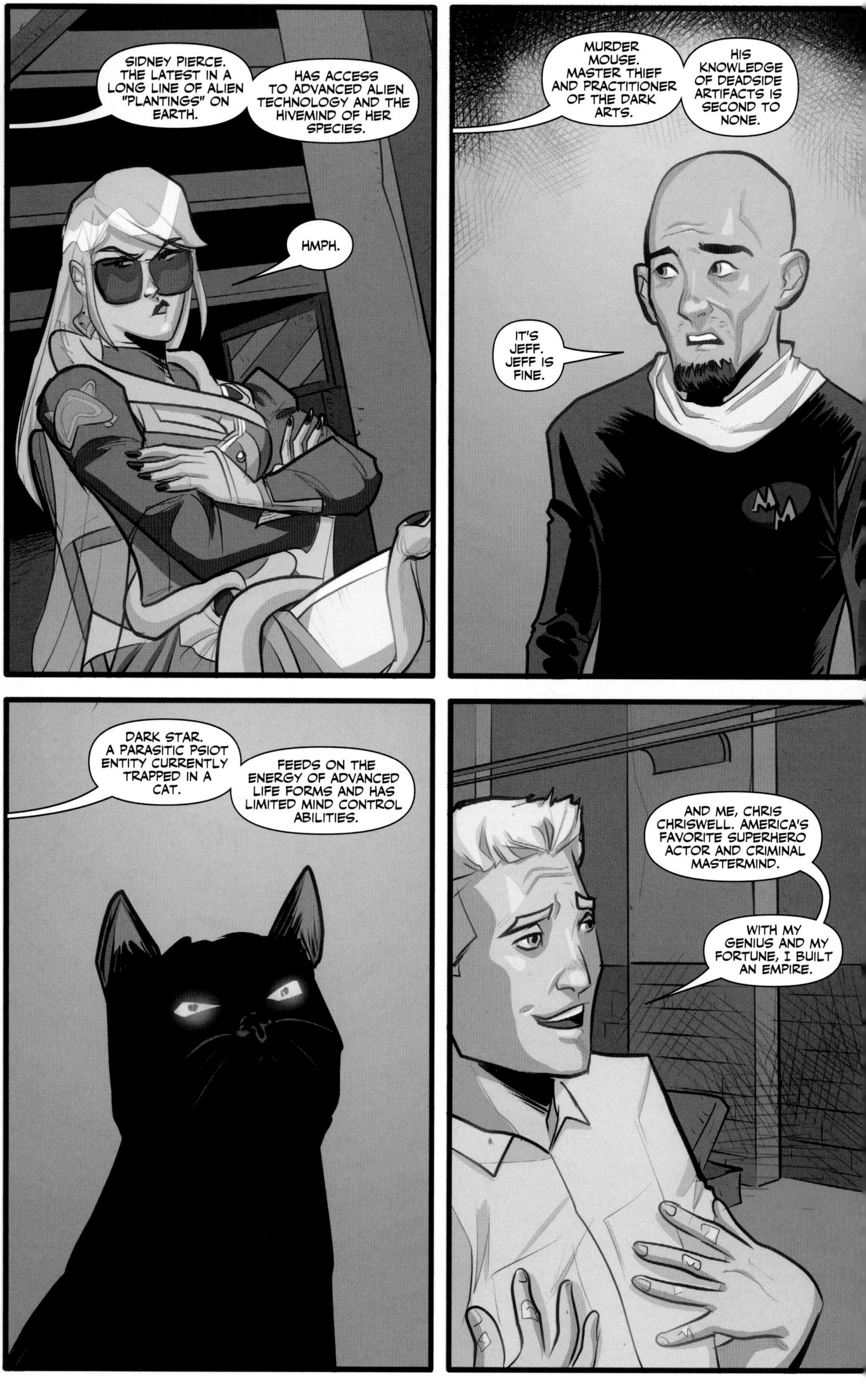
SIDNEY PIERCE. THE LATEST IN A LONG LINE OF ALIEN "PLANTINGS" ON EARTH.
HAS ACCESS TO ADVANCED ALIEN TECHNOLOGY AND THE HIVEMIND OF HER SPECIES.
HMPH.
MURDER MOUSE. MASTER THIEF AND PRACTITIONER OF THE DARK ARTS.
HIS KNOWLEDGE OF DEADSIDE ARTIFACTS IS SECOND TO NONE.
IT'S JEFF. JEFF IS FINE.
DARK STAR. A PARASITIC PSIOT ENTITY CURRENTLY TRAPPED IN A CAT.
FEEDS ON THE ENERGY OF ADVANCED LIFE FORMS AND HAS LIMITED MIND CONTROL ABILITIES.
AND ME, CHRIS CHRISWELL. AMERICA'S FAVORITE SUPERHERO ACTOR AND CRIMINAL MASTERMIND.
WITH MY GENIUS AND MY FORTUNE, I BUILT AN EMPIRE.

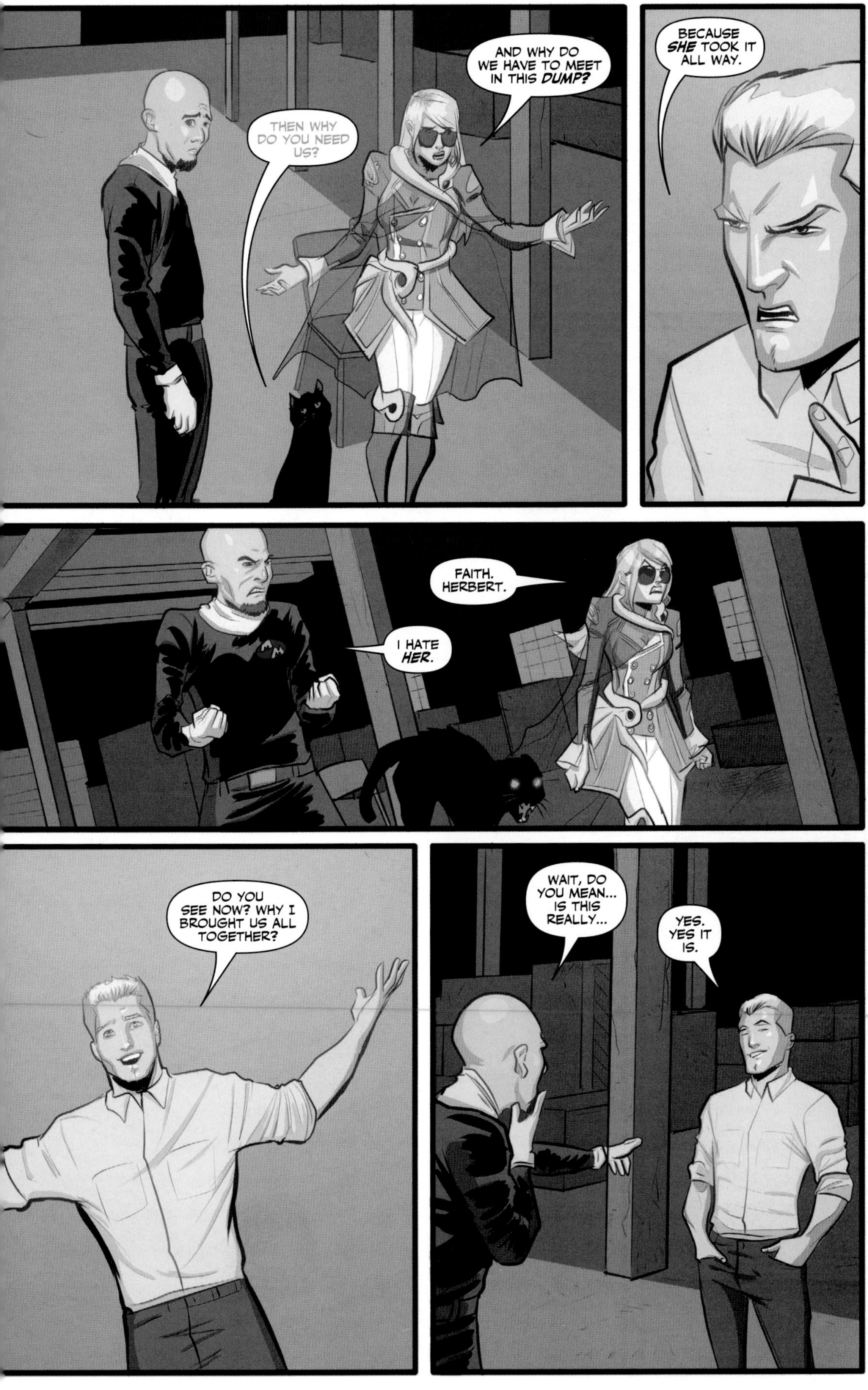
THEN WHY DO YOU NEED US?
AND WHY DO WE HAVE TO MEET IN THIS DUMP?
BECAUSE SHE TOOK IT ALL WAY.
FAITH. HERBERT.
I HATE HER.
DO YOU SEE NOW? WHY I BROUGHT US ALL TOGETHER?
WAIT, DO YOU MEAN... IS THIS REALLY...
YES. YES IT IS.

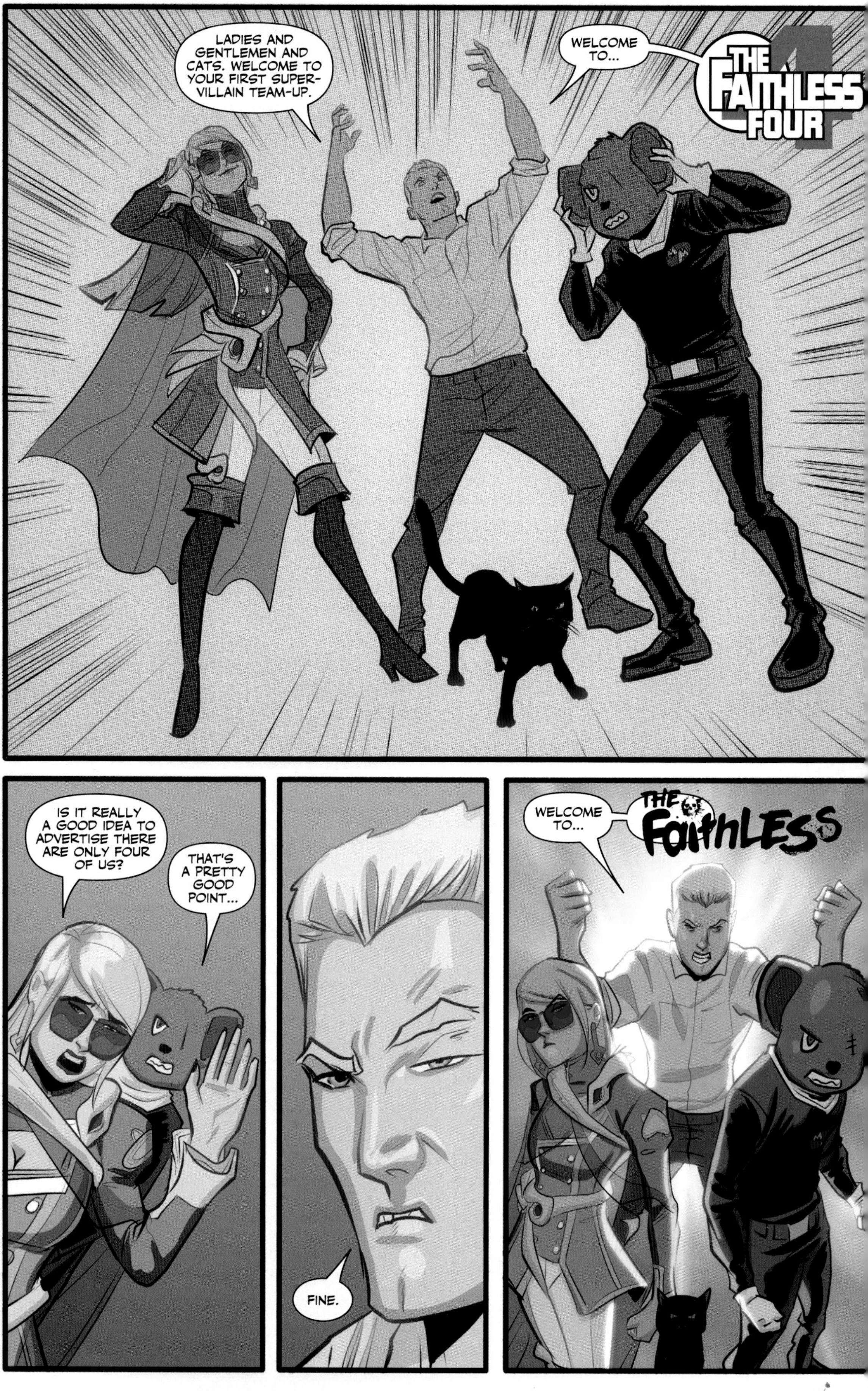
LADIES AND GENTLEMEN AND CATS. WELCOME TO YOUR FIRST SUPER-VILLAIN TEAM-UP.
WELCOME TO...
THE FAITHLESS FOUR
IS IT REALLY A GOOD IDEA TO ADVERTISE THERE ARE ONLY FOUR OF US?
THAT'S A PRETTY GOOD POINT...
FINE.
WELCOME TO...
THE Faithless

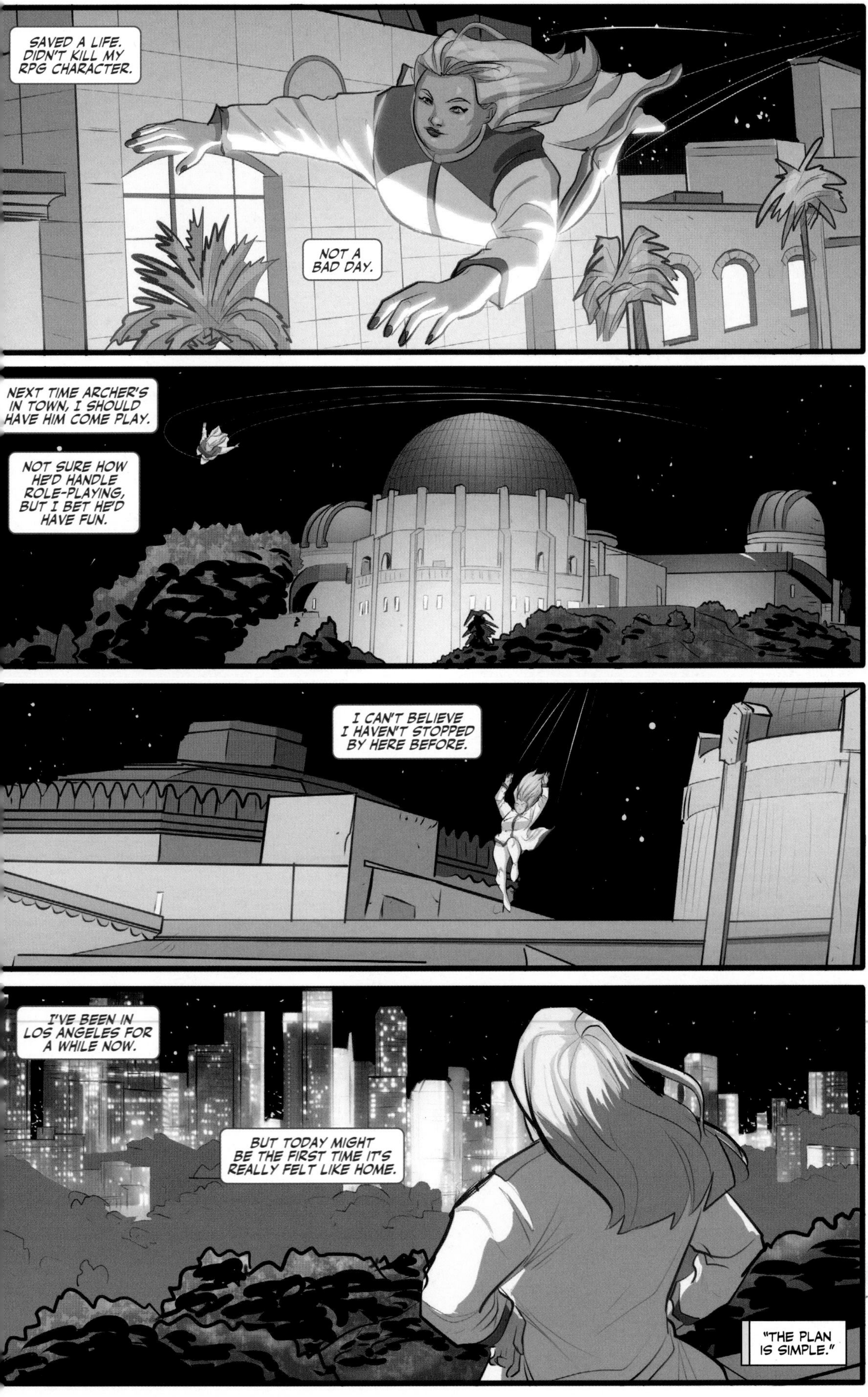
SAVED A LIFE. DIDN'T KILL MY RPG CHARACTER.
NOT A BAD DAY.
NEXT TIME ARCHER'S IN TOWN, I SHOULD HAVE HIM COME PLAY.
NOT SURE HOW HE'D HANDLE ROLE-PLAYING, BUT I BET HE'D HAVE FUN.
I CAN'T BELIEVE I HAVEN'T STOPPED BY HERE BEFORE.
I'VE BEEN IN LOS ANGELES FOR A WHILE NOW.
BUT TODAY MIGHT BE THE FIRST TIME IT'S REALLY FELT LIKE HOME.
"THE PLAN IS SIMPLE."

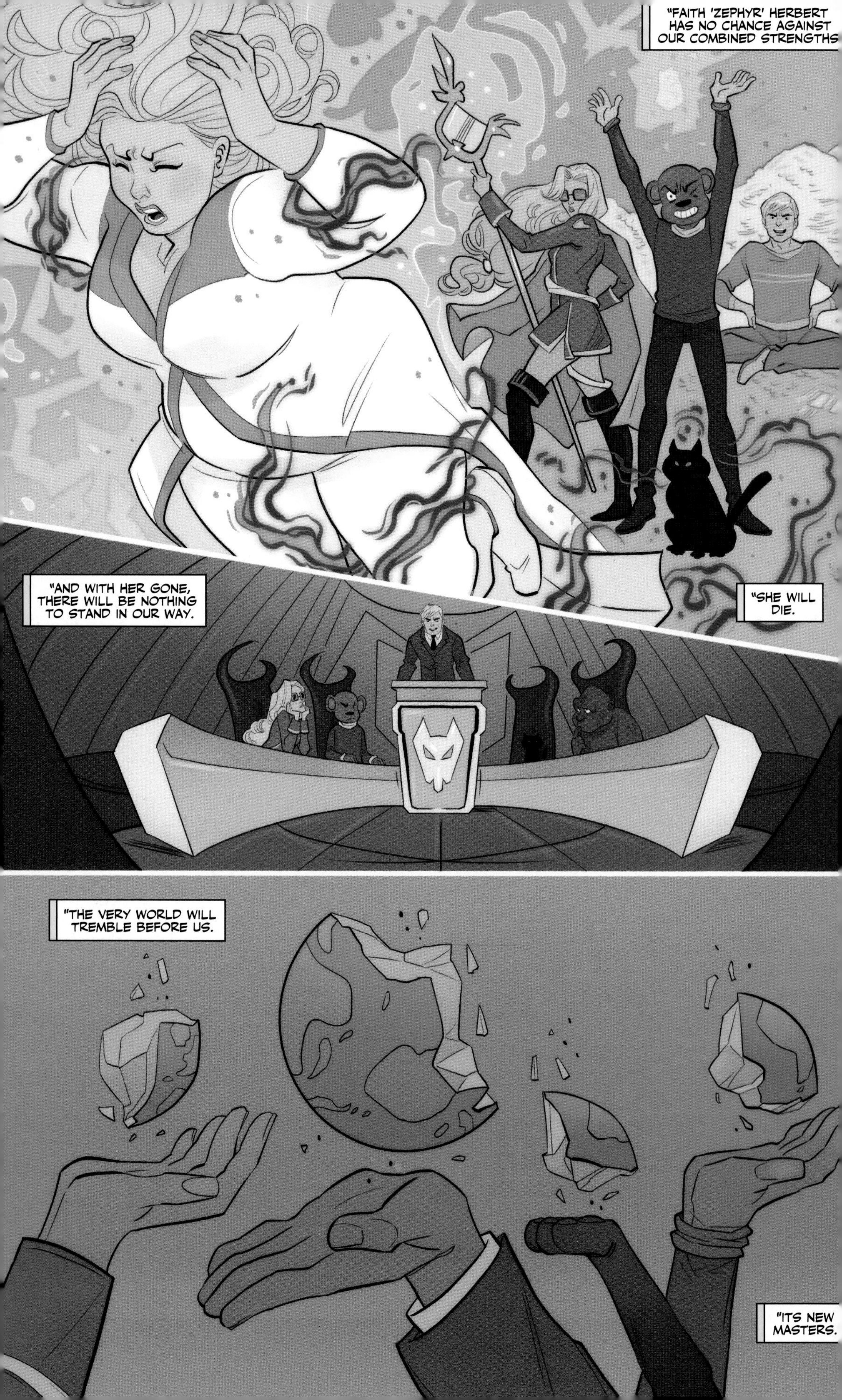
"FAITH 'ZEPHYR' HERBERT HAS NO CHANCE AGAINST OUR COMBINED STRENGTHS
"SHE WILL DIE.
"AND WITH HER GONE, THERE WILL BE NOTHING TO STAND IN OUR WAY.
"THE VERY WORLD WILL TREMBLE BEFORE US.
"ITS NEW MASTERS.

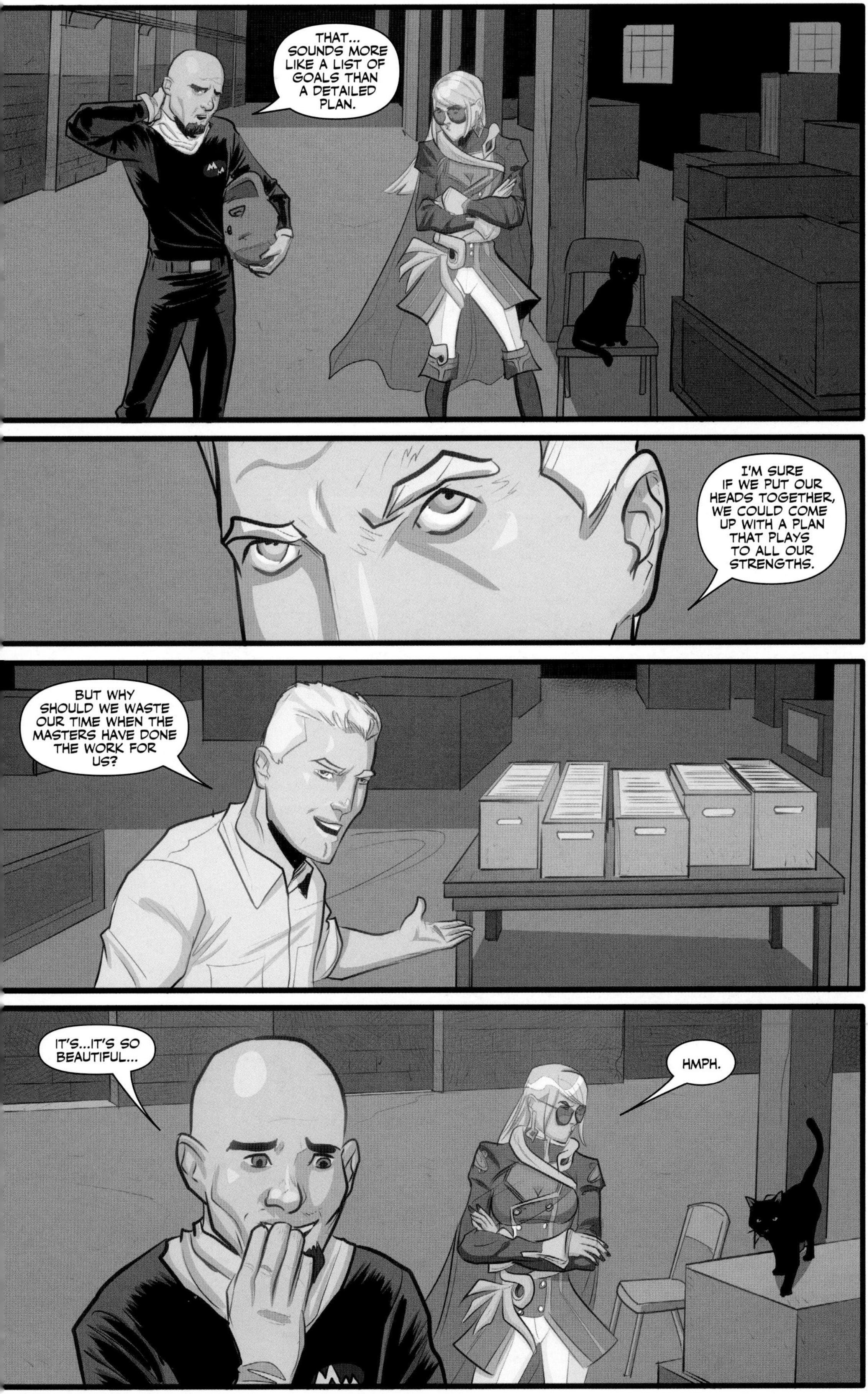
THAT... SOUNDS MORE LIKE A LIST OF GOALS THAN A DETAILED PLAN.
I'M SURE IF WE PUT OUR HEADS TOGETHER, WE COULD COME UP WITH A PLAN THAT PLAYS TO ALL OUR STRENGTHS.
BUT WHY SHOULD WE WASTE OUR TIME WHEN THE MASTERS HAVE DONE THE WORK FOR US?
IT'S...IT'S SO BEAUTIFUL...
HMPH.

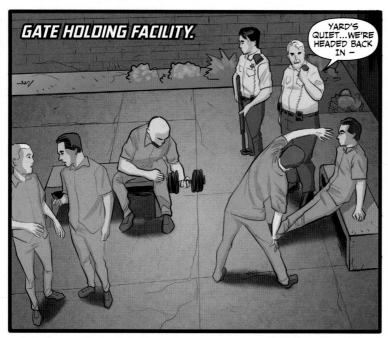

GATE HOLDING FACILITY.

YARD'S QUIET...WE'RE HEADED BACK IN —

GAAAAAH!

NOOOOO!

WHERE DID YOU SEND THEM?

SID... SIDNEY?!

TAHITI. GIVE OR TAKE FIFTY MILES.

HELLO, DIRECTOR. FANCY SEEING YOU HERE.

UP FOR A LITTLE REVENGE?

VALIANT
MARGUERITE SAUVAGE | ANDREW DALHOUSE
Faith
HE
FaithLESS

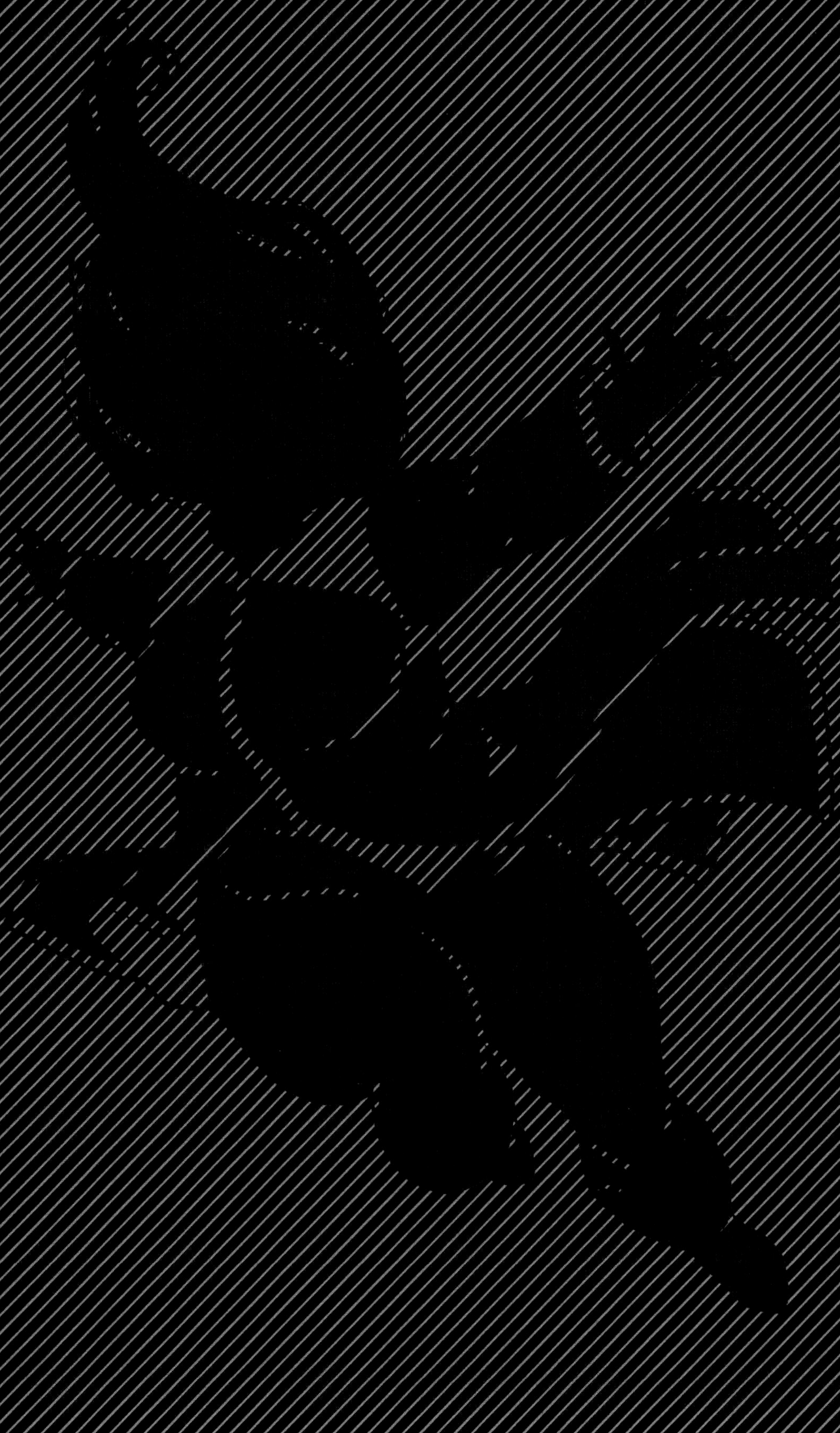

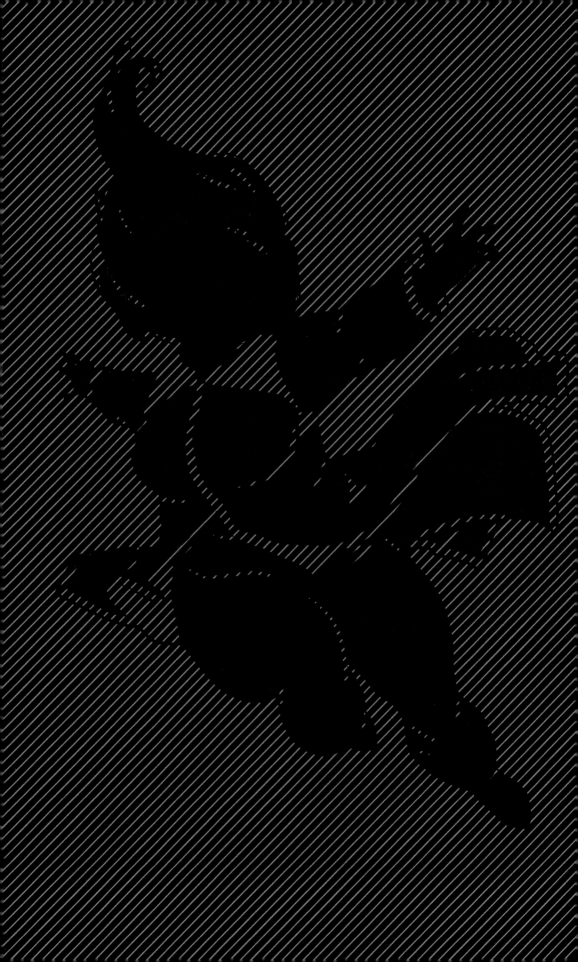

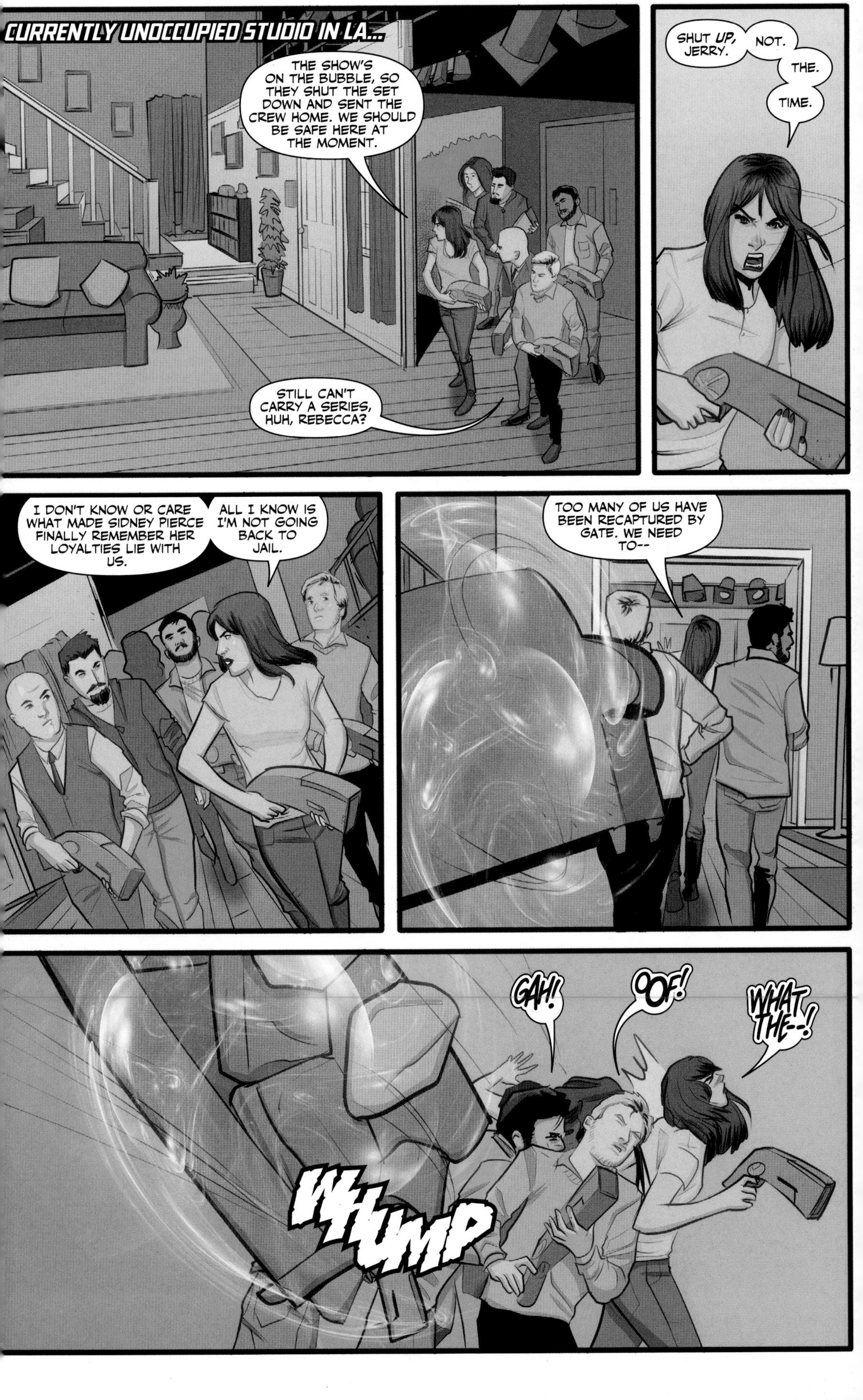
CURRENTLY UNOCCUPIED STUDIO IN LA...
THE SHOW'S ON THE BUBBLE, SO THEY SHUT THE SET DOWN AND SENT THE CREW HOME. WE SHOULD BE SAFE HERE AT THE MOMENT.
STILL CAN'T CARRY A SERIES, HUH, REBECCA?
SHUT UP, JERRY.
NOT.
THE.
TIME.
I DON'T KNOW OR CARE WHAT MADE SIDNEY PIERCE FINALLY REMEMBER HER LOYALTIES LIE WITH US.
ALL I KNOW IS I'M NOT GOING BACK TO JAIL.
TOO MANY OF US HAVE BEEN RECAPTURED BY GATE. WE NEED TO--
GAH!
OOF!
WHAT THE--!
WHUMP

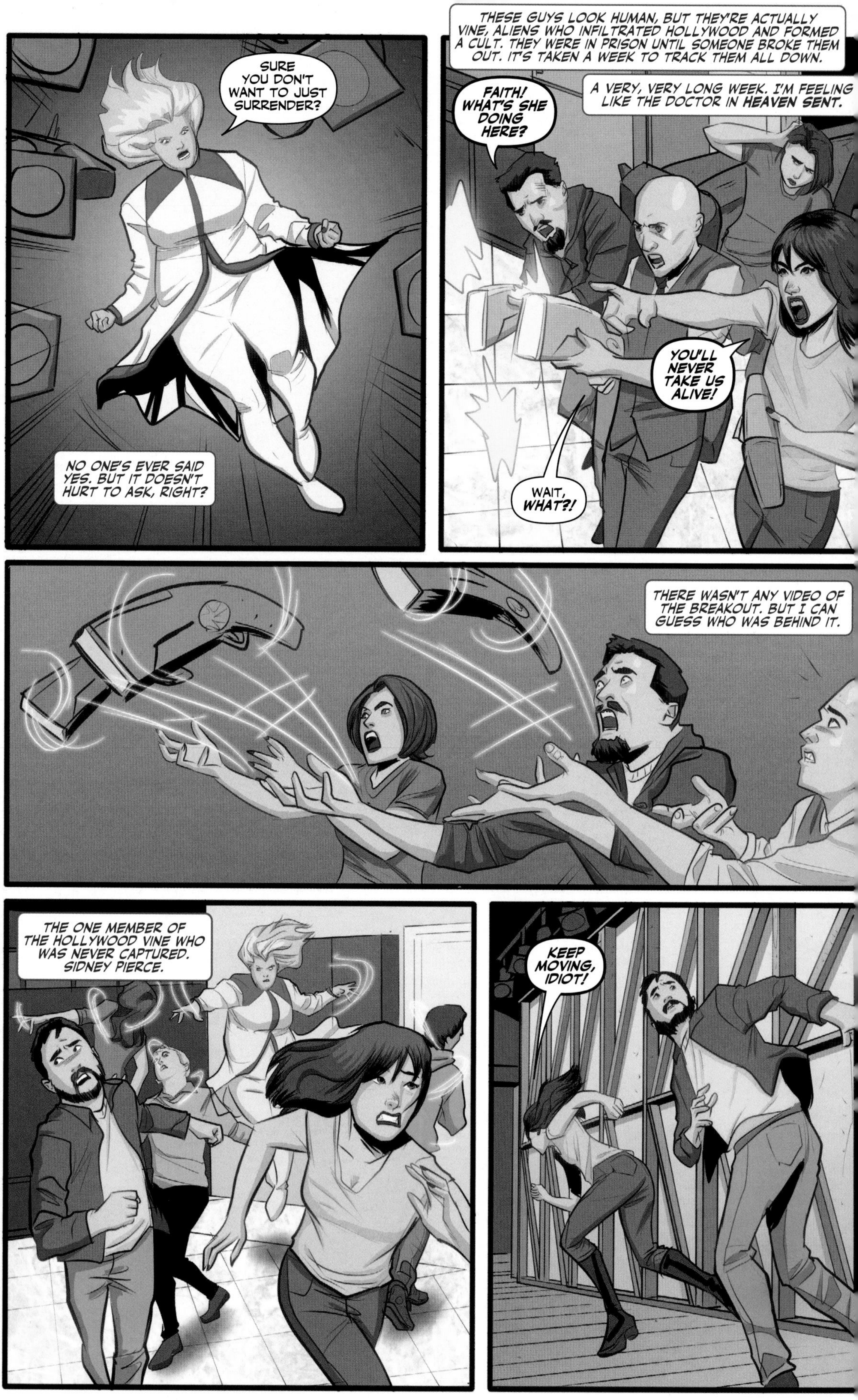

SURE YOU DON'T WANT TO JUST SURRENDER?
NO ONE'S EVER SAID YES. BUT IT DOESN'T HURT TO ASK, RIGHT?
THESE GUYS LOOK HUMAN, BUT THEY'RE ACTUALLY VINE, ALIENS WHO INFILTRATED HOLLYWOOD AND FORMED A CULT. THEY WERE IN PRISON UNTIL SOMEONE BROKE THEM OUT. IT'S TAKEN A WEEK TO TRACK THEM ALL DOWN.
A VERY, VERY LONG WEEK. I'M FEELING LIKE THE DOCTOR IN HEAVEN SENT.
FAITH! WHAT'S SHE DOING HERE?
YOU'LL NEVER TAKE US ALIVE!
WAIT, WHAT?!
THERE WASN'T ANY VIDEO OF THE BREAKOUT. BUT I CAN GUESS WHO WAS BEHIND IT.
THE ONE MEMBER OF THE HOLLYWOOD VINE WHO WAS NEVER CAPTURED. SIDNEY PIERCE.
KEEP MOVING, IDIOT!

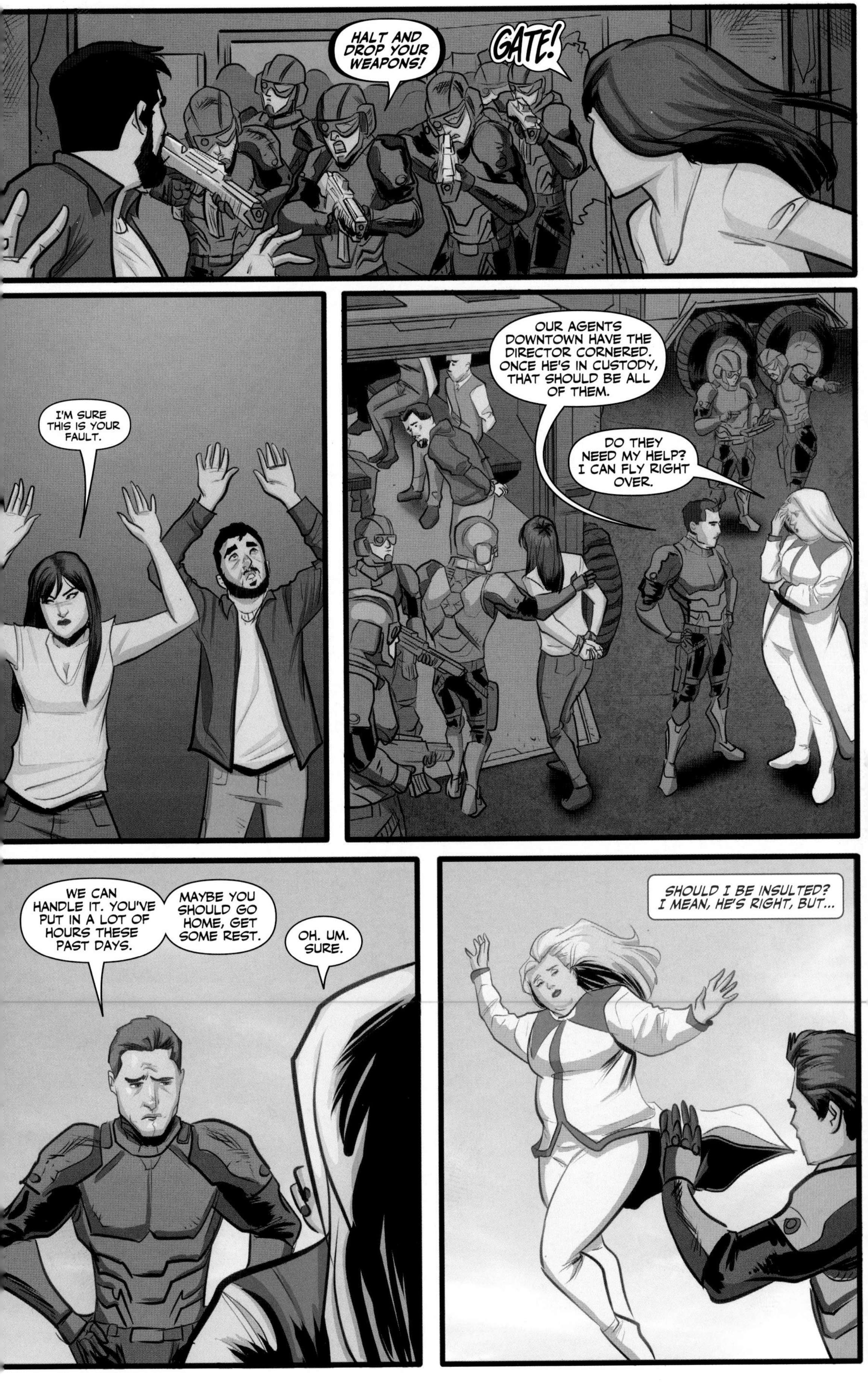
HALT AND DROP YOUR WEAPONS!
GATE!
I'M SURE THIS IS YOUR FAULT.
OUR AGENTS DOWNTOWN HAVE THE DIRECTOR CORNERED. ONCE HE'S IN CUSTODY, THAT SHOULD BE ALL OF THEM.
DO THEY NEED MY HELP? I CAN FLY RIGHT OVER.
WE CAN HANDLE IT. YOU'VE PUT IN A LOT OF HOURS THESE PAST DAYS.
MAYBE YOU SHOULD GO HOME, GET SOME REST.
OH. UM. SURE.
SHOULD I BE INSULTED? I MEAN, HE'S RIGHT, BUT...

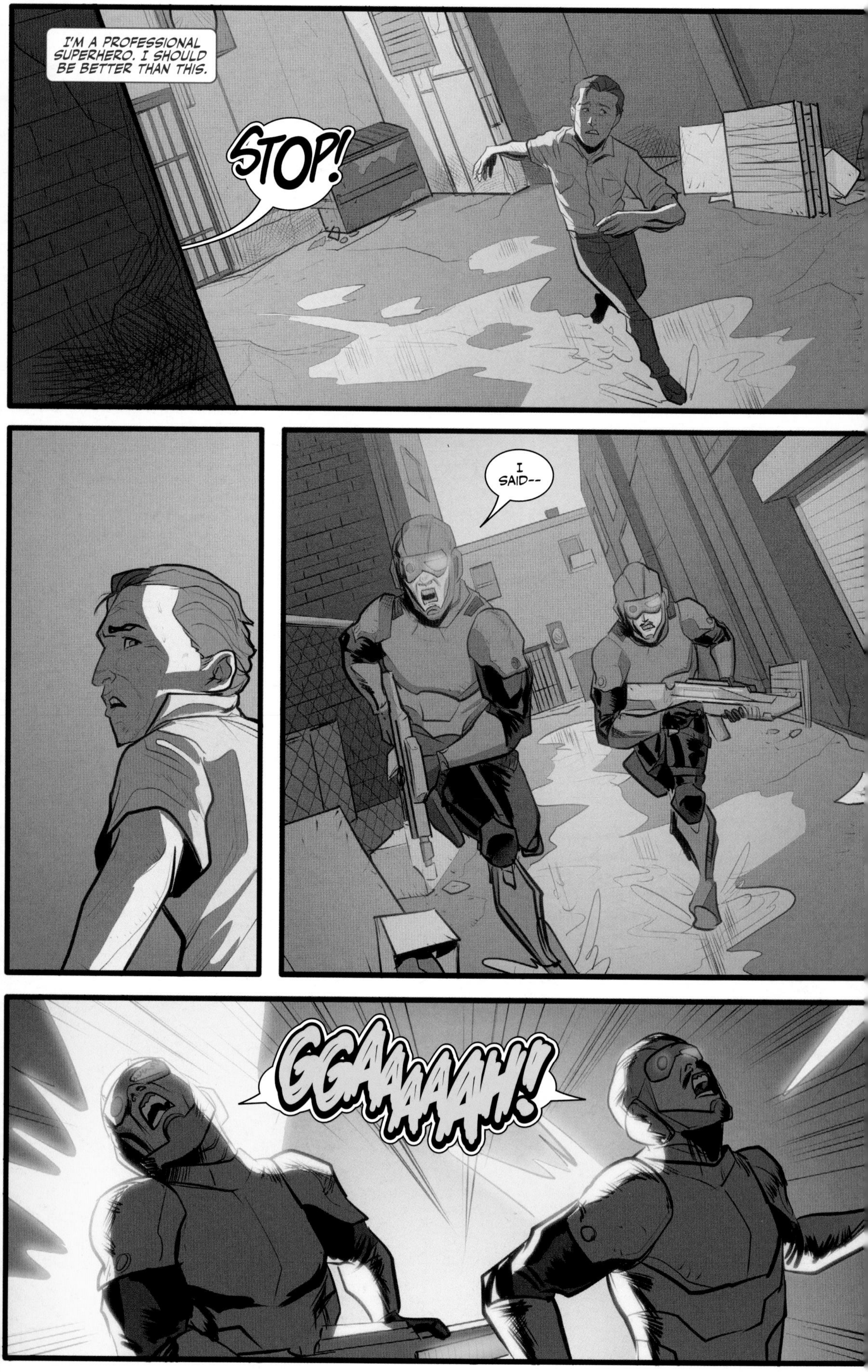
I'M A PROFESSIONAL SUPERHERO. I SHOULD BE BETTER THAN THIS.
STOP!
I SAID--
GGAAAAAH!

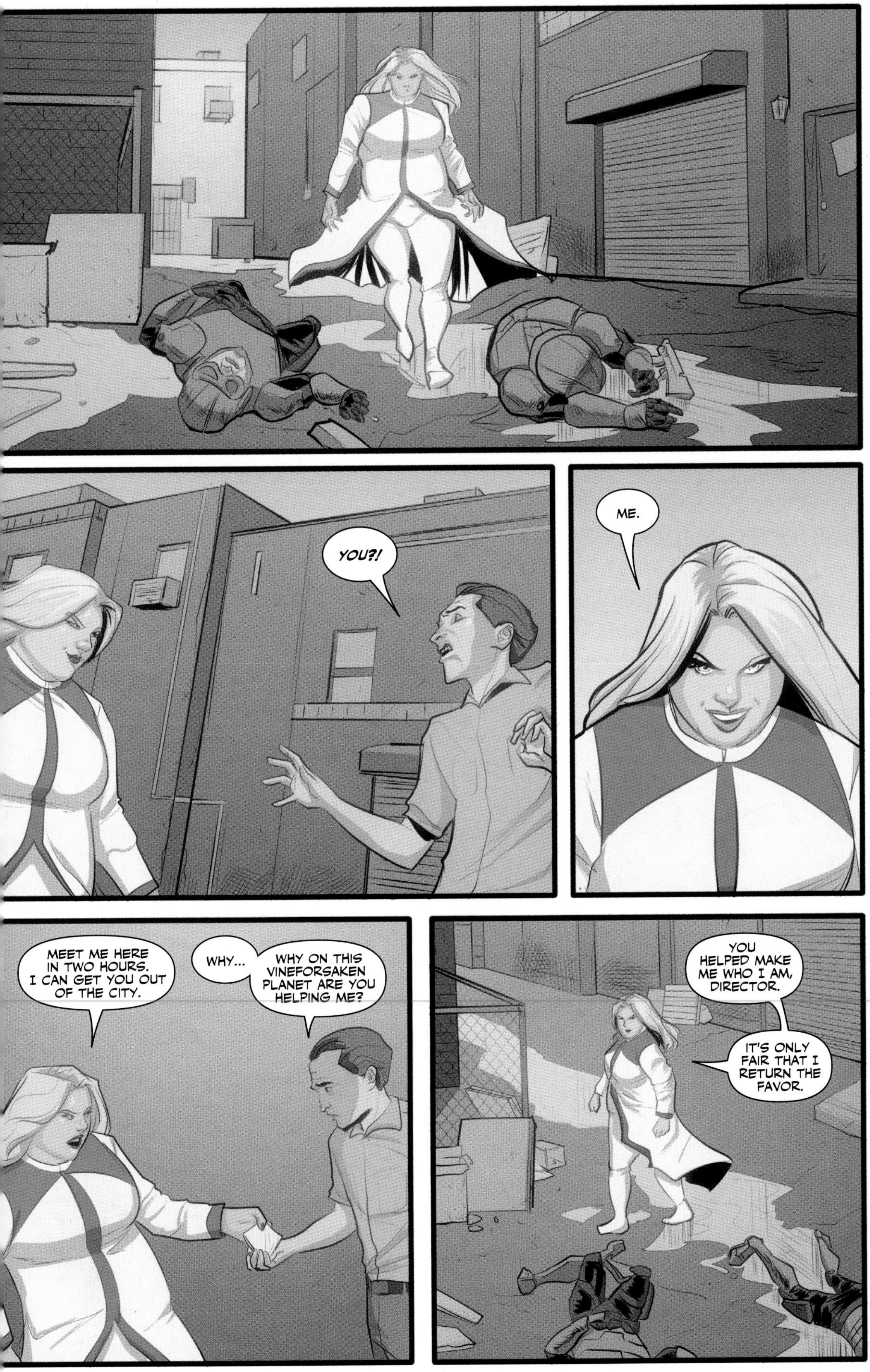
YOU?!
ME.
MEET ME HERE IN TWO HOURS. I CAN GET YOU OUT OF THE CITY.
WHY...
WHY ON THIS VINEFORSAKEN PLANET ARE YOU HELPING ME?
YOU HELPED MAKE ME WHO I AM, DIRECTOR.
IT'S ONLY FAIR THAT I RETURN THE FAVOR.

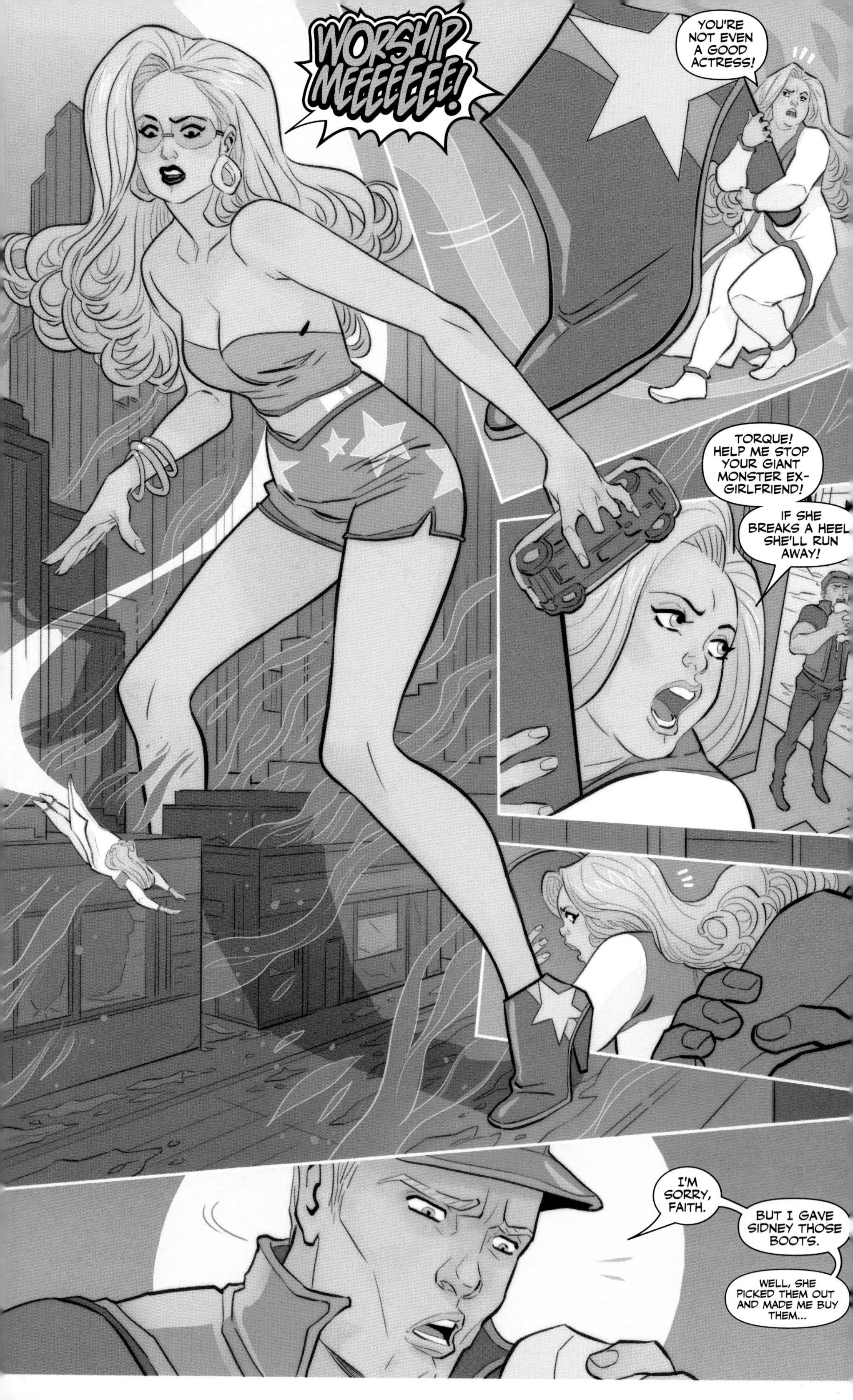
WORSHIP MEEEEEEE!
YOU'RE NOT EVEN A GOOD ACTRESS!
TORQUE! HELP ME STOP YOUR GIANT MONSTER EX-GIRLFRIEND!
IF SHE BREAKS A HEEL SHE'LL RUN AWAY!
I'M SORRY, FAITH.
BUT I GAVE SIDNEY THOSE BOOTS.
WELL, SHE PICKED THEM OUT AND MADE ME BUY THEM...

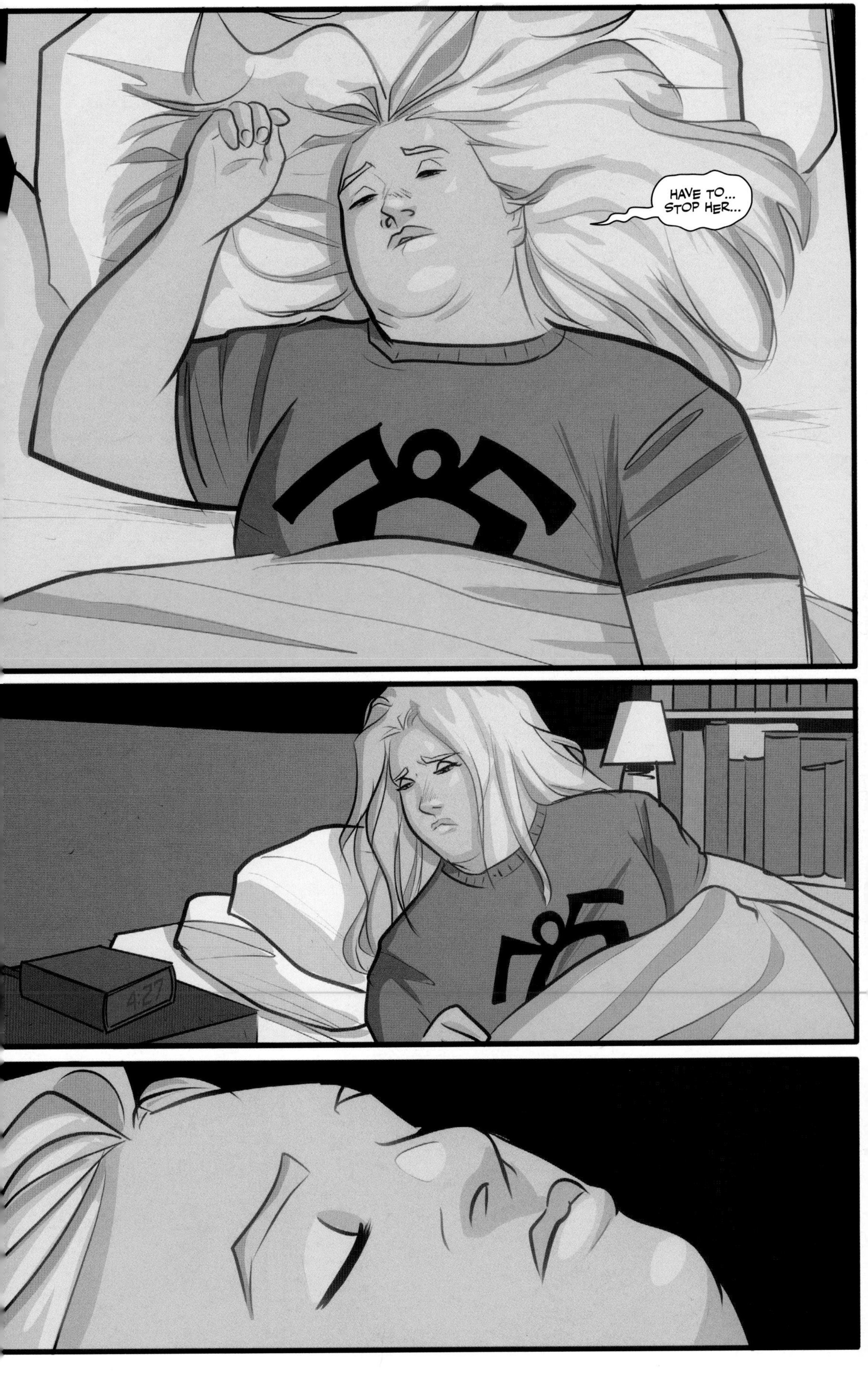
HAVE TO... STOP HER...

IS IT DONE?

EVERYTHING IS IN PLACE, CHRISWELL.

I CAN'T BELIEVE I WENT OUT IN PUBLIC LOOKING LIKE THAT.

IT'S CERTAINLY AN IMPROVEMENT.

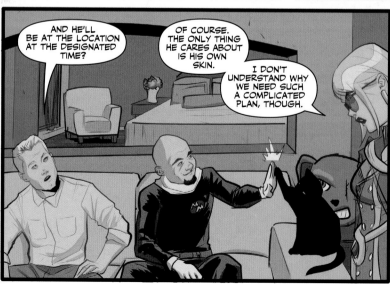

AND HE'LL BE AT THE LOCATION AT THE DESIGNATED TIME?

OF COURSE. THE ONLY THING HE CARES ABOUT IS HIS OWN SKIN.

I DON'T UNDERSTAND WHY WE NEED SUCH A COMPLICATED PLAN, THOUGH.

IF WE'RE GOING TO KILL A SUPERHERO, WE'RE GOING TO DO IT RIGHT.

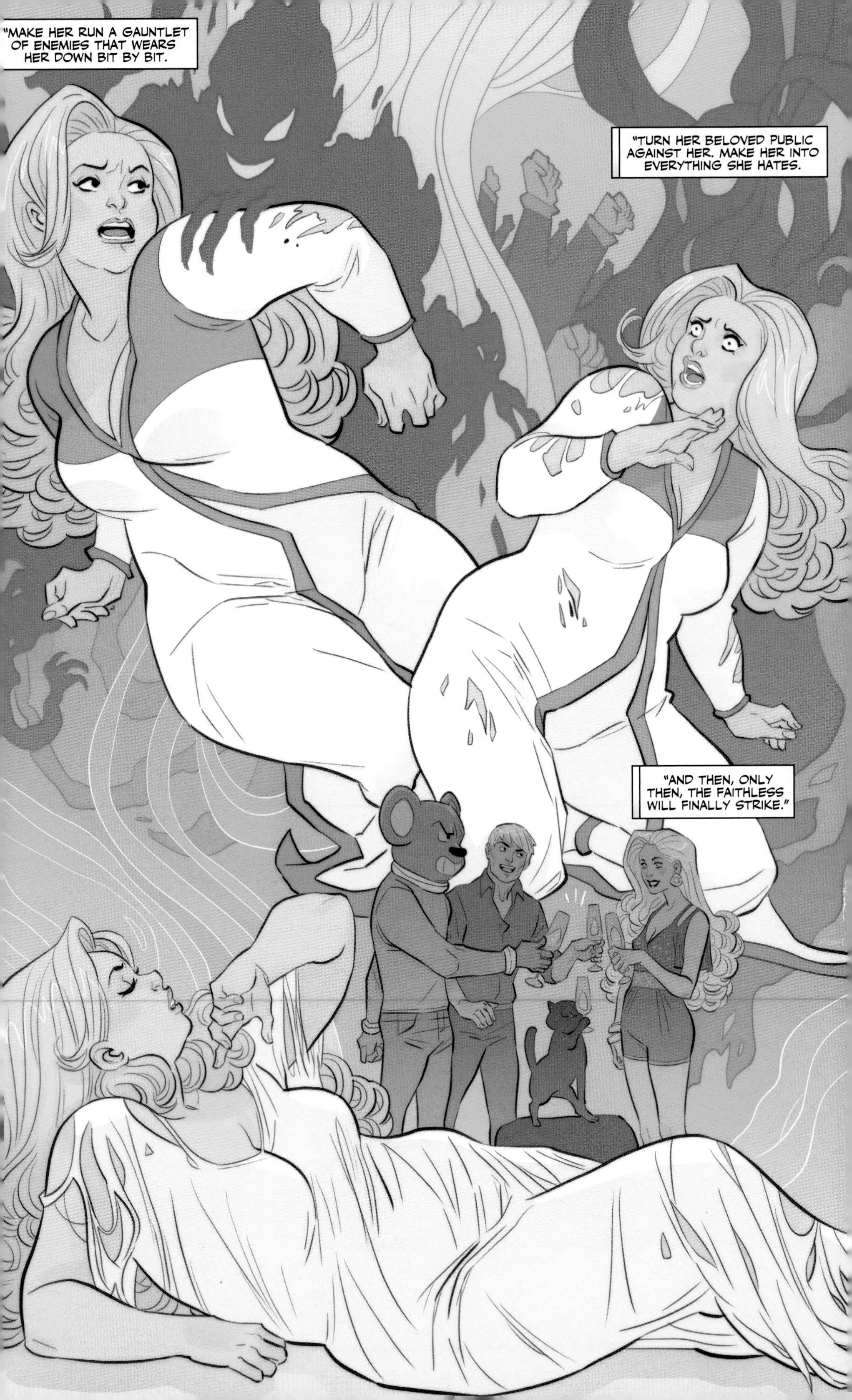
"MAKE HER RUN A GAUNTLET OF ENEMIES THAT WEARS HER DOWN BIT BY BIT.
"TURN HER BELOVED PUBLIC AGAINST HER. MAKE HER INTO EVERYTHING SHE HATES.
"AND THEN, ONLY THEN, THE FAITHLESS WILL FINALLY STRIKE."

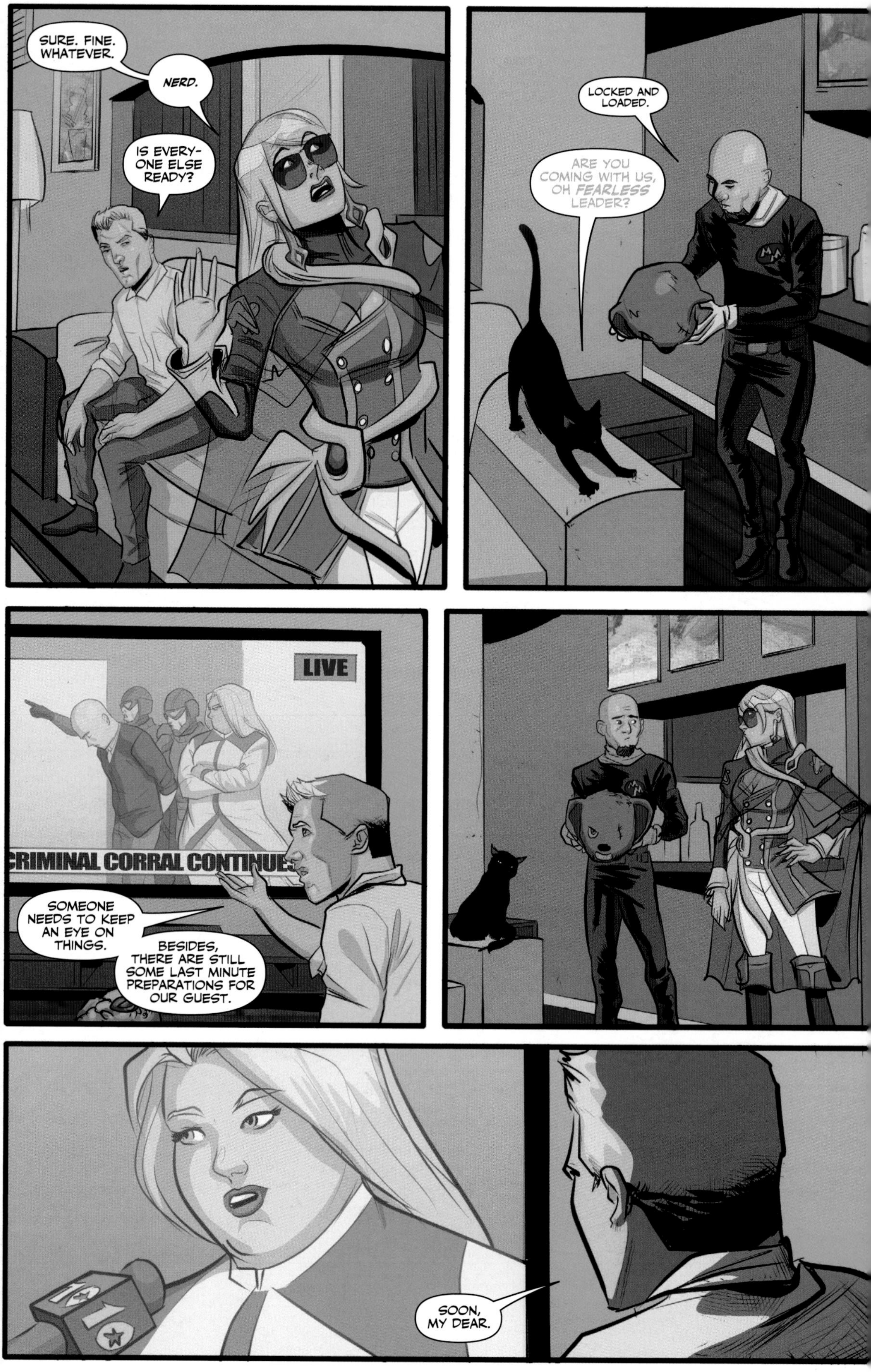
SURE. FINE. WHATEVER.
NERD.
IS EVERY-ONE ELSE READY?
LOCKED AND LOADED.
ARE YOU COMING WITH US, OH FEARLESS LEADER?
LIVE
CRIMINAL CORRAL CONTINUES
SOMEONE NEEDS TO KEEP AN EYE ON THINGS.
BESIDES, THERE ARE STILL SOME LAST MINUTE PREPARATIONS FOR OUR GUEST.
SOON, MY DEAR.

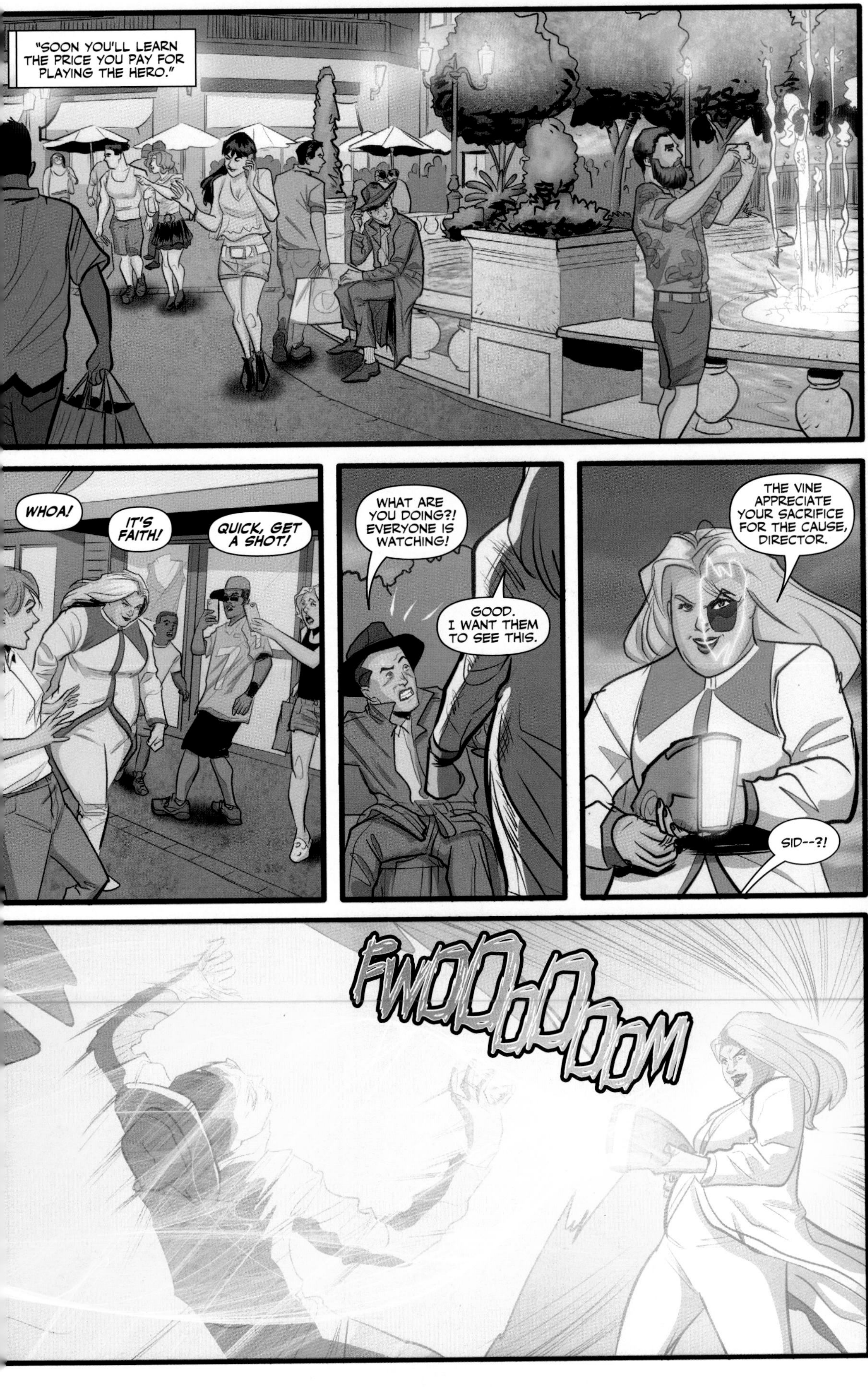
"SOON YOU'LL LEARN THE PRICE YOU PAY FOR PLAYING THE HERO."
WHOA!
IT'S FAITH!
QUICK, GET A SHOT!
WHAT ARE YOU DOING?! EVERYONE IS WATCHING!
GOOD. I WANT THEM TO SEE THIS.
THE VINE APPRECIATE YOUR SACRIFICE FOR THE CAUSE, DIRECTOR.
SID--?!
FWOOOOOOOM

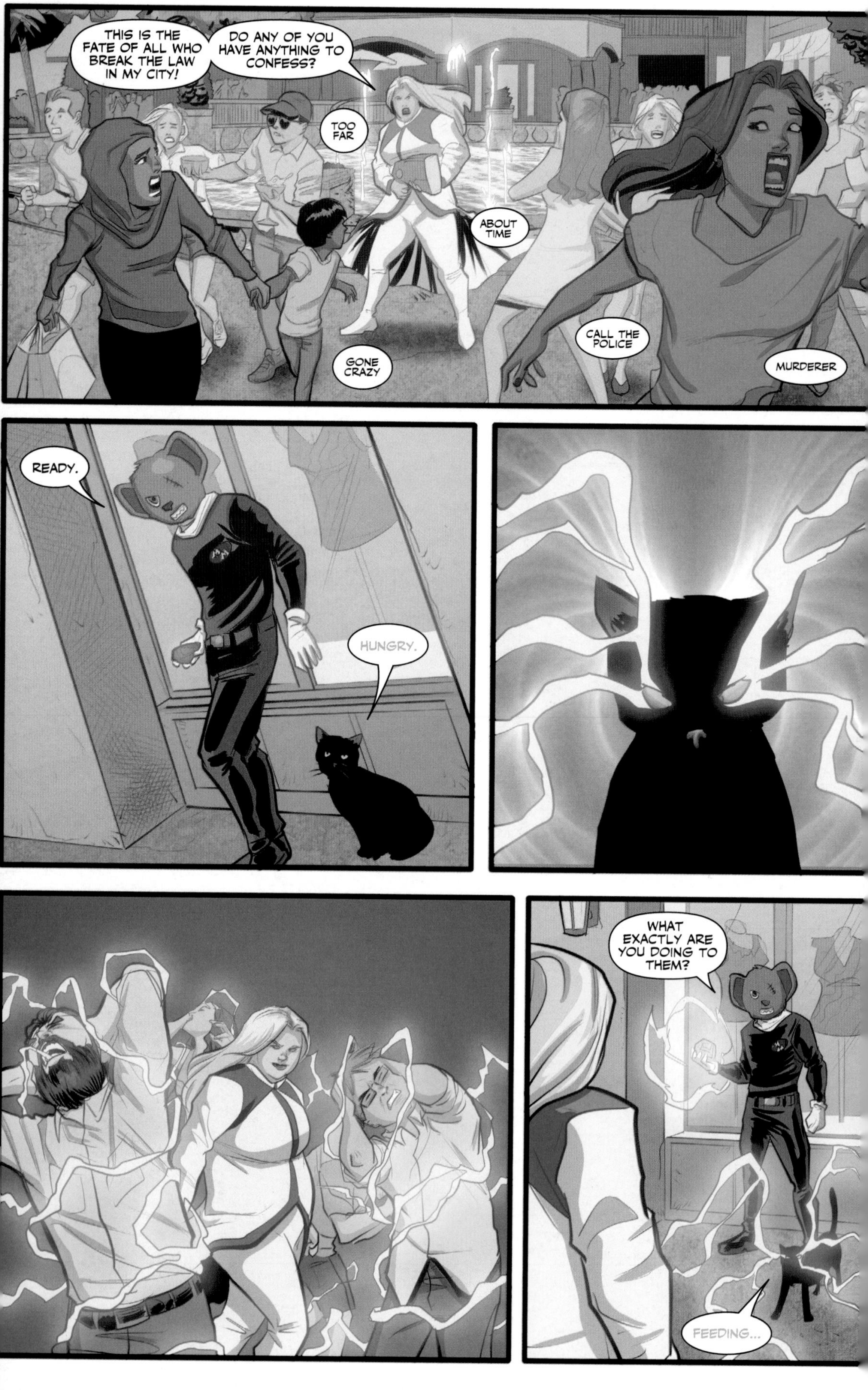
THIS IS THE FATE OF ALL WHO BREAK THE LAW IN MY CITY!
DO ANY OF YOU HAVE ANYTHING TO CONFESS?
TOO FAR
ABOUT TIME
GONE CRAZY
CALL THE POLICE
MURDERER
READY.
HUNGRY.
WHAT EXACTLY ARE YOU DOING TO THEM?
FEEDING...

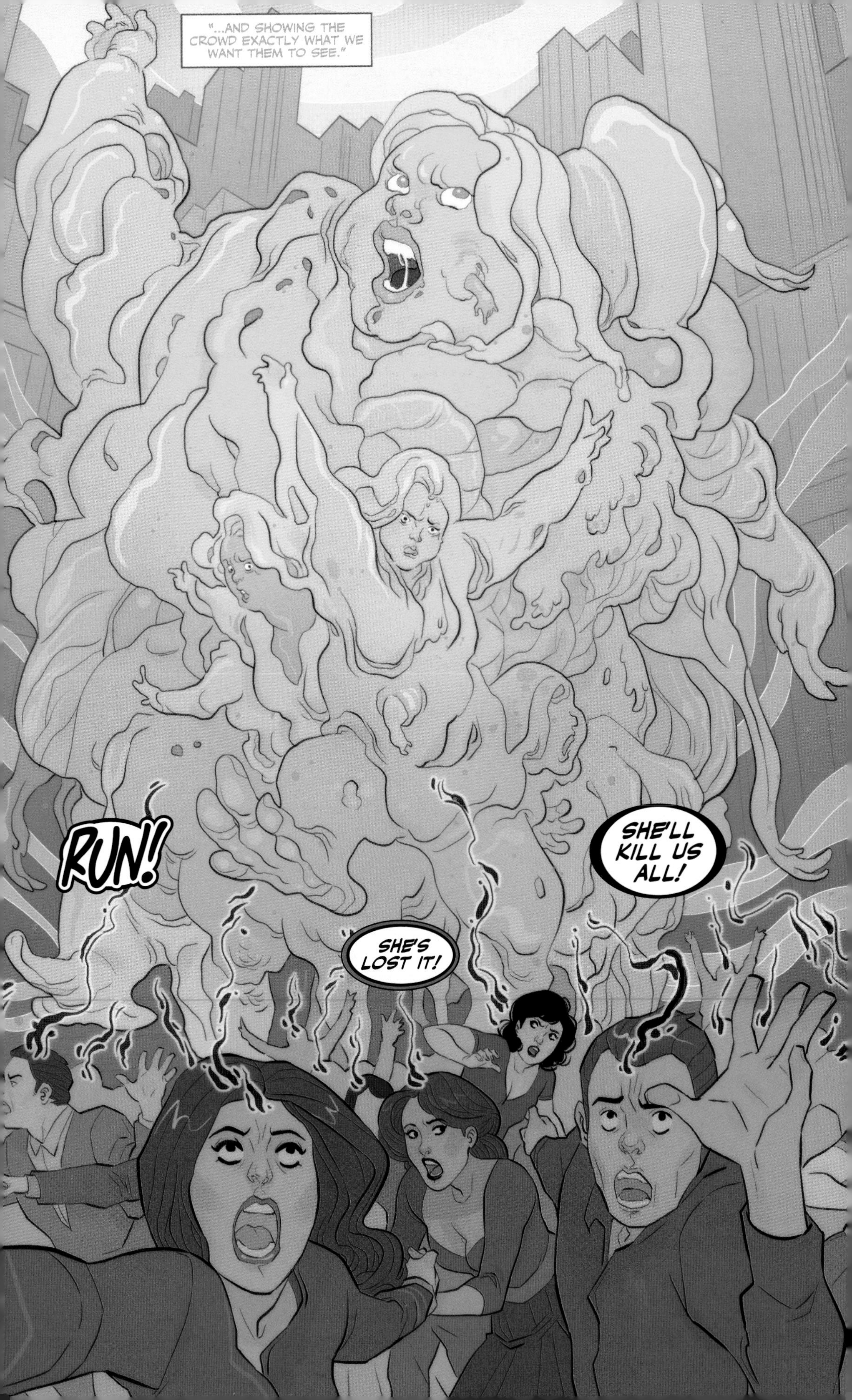
"...AND SHOWING THE CROWD EXACTLY WHAT WE WANT THEM TO SEE."
RUN!
SHE'LL KILL US ALL!
SHE'S LOST IT!

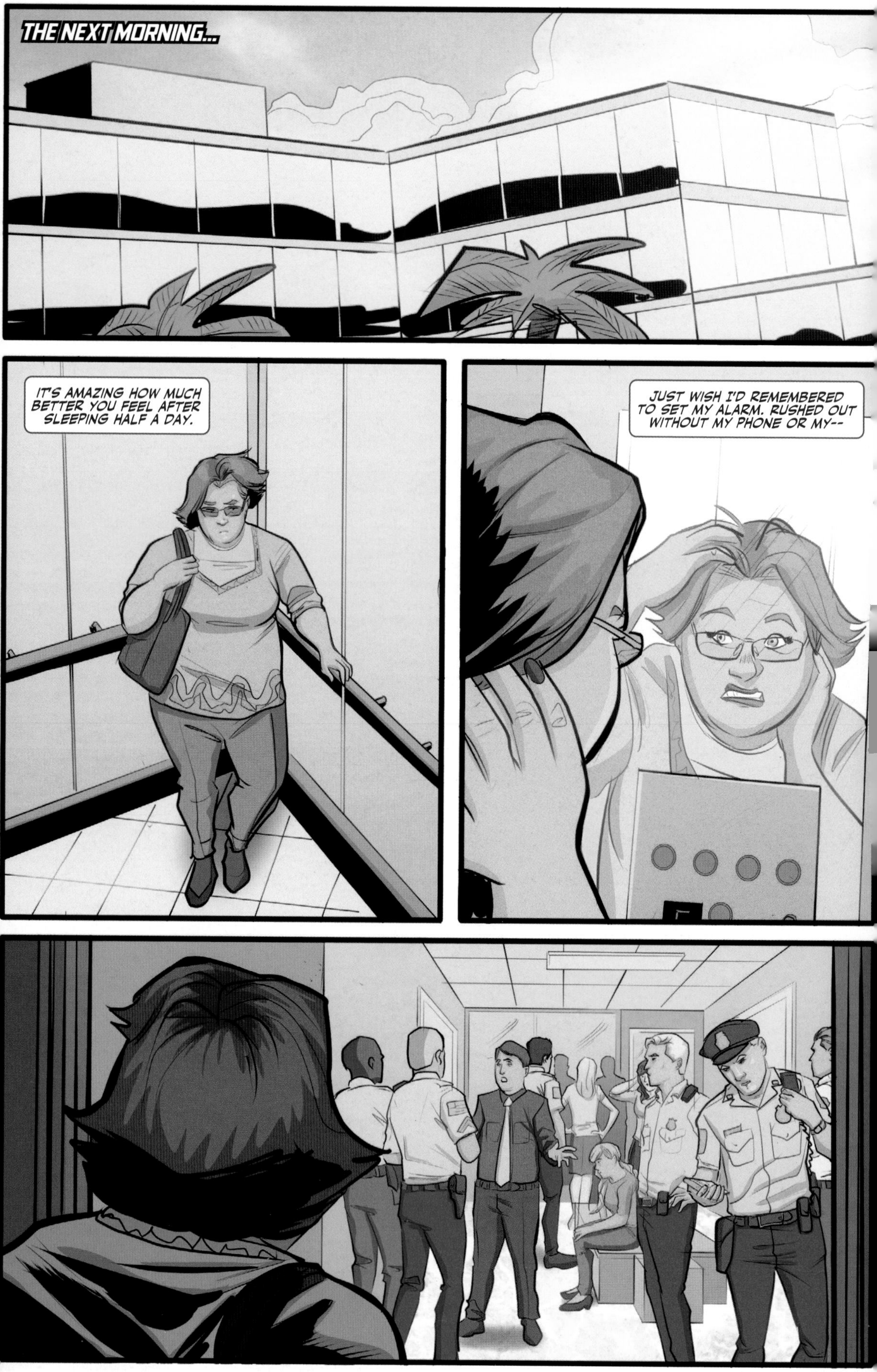
THE NEXT MORNING...
IT'S AMAZING HOW MUCH BETTER YOU FEEL AFTER SLEEPING HALF A DAY.
JUST WISH I'D REMEMBERED TO SET MY ALARM. RUSHED OUT WITHOUT MY PHONE OR MY--

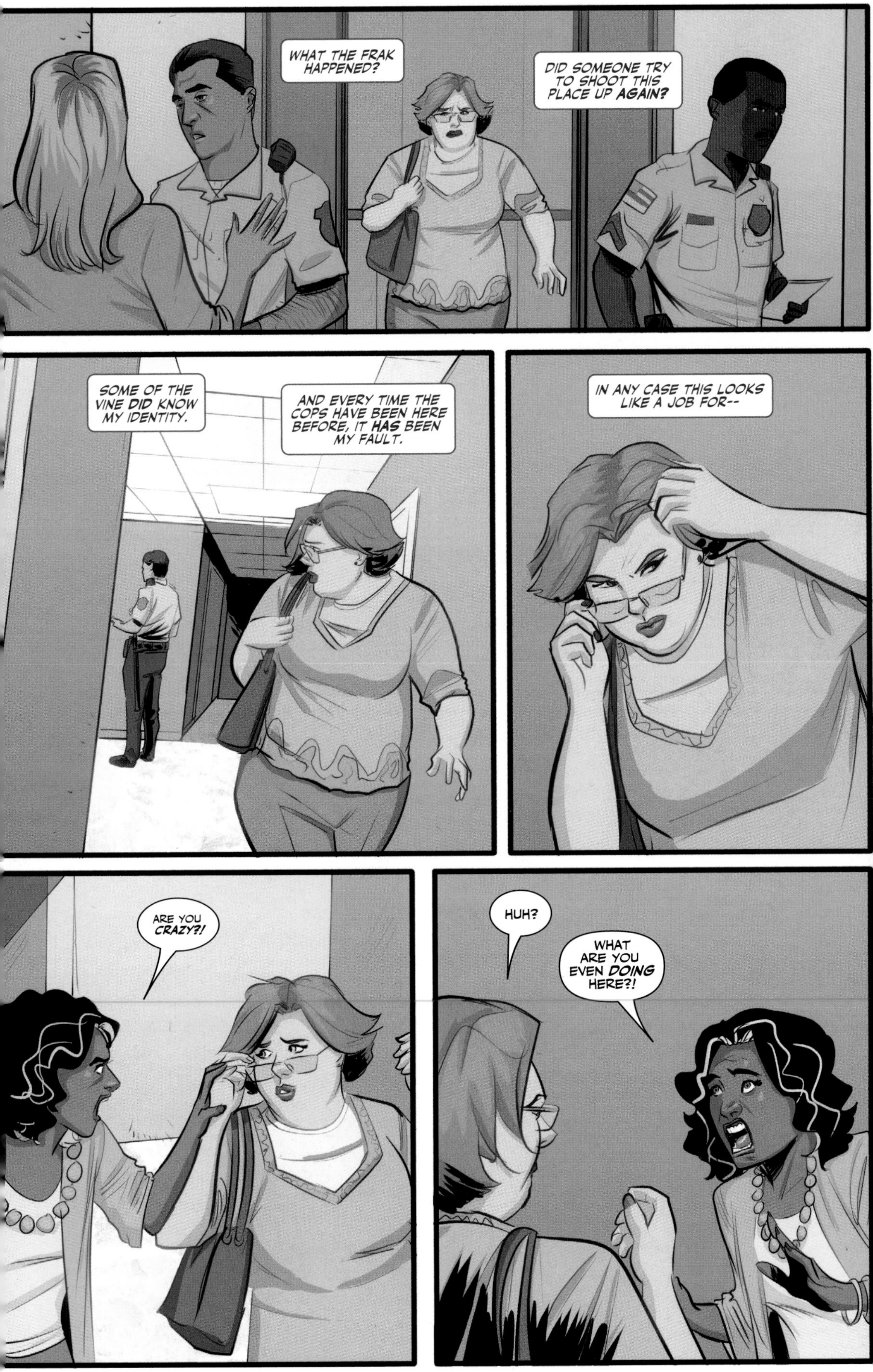
WHAT THE FRAK HAPPENED?
DID SOMEONE TRY TO SHOOT THIS PLACE UP AGAIN?
SOME OF THE VINE DID KNOW MY IDENTITY.
AND EVERY TIME THE COPS HAVE BEEN HERE BEFORE, IT HAS BEEN MY FAULT.
IN ANY CASE THIS LOOKS LIKE A JOB FOR--
ARE YOU CRAZY?!
HUH?
WHAT ARE YOU EVEN DOING HERE?!

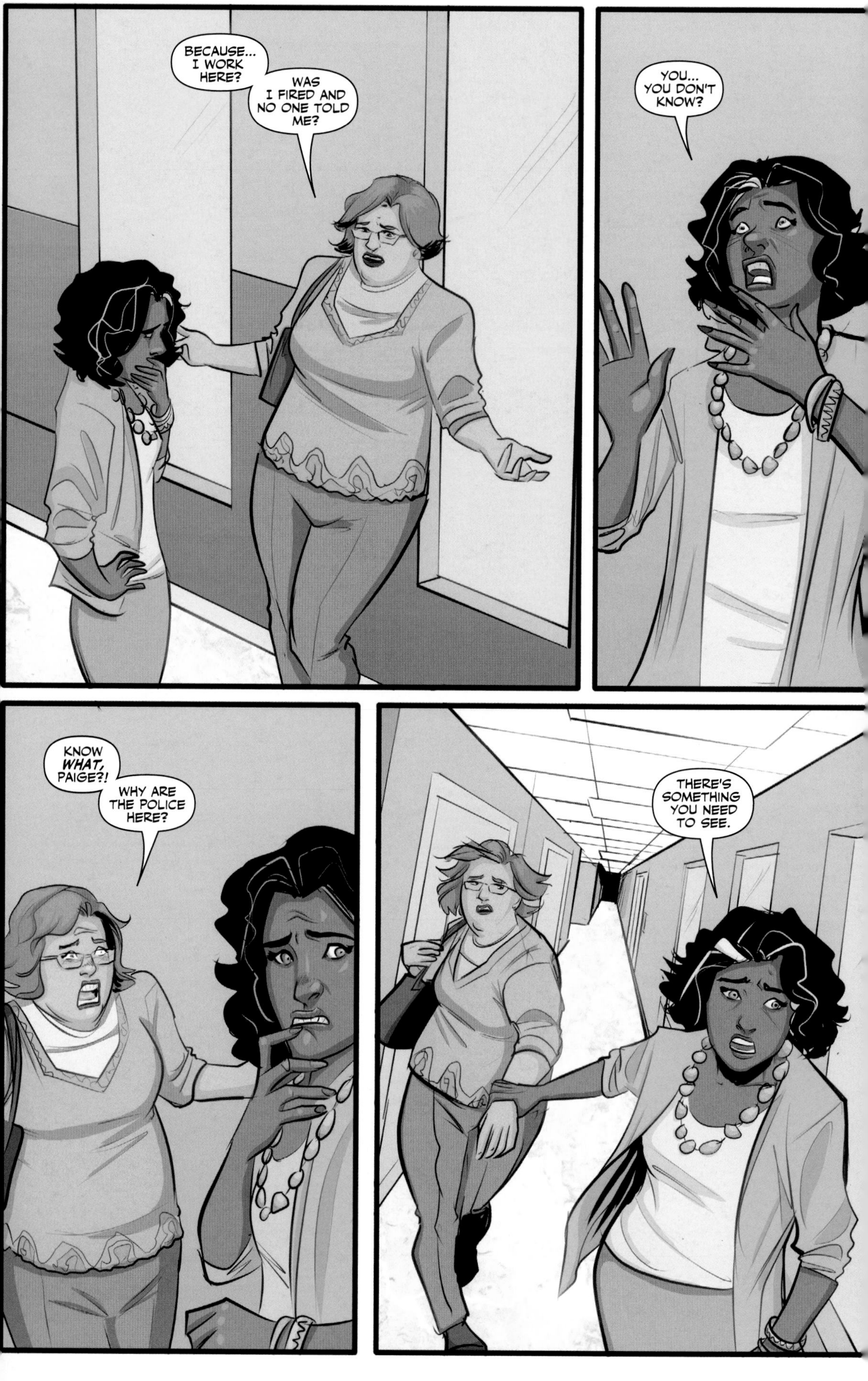
BECAUSE... I WORK HERE?
WAS I FIRED AND NO ONE TOLD ME?
YOU... YOU DON'T KNOW?
KNOW *WHAT*, PAIGE?!
WHY ARE THE POLICE HERE?
THERE'S SOMETHING YOU NEED TO SEE.

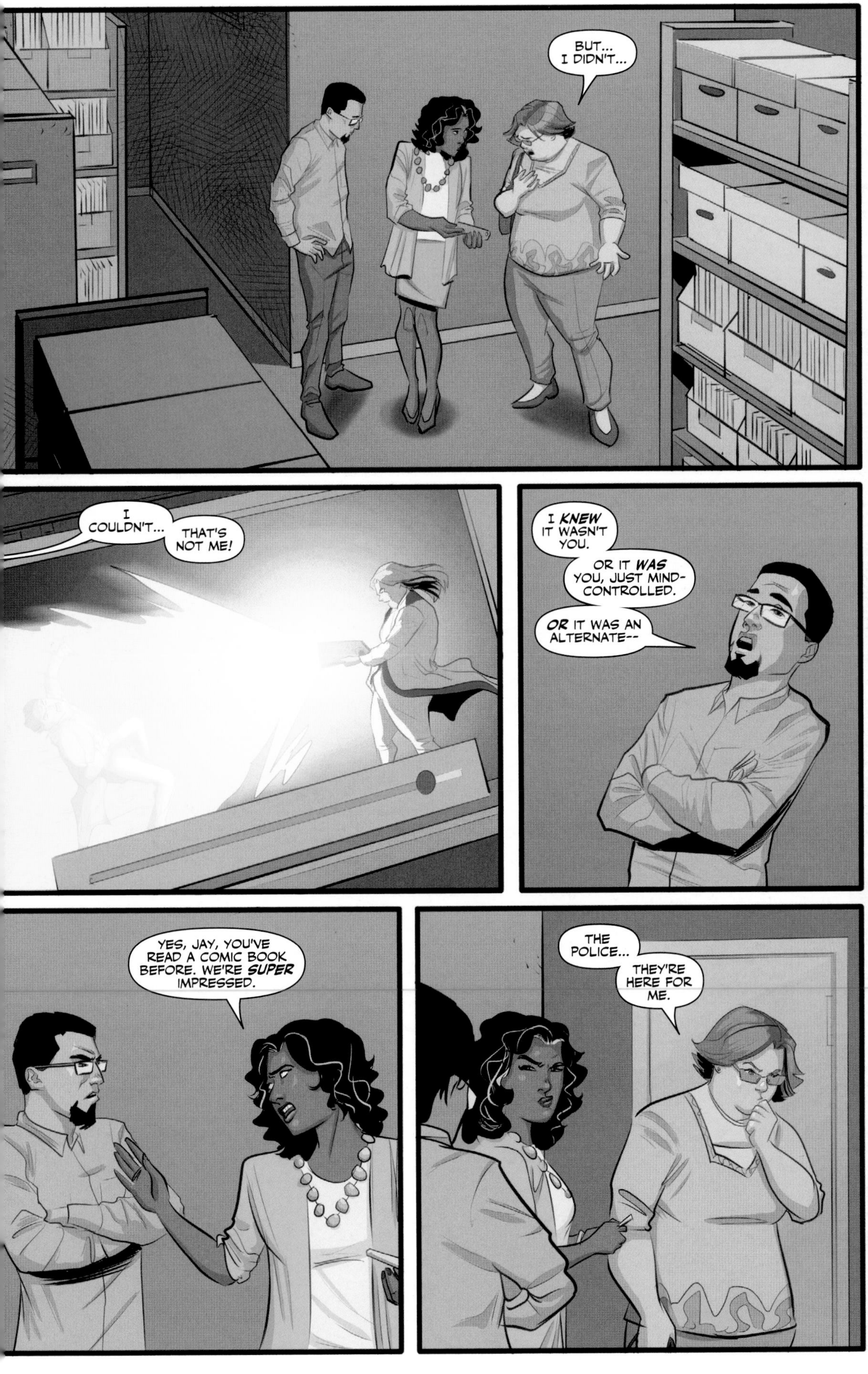
BUT... I DIDN'T...
I COULDN'T...
THAT'S NOT ME!
I KNEW IT WASN'T YOU.
OR IT WAS YOU, JUST MIND-CONTROLLED.
OR IT WAS AN ALTERNATE--
YES, JAY, YOU'VE READ A COMIC BOOK BEFORE. WE'RE SUPER IMPRESSED.
THE POLICE...
THEY'RE HERE FOR ME.

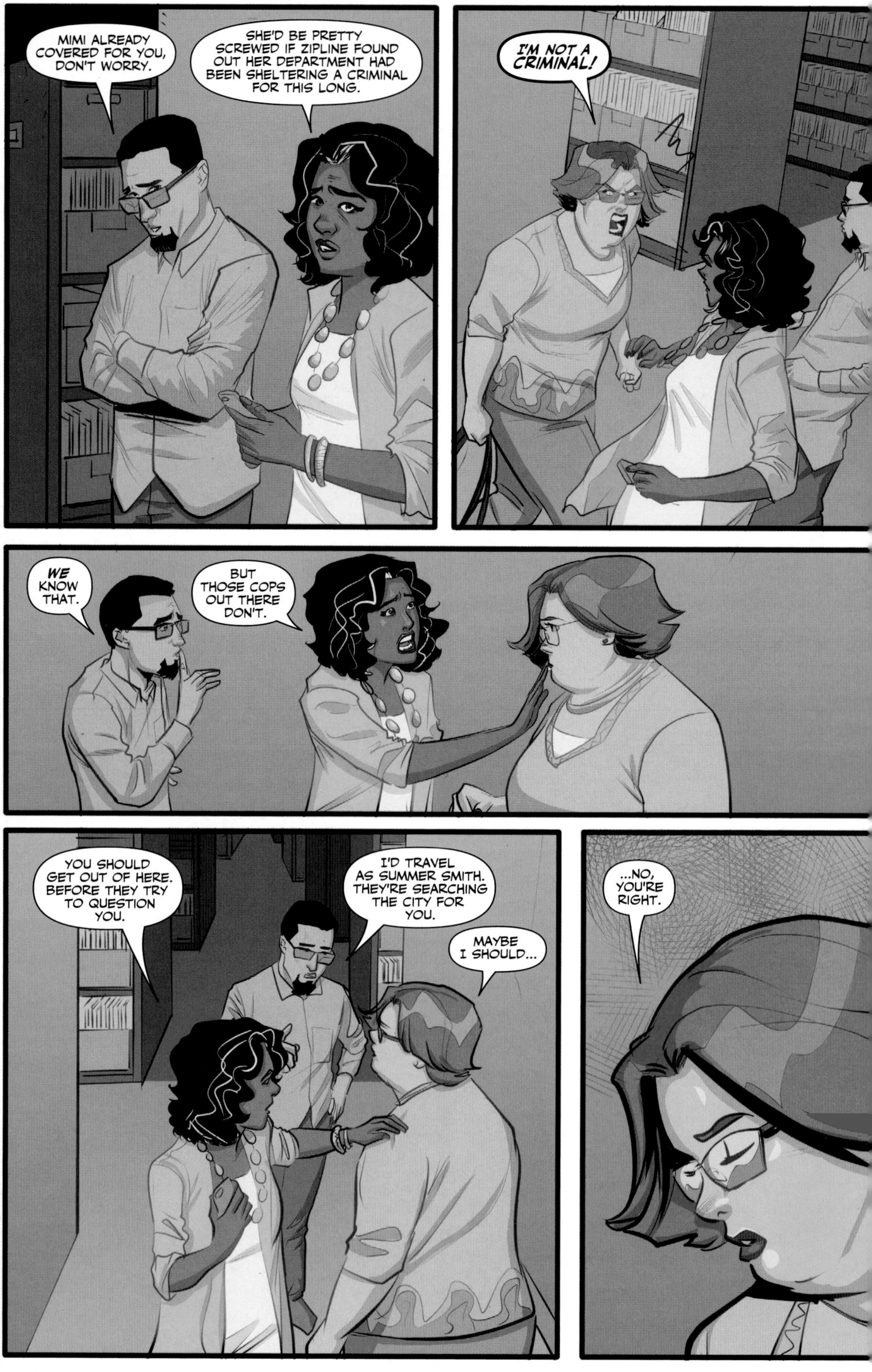

MIMI ALREADY COVERED FOR YOU, DON'T WORRY.
SHE'D BE PRETTY SCREWED IF ZIPLINE FOUND OUT HER DEPARTMENT HAD BEEN SHELTERING A CRIMINAL FOR THIS LONG.
I'M NOT A CRIMINAL!
WE KNOW THAT.
BUT THOSE COPS OUT THERE DON'T.
YOU SHOULD GET OUT OF HERE. BEFORE THEY TRY TO QUESTION YOU.
I'D TRAVEL AS SUMMER SMITH. THEY'RE SEARCHING THE CITY FOR YOU.
MAYBE I SHOULD...
...NO, YOU'RE RIGHT.

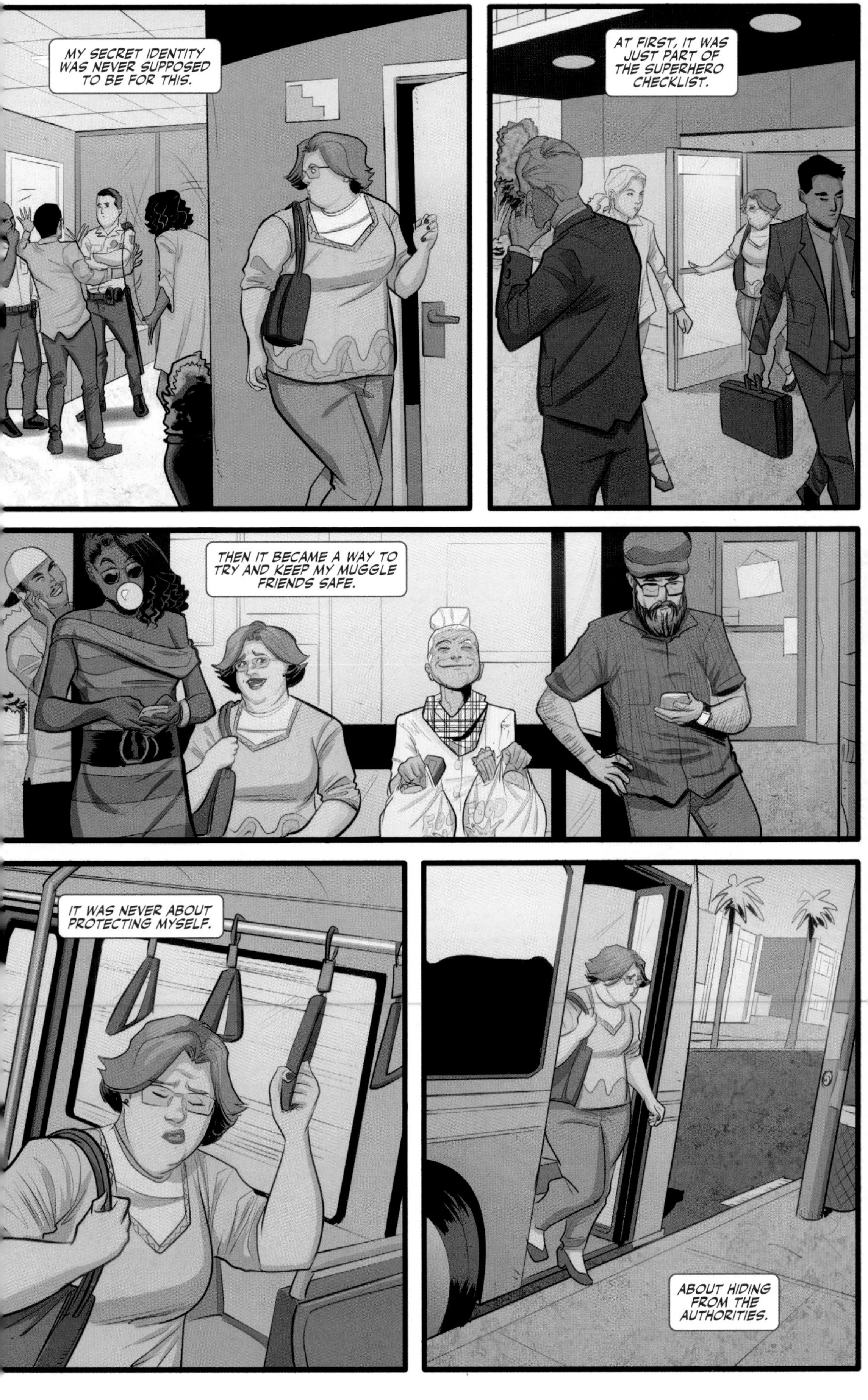
MY SECRET IDENTITY WAS NEVER SUPPOSED TO BE FOR THIS.
AT FIRST, IT WAS JUST PART OF THE SUPERHERO CHECKLIST.
THEN IT BECAME A WAY TO TRY AND KEEP MY MUGGLE FRIENDS SAFE.
FOOD
FOOD
IT WAS NEVER ABOUT PROTECTING MYSELF.
ABOUT HIDING FROM THE AUTHORITIES.

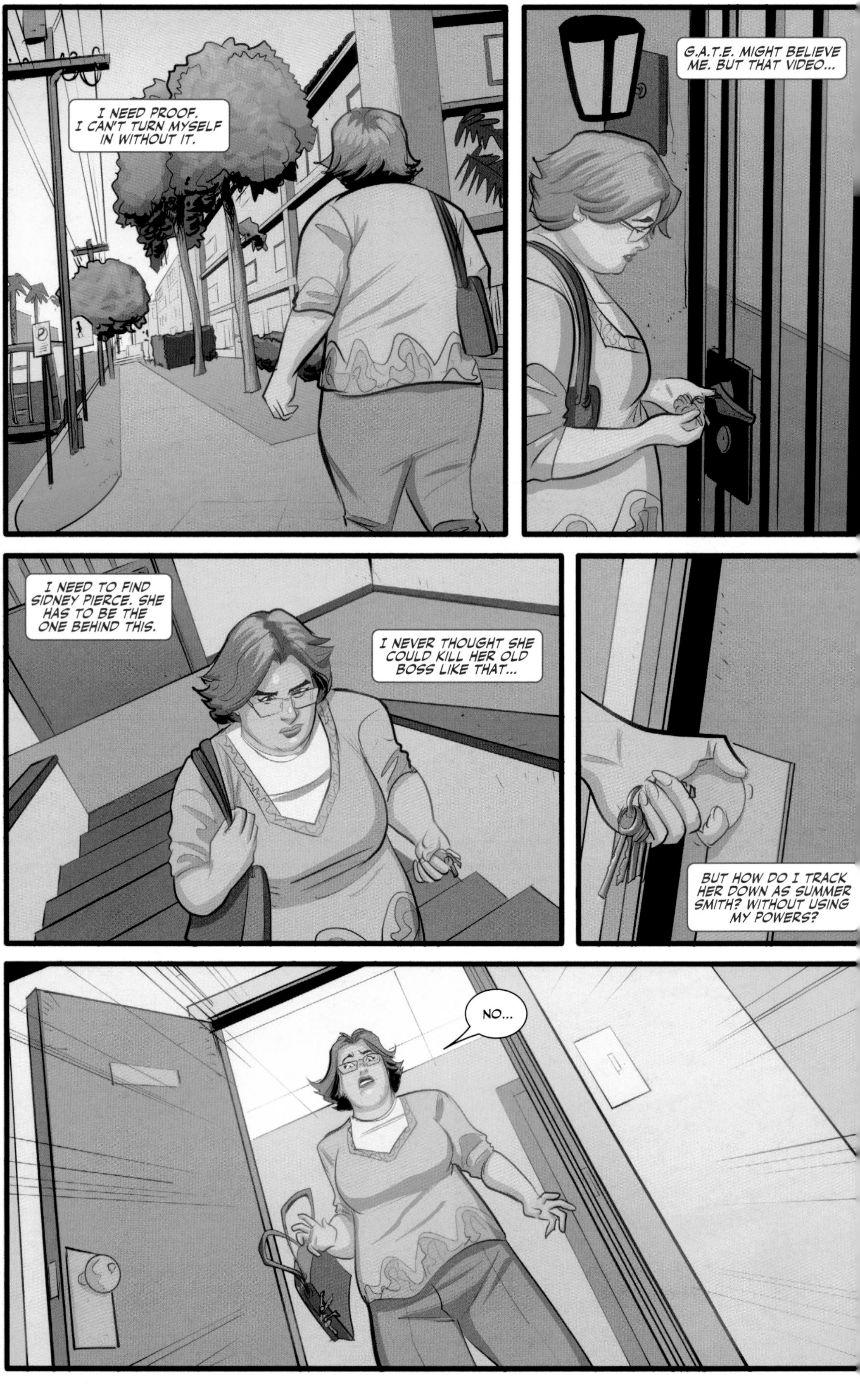
I NEED PROOF. I CAN'T TURN MYSELF IN WITHOUT IT.
G.A.T.E. MIGHT BELIEVE ME. BUT THAT VIDEO...
I NEED TO FIND SIDNEY PIERCE. SHE HAS TO BE THE ONE BEHIND THIS.
I NEVER THOUGHT SHE COULD KILL HER OLD BOSS LIKE THAT...
BUT HOW DO I TRACK HER DOWN AS SUMMER SMITH? WITHOUT USING MY POWERS?
NO...

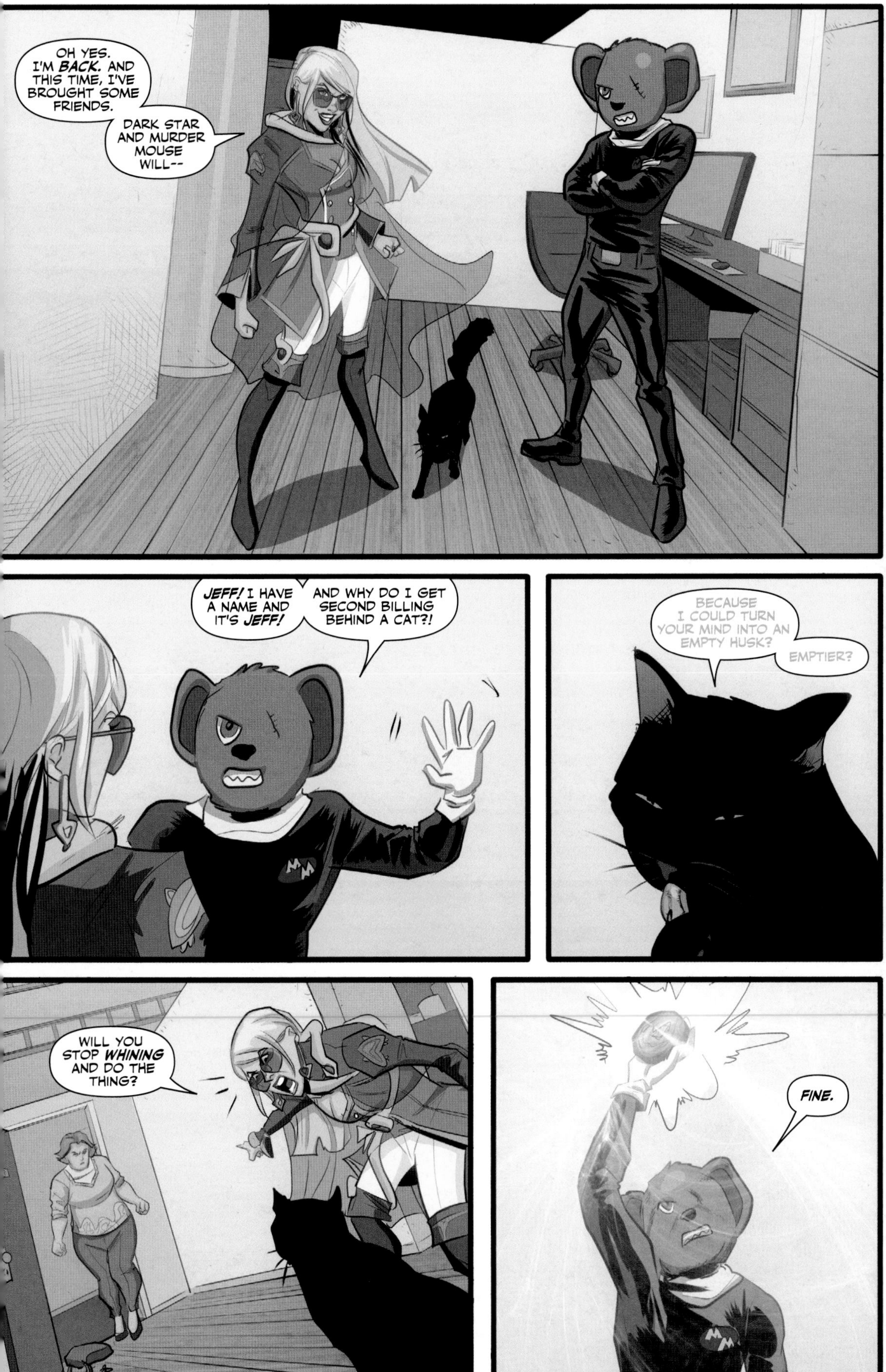
OH YES. I'M *BACK.* AND THIS TIME, I'VE BROUGHT SOME FRIENDS.
DARK STAR AND MURDER MOUSE WILL--
JEFF! I HAVE A NAME AND IT'S *JEFF!*
AND WHY DO I GET SECOND BILLING BEHIND A CAT?!
BECAUSE I COULD TURN YOUR MIND INTO AN EMPTY HUSK?
EMPTIER?
WILL YOU STOP *WHINING* AND DO THE THING?
FINE.

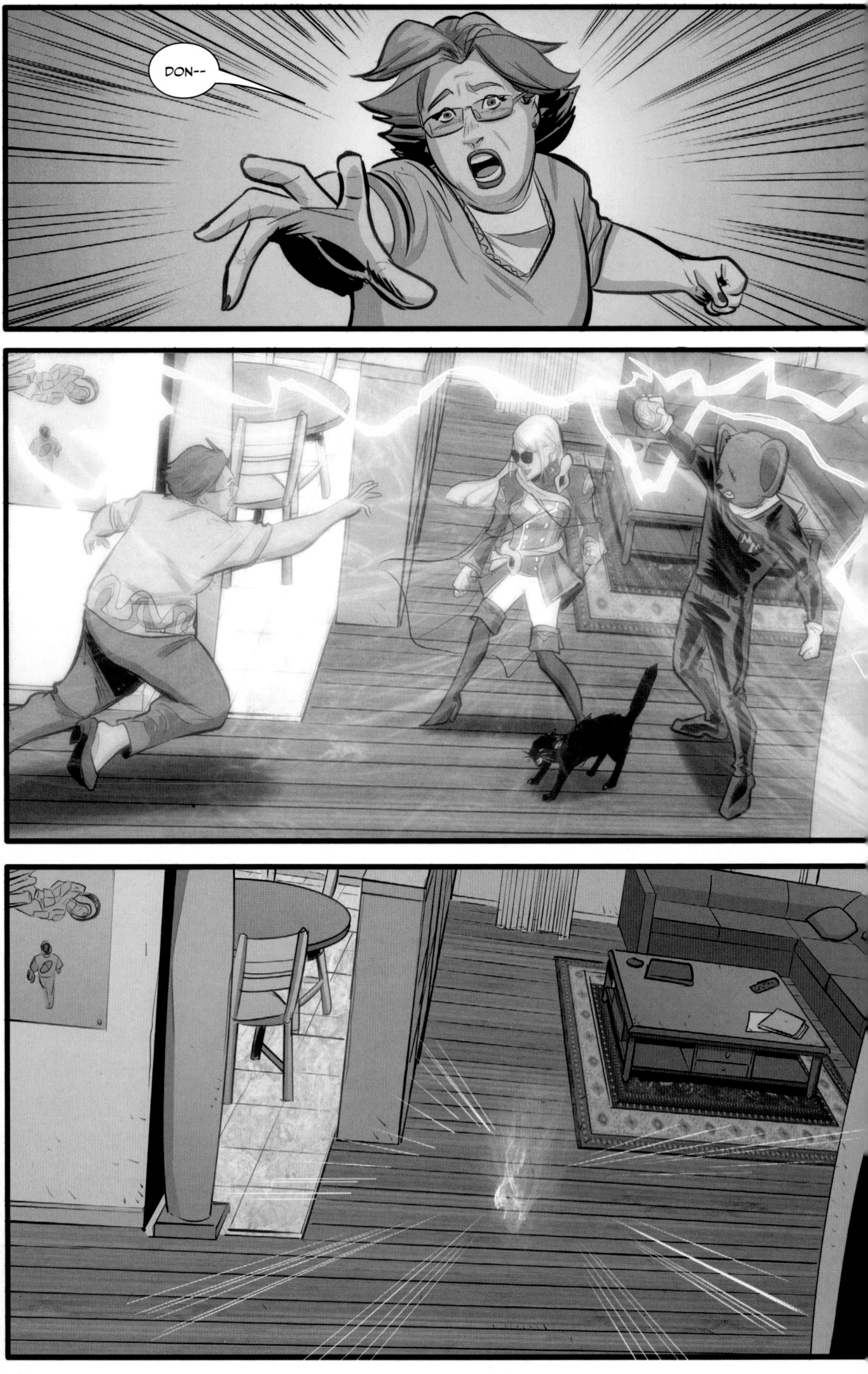
DON--

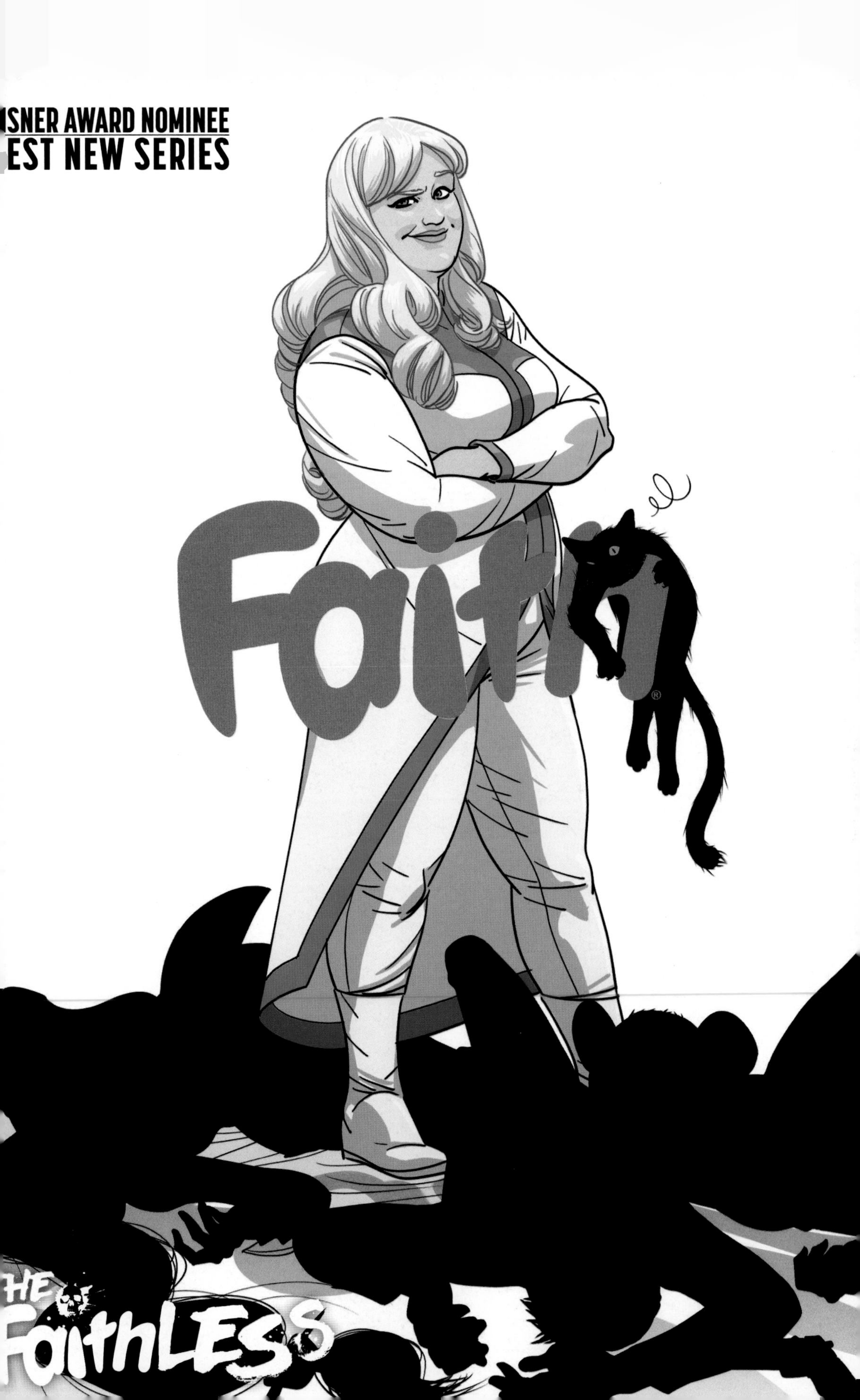
ISNER AWARD NOMINEE
EST NEW SERIES
HE
aithLESS

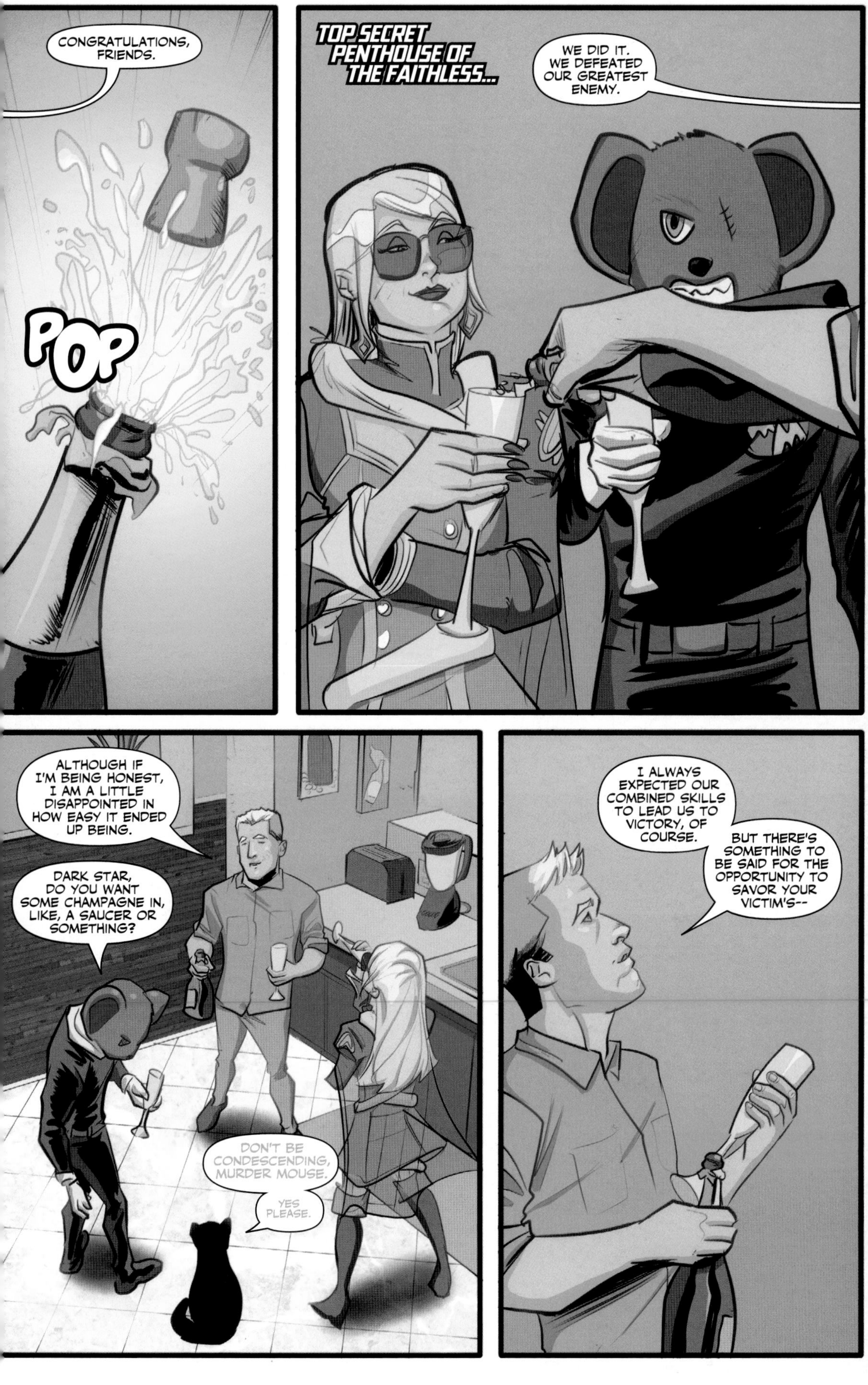
CONGRATULATIONS, FRIENDS.
POP
TOP SECRET PENTHOUSE OF THE FAITHLESS...
WE DID IT. WE DEFEATED OUR GREATEST ENEMY.
ALTHOUGH IF I'M BEING HONEST, I AM A LITTLE DISAPPOINTED IN HOW EASY IT ENDED UP BEING.
DARK STAR, DO YOU WANT SOME CHAMPAGNE IN, LIKE, A SAUCER OR SOMETHING?
DON'T BE CONDESCENDING, MURDER MOUSE.
YES PLEASE.
I ALWAYS EXPECTED OUR COMBINED SKILLS TO LEAD US TO VICTORY, OF COURSE.
BUT THERE'S SOMETHING TO BE SAID FOR THE OPPORTUNITY TO SAVOR YOUR VICTIM'S--

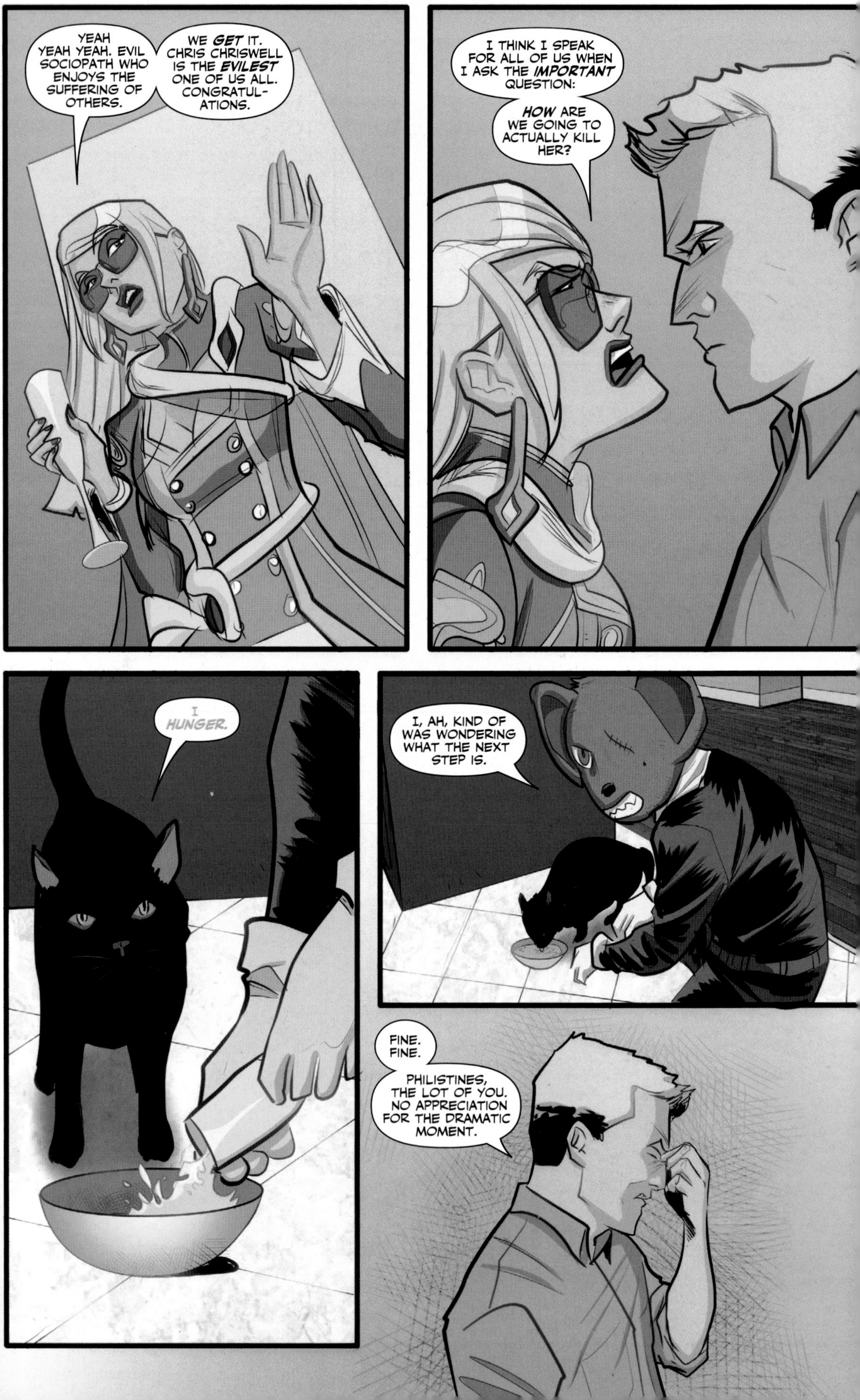
YEAH YEAH YEAH. EVIL SOCIOPATH WHO ENJOYS THE SUFFERING OF OTHERS.
WE *GET* IT. CHRIS CHRISWELL IS THE *EVILEST* ONE OF US ALL. CONGRATUL-ATIONS.
I THINK I SPEAK FOR ALL OF US WHEN I ASK THE *IMPORTANT* QUESTION:
HOW ARE WE GOING TO ACTUALLY KILL HER?
I *HUNGER.*
I, AH, KIND OF WAS WONDERING WHAT THE NEXT STEP IS.
FINE. FINE.
PHILISTINES, THE LOT OF YOU. NO APPRECIATION FOR THE DRAMATIC MOMENT.

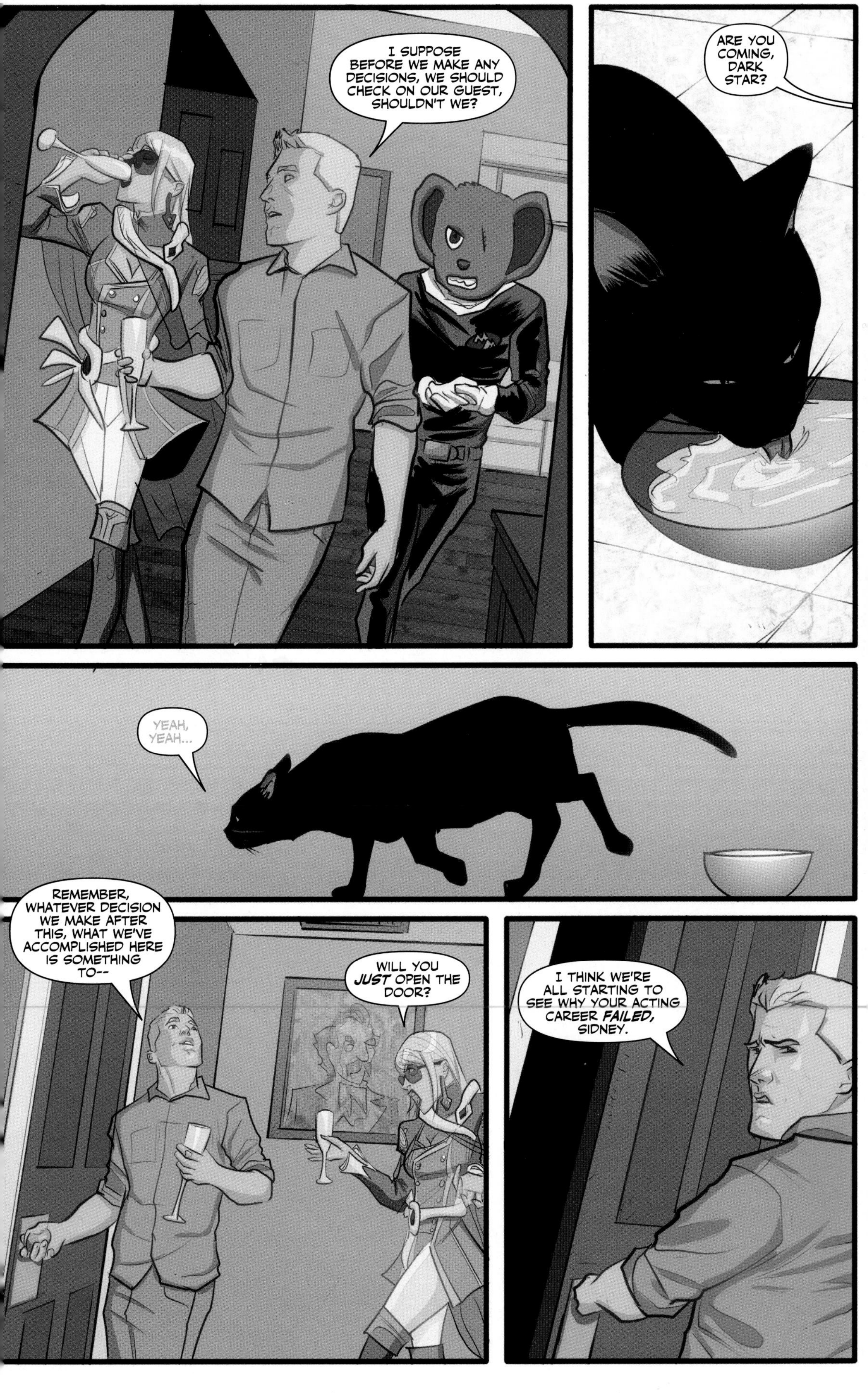
I SUPPOSE BEFORE WE MAKE ANY DECISIONS, WE SHOULD CHECK ON OUR GUEST, SHOULDN'T WE?
ARE YOU COMING, DARK STAR?
YEAH, YEAH...
REMEMBER, WHATEVER DECISION WE MAKE AFTER THIS, WHAT WE'VE ACCOMPLISHED HERE IS SOMETHING TO--
WILL YOU *JUST* OPEN THE DOOR?
I THINK WE'RE ALL STARTING TO SEE WHY YOUR ACTING CAREER *FAILED,* SIDNEY.

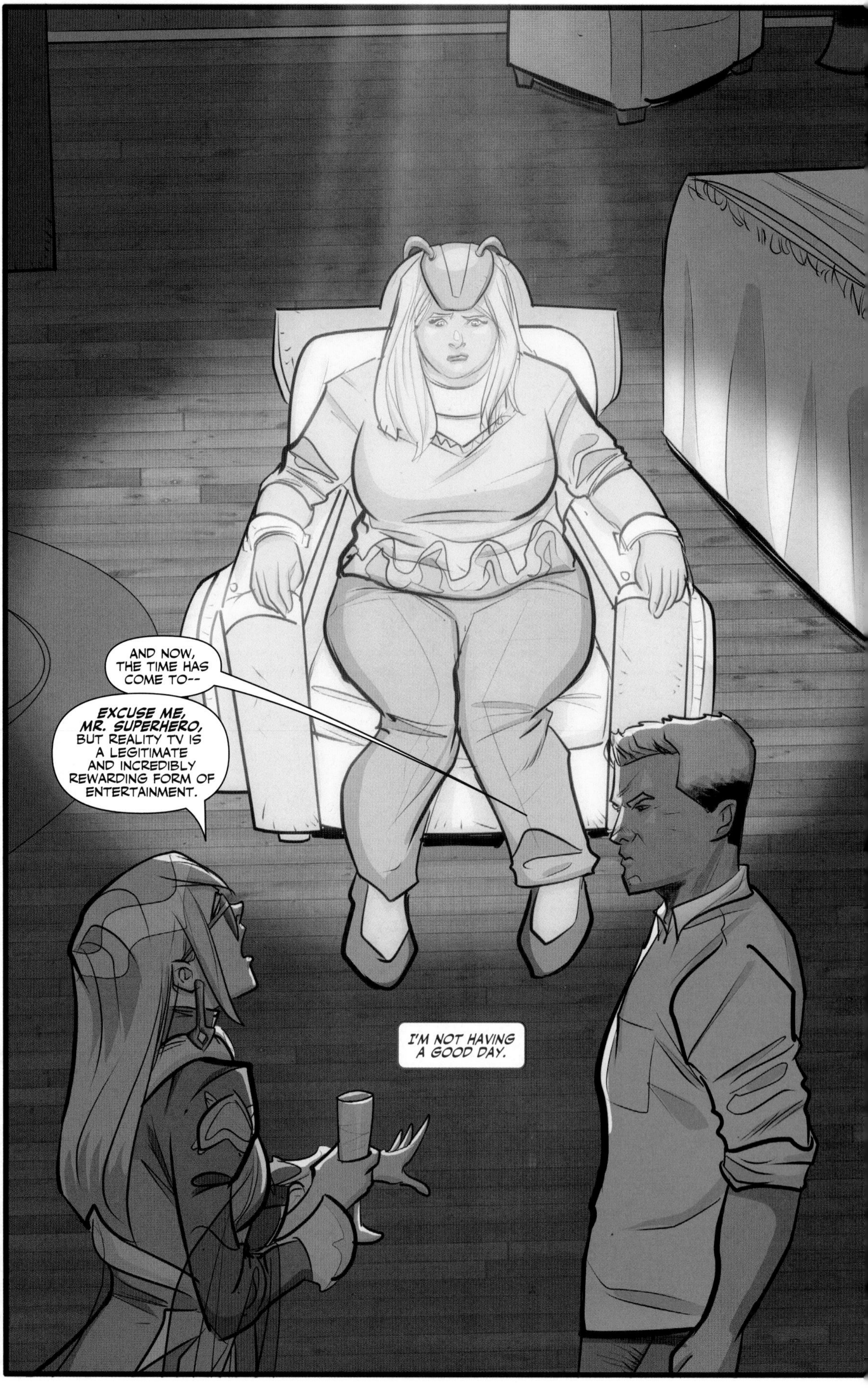
AND NOW, THE TIME HAS COME TO--
EXCUSE ME, MR. SUPERHERO, BUT REALITY TV IS A LEGITIMATE AND INCREDIBLY REWARDING FORM OF ENTERTAINMENT.
I'M NOT HAVING A GOOD DAY.

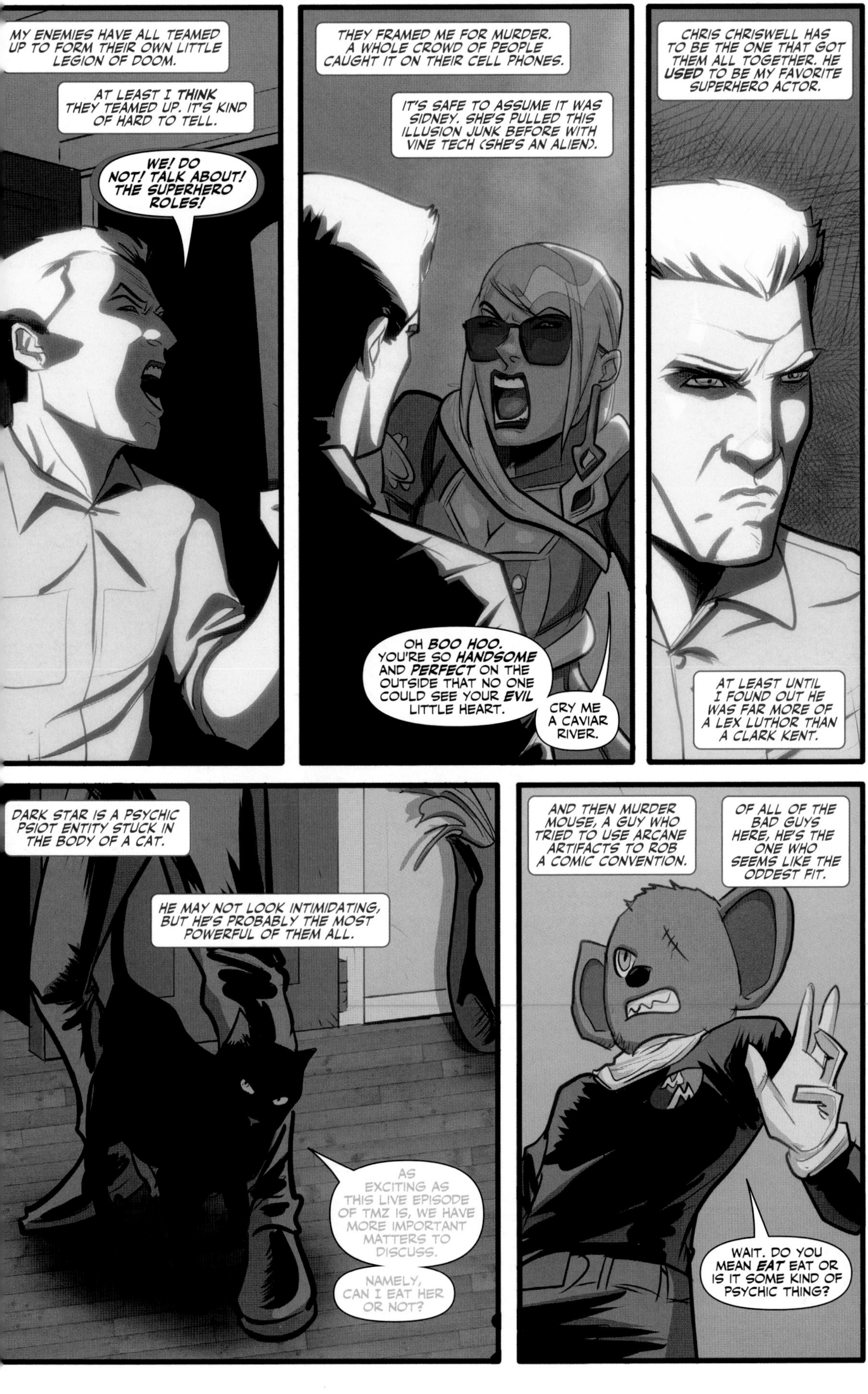
MY ENEMIES HAVE ALL TEAMED UP TO FORM THEIR OWN LITTLE LEGION OF DOOM.
AT LEAST I THINK THEY TEAMED UP. IT'S KIND OF HARD TO TELL.
WE! DO NOT! TALK ABOUT! THE SUPERHERO ROLES!
THEY FRAMED ME FOR MURDER. A WHOLE CROWD OF PEOPLE CAUGHT IT ON THEIR CELL PHONES.
IT'S SAFE TO ASSUME IT WAS SIDNEY. SHE'S PULLED THIS ILLUSION JUNK BEFORE WITH VINE TECH (SHE'S AN ALIEN).
OH BOO HOO. YOU'RE SO HANDSOME AND PERFECT ON THE OUTSIDE THAT NO ONE COULD SEE YOUR EVIL LITTLE HEART.
CRY ME A CAVIAR RIVER.
CHRIS CHRISWELL HAS TO BE THE ONE THAT GOT THEM ALL TOGETHER. HE USED TO BE MY FAVORITE SUPERHERO ACTOR.
AT LEAST UNTIL I FOUND OUT HE WAS FAR MORE OF A LEX LUTHOR THAN A CLARK KENT.
DARK STAR IS A PSYCHIC PSIOT ENTITY STUCK IN THE BODY OF A CAT.
HE MAY NOT LOOK INTIMIDATING, BUT HE'S PROBABLY THE MOST POWERFUL OF THEM ALL.
AS EXCITING AS THIS LIVE EPISODE OF TMZ IS, WE HAVE MORE IMPORTANT MATTERS TO DISCUSS.
NAMELY, CAN I EAT HER OR NOT?
AND THEN MURDER MOUSE, A GUY WHO TRIED TO USE ARCANE ARTIFACTS TO ROB A COMIC CONVENTION.
OF ALL OF THE BAD GUYS HERE, HE'S THE ONE WHO SEEMS LIKE THE ODDEST FIT.
WAIT. DO YOU MEAN EAT EAT OR IS IT SOME KIND OF PSYCHIC THING?

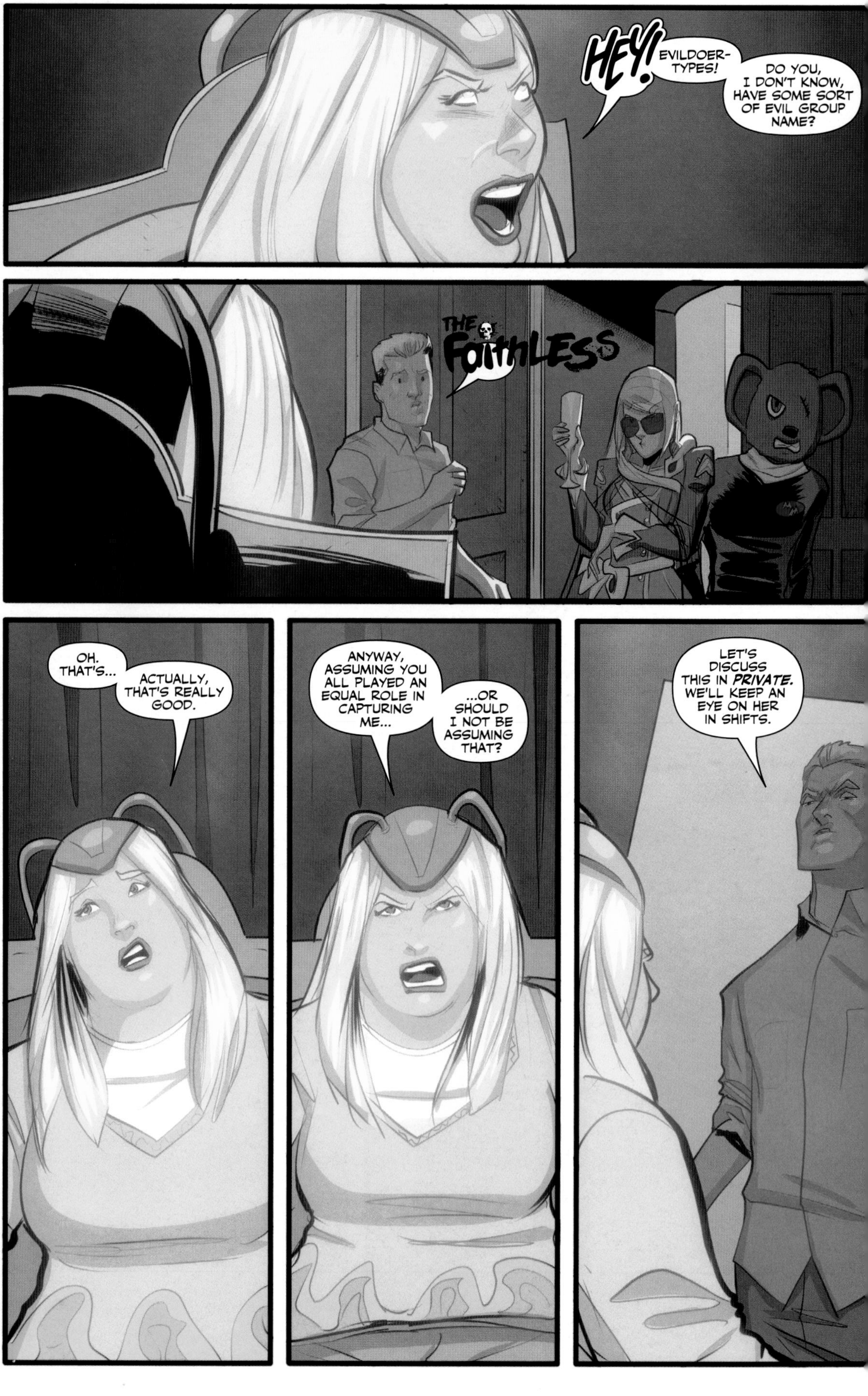
HEY!
EVILDOER-TYPES!
DO YOU, I DON'T KNOW, HAVE SOME SORT OF EVIL GROUP NAME?
THE FAITHLESS
OH. THAT'S...
ACTUALLY, THAT'S REALLY GOOD.
ANYWAY, ASSUMING YOU ALL PLAYED AN EQUAL ROLE IN CAPTURING ME...
...OR SHOULD I NOT BE ASSUMING THAT?
LET'S DISCUSS THIS IN PRIVATE. WE'LL KEEP AN EYE ON HER IN SHIFTS.

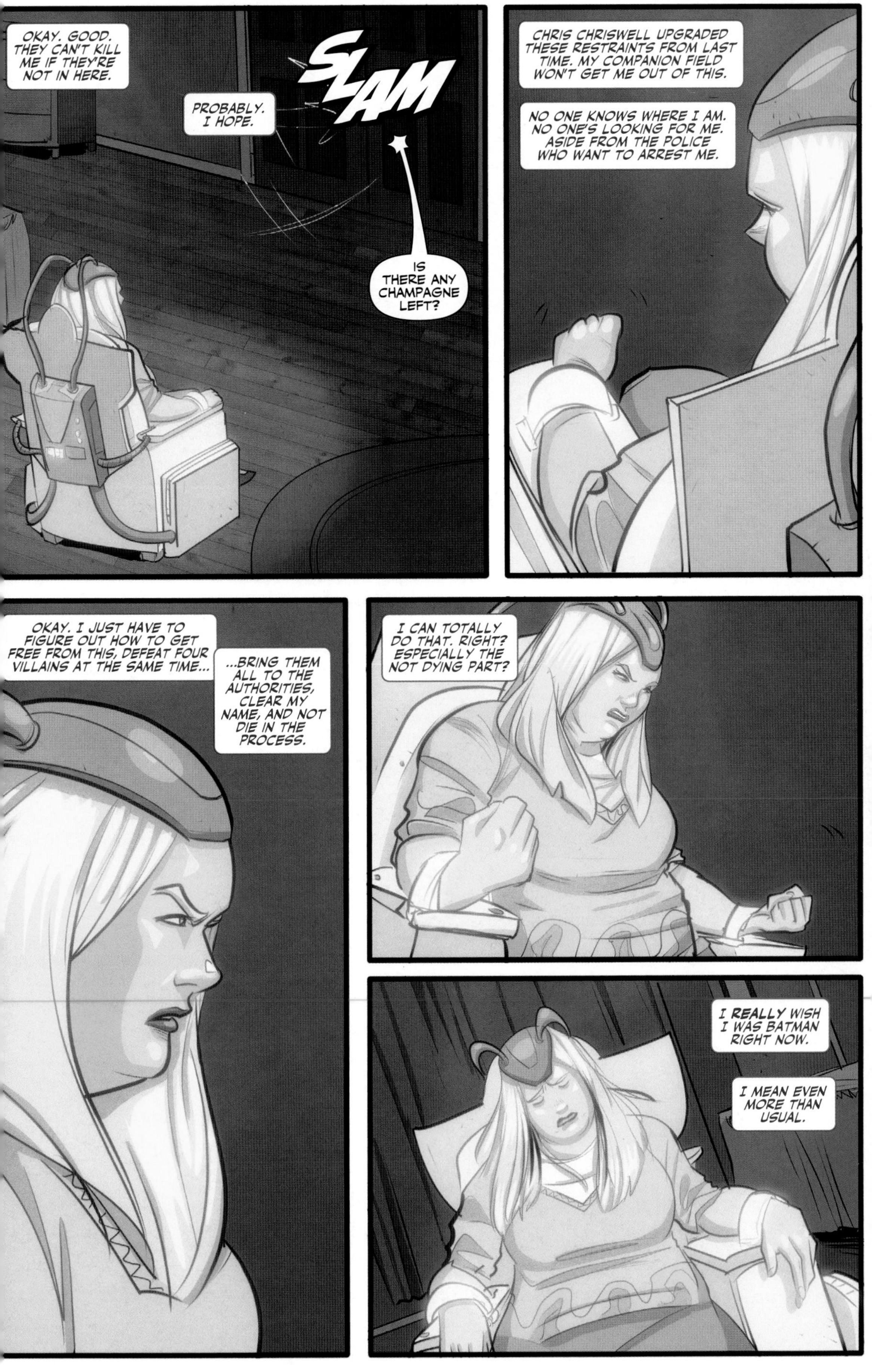
OKAY. GOOD. THEY CAN'T KILL ME IF THEY'RE NOT IN HERE.
PROBABLY. I HOPE.
SLAM
IS THERE ANY CHAMPAGNE LEFT?
CHRIS CHRISWELL UPGRADED THESE RESTRAINTS FROM LAST TIME. MY COMPANION FIELD WON'T GET ME OUT OF THIS.
NO ONE KNOWS WHERE I AM. NO ONE'S LOOKING FOR ME. ASIDE FROM THE POLICE WHO WANT TO ARREST ME.
OKAY. I JUST HAVE TO FIGURE OUT HOW TO GET FREE FROM THIS, DEFEAT FOUR VILLAINS AT THE SAME TIME...
...BRING THEM ALL TO THE AUTHORITIES, CLEAR MY NAME, AND NOT DIE IN THE PROCESS.
I CAN TOTALLY DO THAT. RIGHT? ESPECIALLY THE NOT DYING PART?
I REALLY WISH I WAS BATMAN RIGHT NOW.
I MEAN EVEN MORE THAN USUAL.

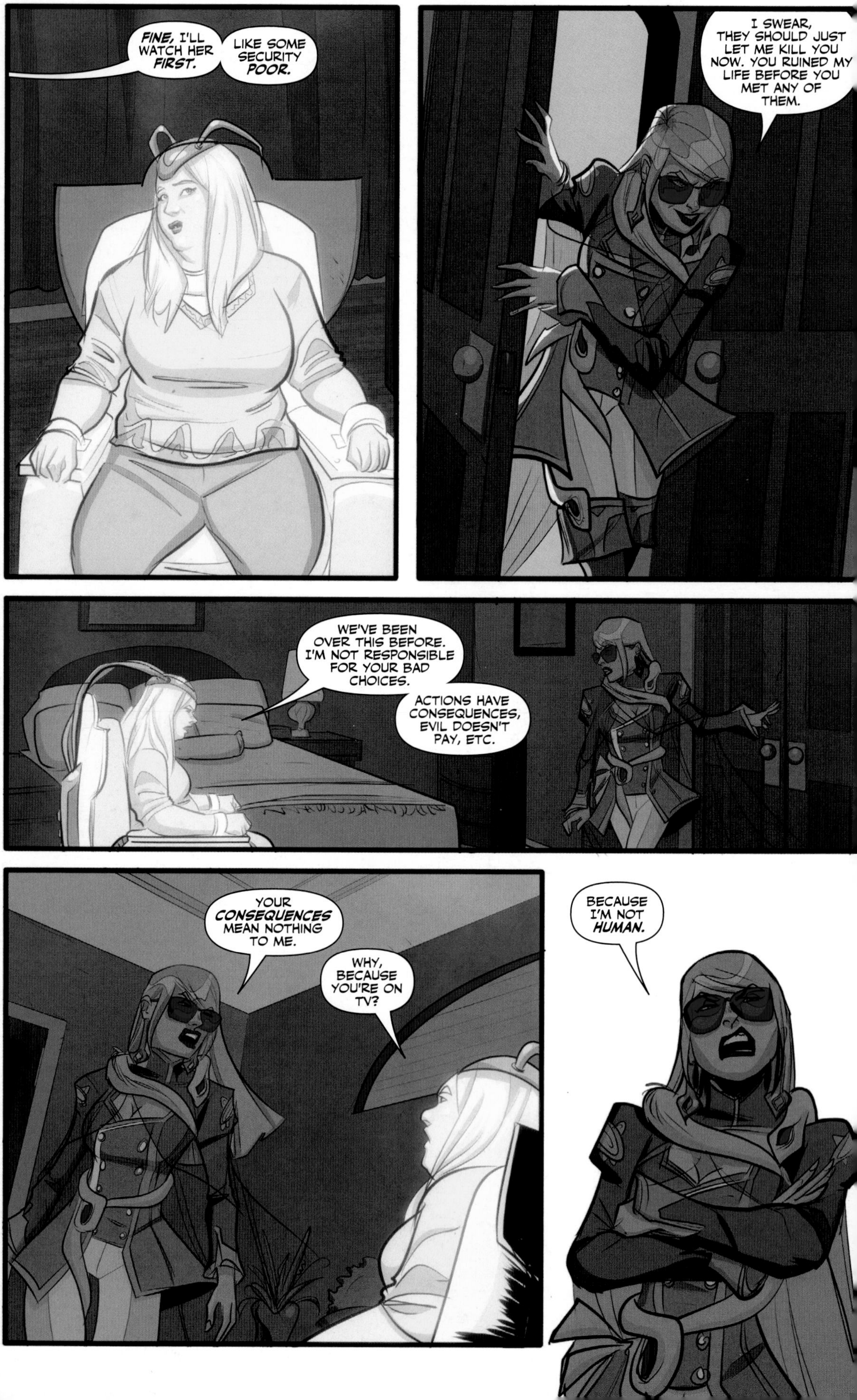
FINE, I'LL WATCH HER FIRST.
LIKE SOME SECURITY POOR.
I SWEAR, THEY SHOULD JUST LET ME KILL YOU NOW. YOU RUINED MY LIFE BEFORE YOU MET ANY OF THEM.
WE'VE BEEN OVER THIS BEFORE. I'M NOT RESPONSIBLE FOR YOUR BAD CHOICES.
ACTIONS HAVE CONSEQUENCES, EVIL DOESN'T PAY, ETC.
YOUR CONSEQUENCES MEAN NOTHING TO ME.
WHY, BECAUSE YOU'RE ON TV?
BECAUSE I'M NOT HUMAN.

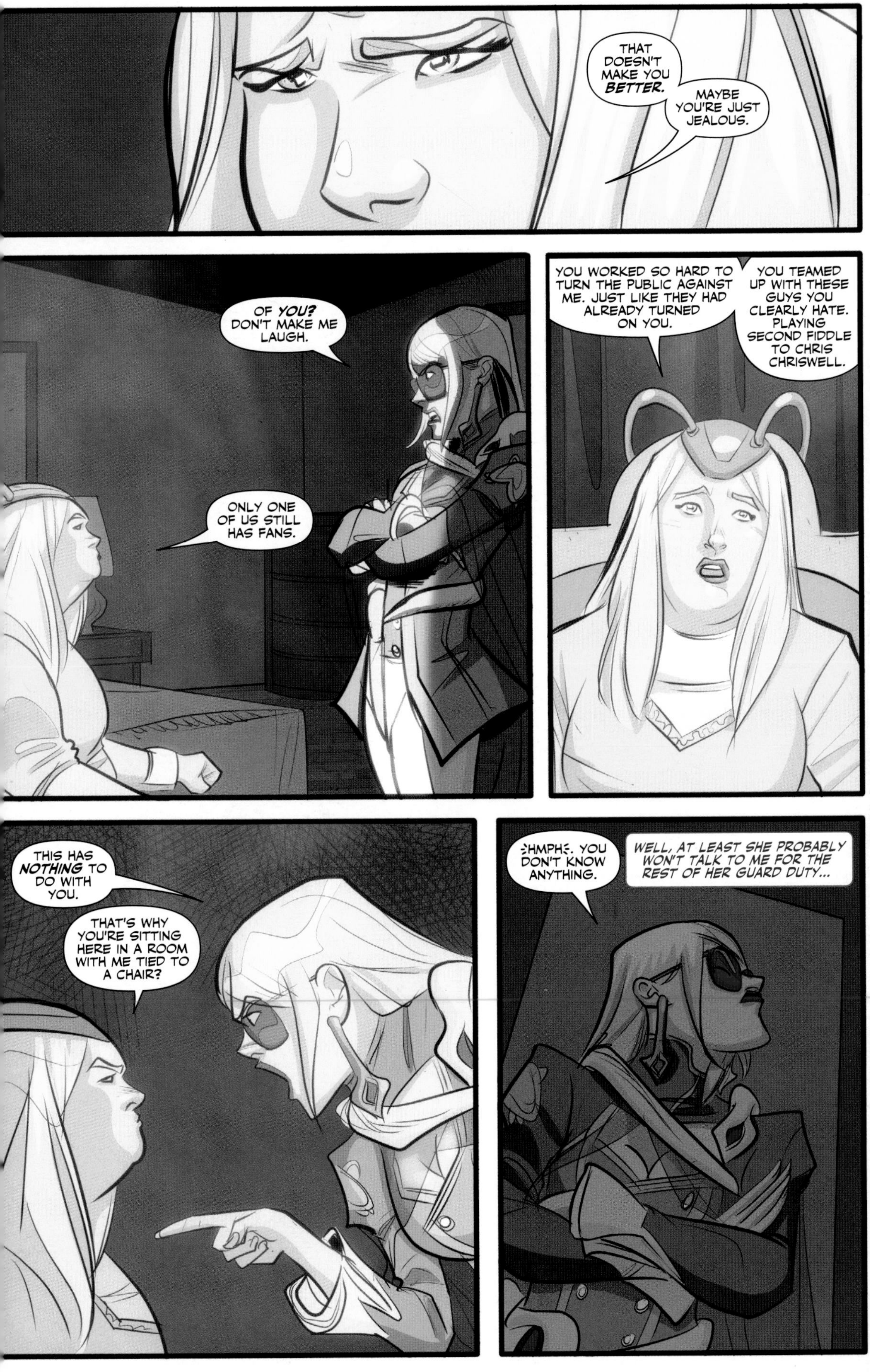
THAT DOESN'T MAKE YOU *BETTER.*
MAYBE YOU'RE JUST JEALOUS.
OF *YOU?* DON'T MAKE ME LAUGH.
ONLY ONE OF US STILL HAS FANS.
YOU WORKED SO HARD TO TURN THE PUBLIC AGAINST ME. JUST LIKE THEY HAD ALREADY TURNED ON YOU.
YOU TEAMED UP WITH THESE GUYS YOU CLEARLY HATE. PLAYING SECOND FIDDLE TO CHRIS CHRISWELL.
THIS HAS *NOTHING* TO DO WITH YOU.
THAT'S WHY YOU'RE SITTING HERE IN A ROOM WITH ME TIED TO A CHAIR?
HMPH. YOU DON'T KNOW ANYTHING.
WELL, AT LEAST SHE PROBABLY WON'T TALK TO ME FOR THE REST OF HER GUARD DUTY...

MY. TURN.

FINALLY.

BET YOU THINK YOU CAN ESCAPE WITH JUST A LITTLE KITTY CAT IN HERE.

WON'T WORK. THAT NEW ANTI-PSIOT STUFF THEY MADE IS REEEEEEALLY STRONG.

I TRIED TOO, YOU KNOW. TRIED AND TRIED AND TRIED.

YOU HUMANS AND YOUR STUPID CAGES.

ARE YOU... ARE YOU DRUNK?

NO!

...MAYBE.

DOESN'T MATTER. AFTER I FEED ON YOU, I'LL BE A NEW CAT.

OR I'LL BE YOU. SOMETHING.

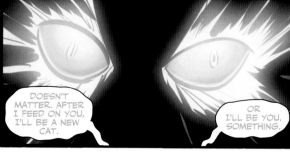

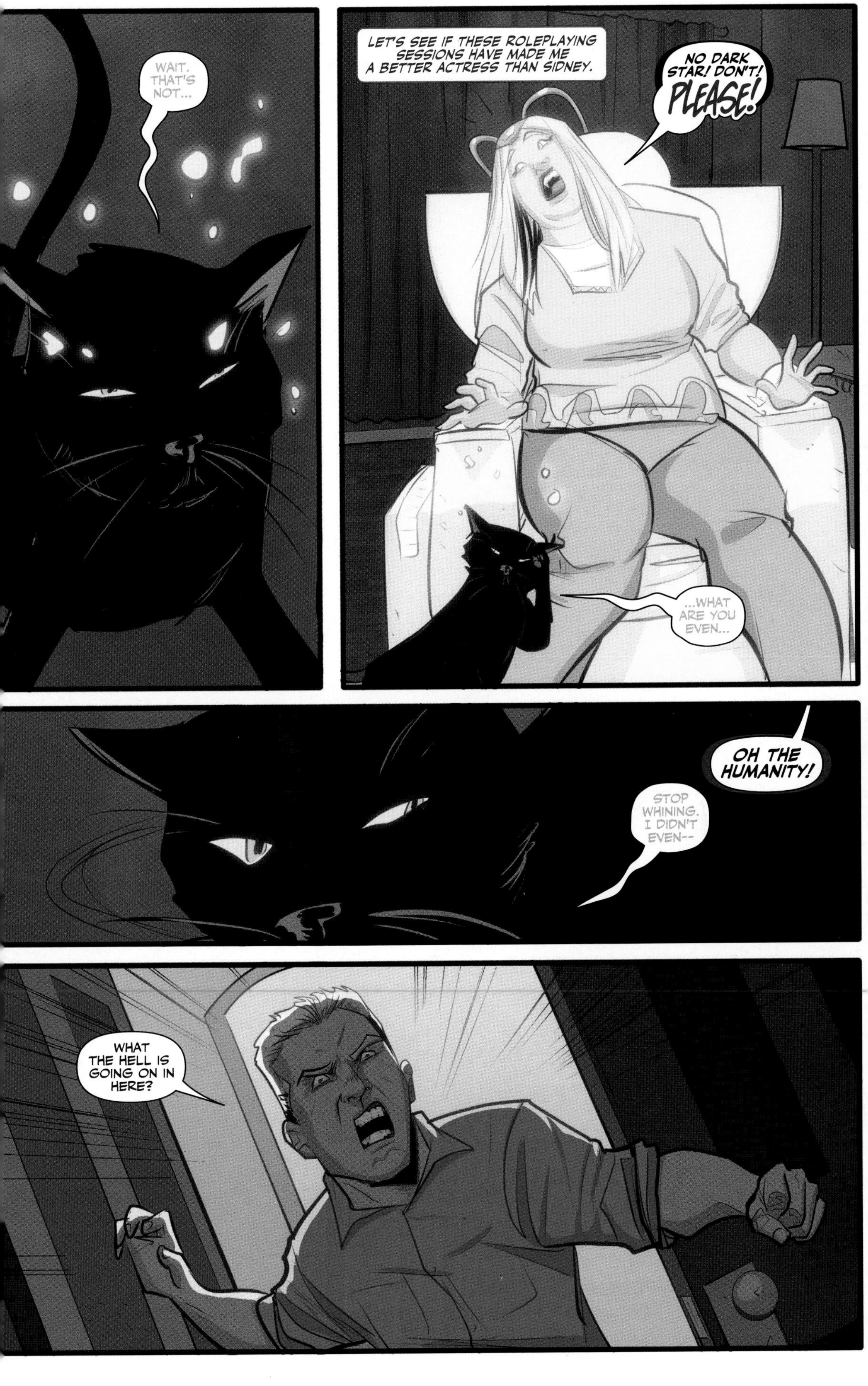
WAIT. THAT'S NOT...
LET'S SEE IF THESE ROLEPLAYING SESSIONS HAVE MADE ME A BETTER ACTRESS THAN SIDNEY.
NO DARK STAR! DON'T! PLEASE!
...WHAT ARE YOU EVEN...
OH THE HUMANITY!
STOP WHINING. I DIDN'T EVEN--
WHAT THE HELL IS GOING ON IN HERE?

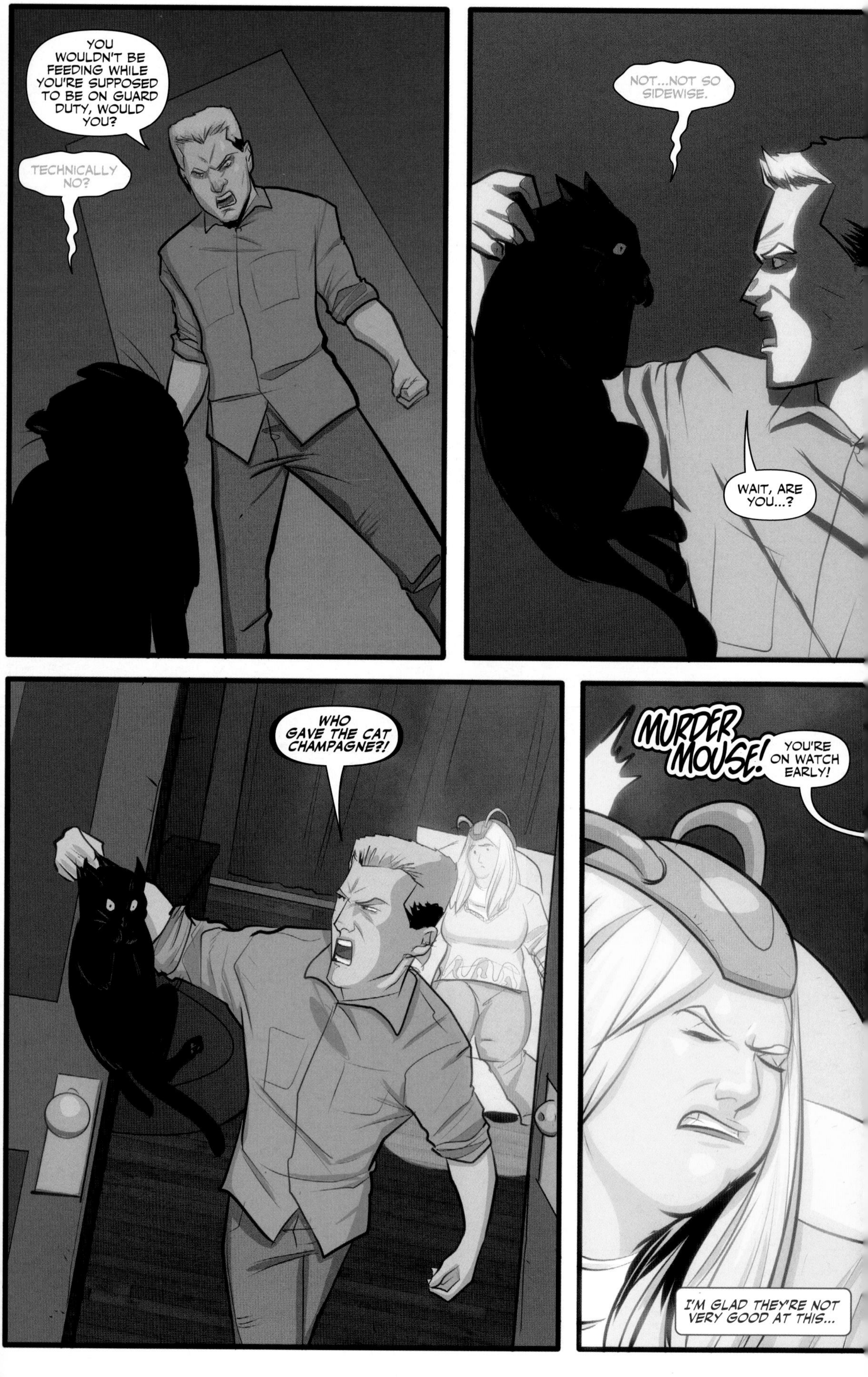
YOU WOULDN'T BE FEEDING WHILE YOU'RE SUPPOSED TO BE ON GUARD DUTY, WOULD YOU?
TECHNICALLY NO?
NOT...NOT SO SIDEWISE.
WAIT, ARE YOU...?
WHO GAVE THE CAT CHAMPAGNE?!
MURDER MOUSE!
YOU'RE ON WATCH EARLY!
I'M GLAD THEY'RE NOT VERY GOOD AT THIS...

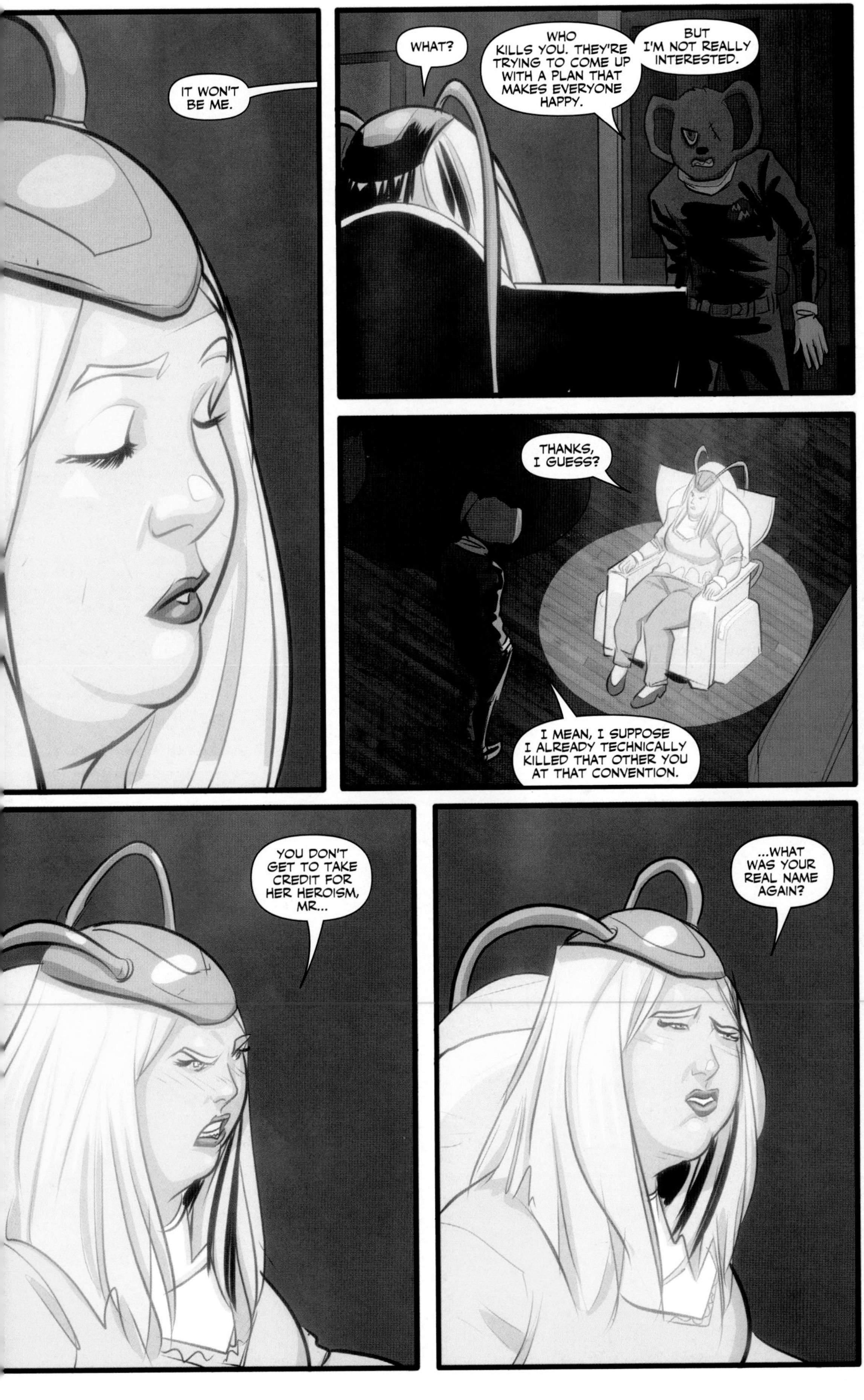
IT WON'T BE ME.
WHAT?
WHO KILLS YOU. THEY'RE TRYING TO COME UP WITH A PLAN THAT MAKES EVERYONE HAPPY.
BUT I'M NOT REALLY INTERESTED.
THANKS, I GUESS?
I MEAN, I SUPPOSE I ALREADY TECHNICALLY KILLED THAT OTHER YOU AT THAT CONVENTION.
YOU DON'T GET TO TAKE CREDIT FOR HER HEROISM, MR...
...WHAT WAS YOUR REAL NAME AGAIN?

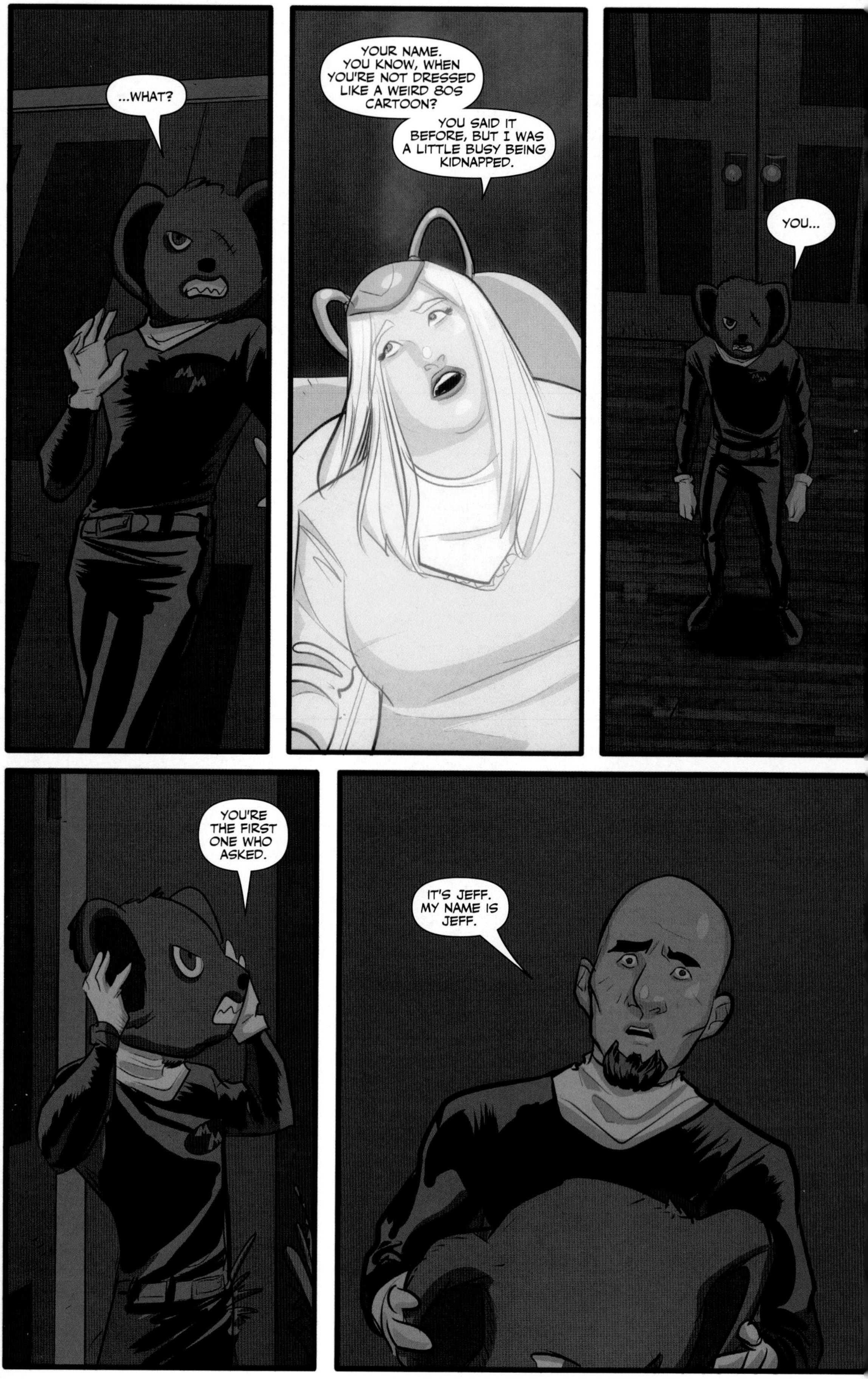

...WHAT?
YOUR NAME. YOU KNOW, WHEN YOU'RE NOT DRESSED LIKE A WEIRD 80S CARTOON?
YOU SAID IT BEFORE, BUT I WAS A LITTLE BUSY BEING KIDNAPPED.
YOU...
YOU'RE THE FIRST ONE WHO ASKED.
IT'S JEFF. MY NAME IS JEFF.

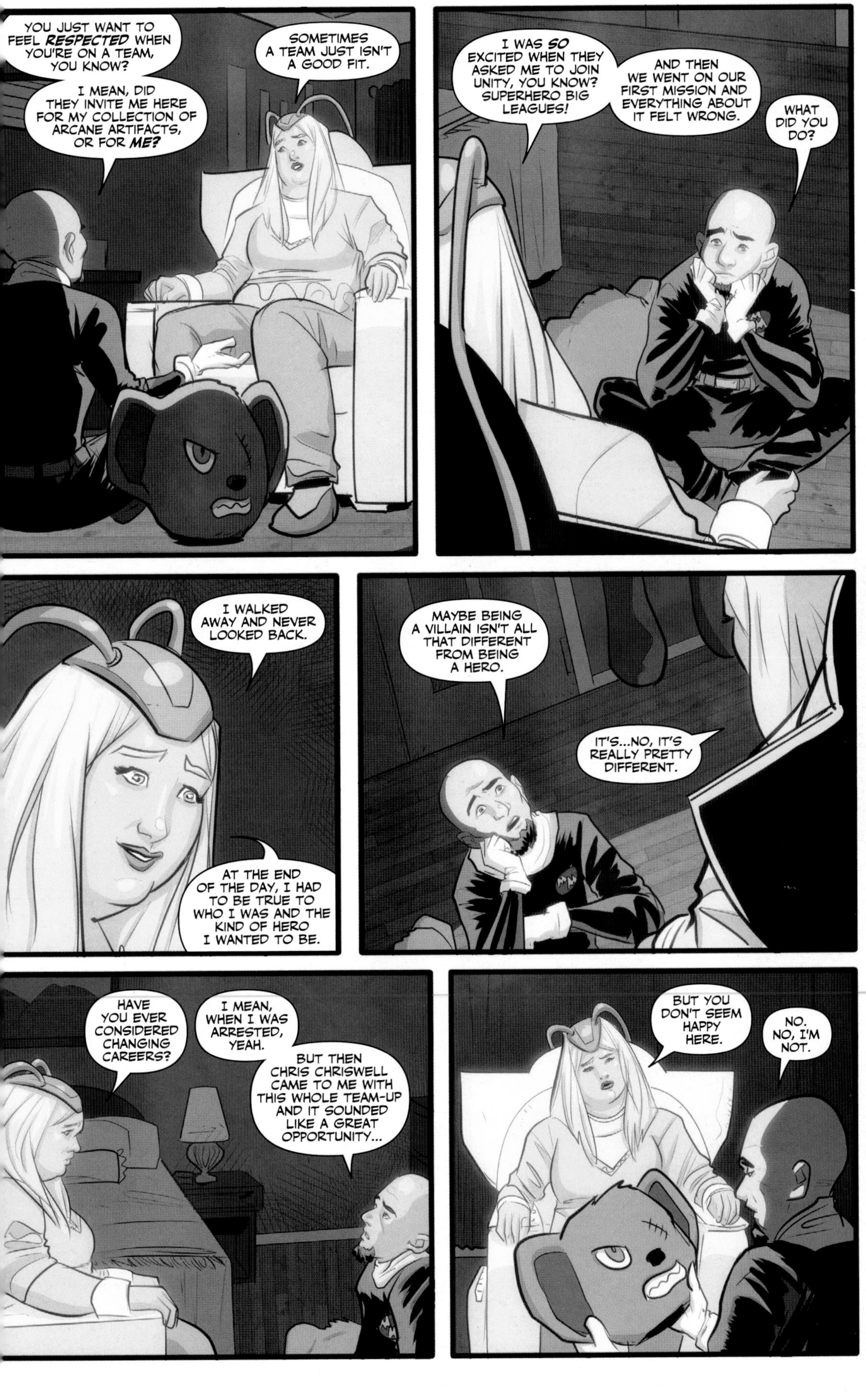
YOU JUST WANT TO FEEL *RESPECTED* WHEN YOU'RE ON A TEAM, YOU KNOW?
I MEAN, DID THEY INVITE ME HERE FOR MY COLLECTION OF ARCANE ARTIFACTS, OR FOR *ME?*
SOMETIMES A TEAM JUST ISN'T A GOOD FIT.
I WAS *SO* EXCITED WHEN THEY ASKED ME TO JOIN UNITY, YOU KNOW? SUPERHERO BIG LEAGUES!
AND THEN WE WENT ON OUR FIRST MISSION AND EVERYTHING ABOUT IT FELT WRONG.
WHAT DID YOU DO?
I WALKED AWAY AND NEVER LOOKED BACK.
AT THE END OF THE DAY, I HAD TO BE TRUE TO WHO I WAS AND THE KIND OF HERO I WANTED TO BE.
MAYBE BEING A VILLAIN ISN'T ALL THAT DIFFERENT FROM BEING A HERO.
IT'S...NO, IT'S REALLY PRETTY DIFFERENT.
HAVE YOU EVER CONSIDERED CHANGING CAREERS?
I MEAN, WHEN I WAS ARRESTED, YEAH.
BUT THEN CHRIS CHRISWELL CAME TO ME WITH THIS WHOLE TEAM-UP AND IT SOUNDED LIKE A GREAT OPPORTUNITY...
BUT YOU DON'T SEEM HAPPY HERE.
NO. NO, I'M NOT.

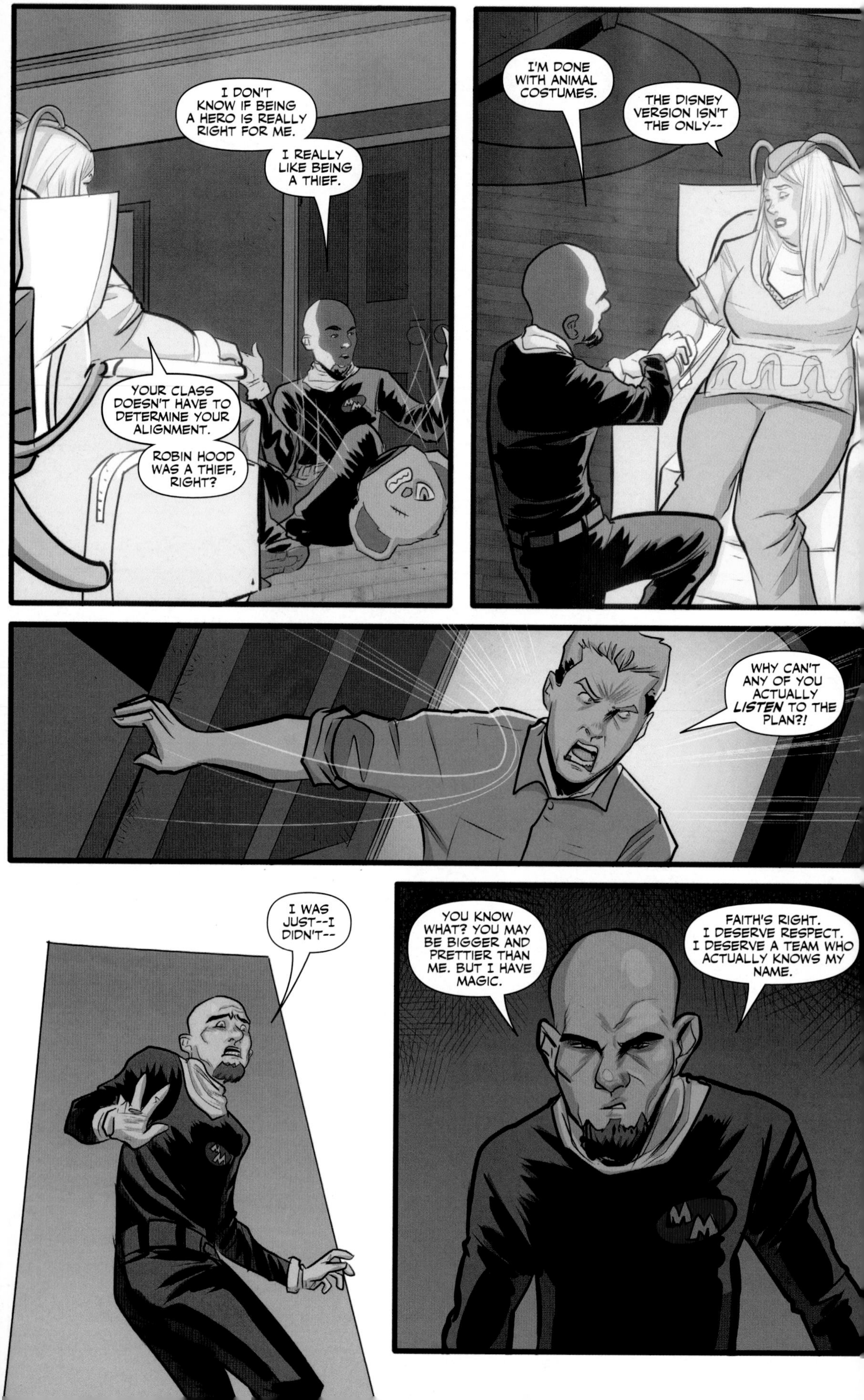
I DON'T KNOW IF BEING A HERO IS REALLY RIGHT FOR ME.
I REALLY LIKE BEING A THIEF.
YOUR CLASS DOESN'T HAVE TO DETERMINE YOUR ALIGNMENT.
ROBIN HOOD WAS A THIEF, RIGHT?
I'M DONE WITH ANIMAL COSTUMES.
THE DISNEY VERSION ISN'T THE ONLY--
WHY CAN'T ANY OF YOU ACTUALLY LISTEN TO THE PLAN?!
I WAS JUST--I DIDN'T--
YOU KNOW WHAT? YOU MAY BE BIGGER AND PRETTIER THAN ME. BUT I HAVE MAGIC.
FAITH'S RIGHT. I DESERVE RESPECT. I DESERVE A TEAM WHO ACTUALLY KNOWS MY NAME.

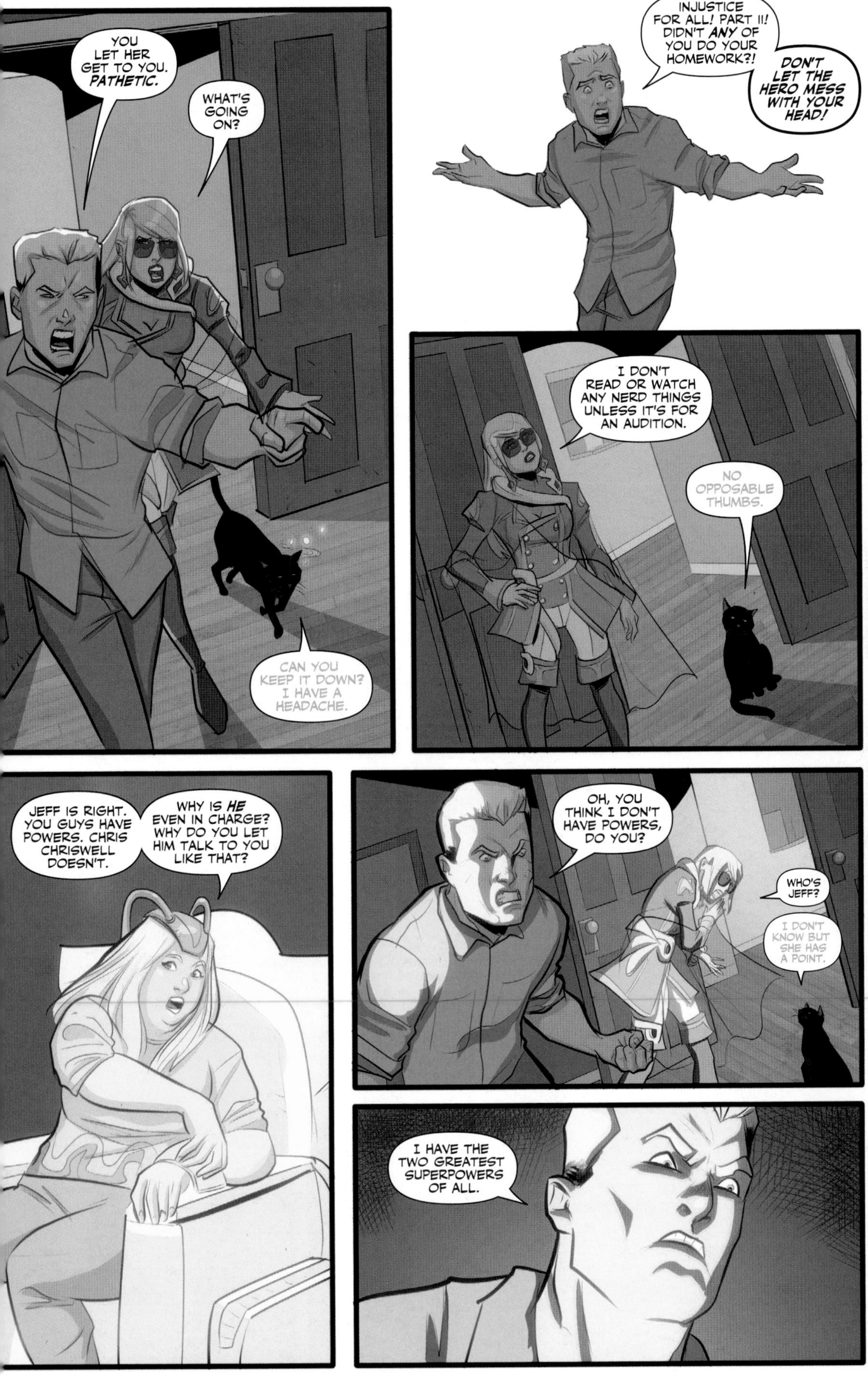
YOU LET HER GET TO YOU. *PATHETIC.*
WHAT'S GOING ON?
CAN YOU KEEP IT DOWN? I HAVE A HEADACHE.
INJUSTICE FOR ALL! PART II! DIDN'T *ANY* OF YOU DO YOUR HOMEWORK?!
DON'T LET THE HERO MESS WITH YOUR HEAD!
I DON'T READ OR WATCH ANY NERD THINGS UNLESS IT'S FOR AN AUDITION.
NO OPPOSABLE THUMBS.
JEFF IS RIGHT. YOU GUYS HAVE POWERS. CHRIS CHRISWELL DOESN'T.
WHY IS *HE* EVEN IN CHARGE? WHY DO YOU LET HIM TALK TO YOU LIKE THAT?
OH, YOU THINK I DON'T HAVE POWERS, DO YOU?
WHO'S JEFF?
I DON'T KNOW BUT SHE HAS A POINT.
I HAVE THE TWO GREATEST SUPERPOWERS OF ALL.

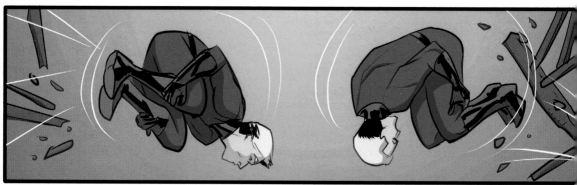

MEET **FAME** AND **FORTUNE.** THE MOST ELITE OF MY STUNT DOUBLES.

THAT'S IT, CHRIS. I'M **DONE** BEING A PART OF YOUR DISTURBED LITTLE CHILDHOOD FANTASY.

SO MANY FACES TO CONSUME.

I WANTED THEM TO TURN ON EACH OTHER. BUT NOT IN A MURDER SORT OF WAY.

TAKE THEM ALL DOWN! AND DON'T LET THE CAT EAT YOUR MIND!

I GUESS I SHOULD HAVE EXPECTED THIS OUTCOME. THEY **ARE** SUPER VILLAINS.

I'VE GOT TO STOP THIS.

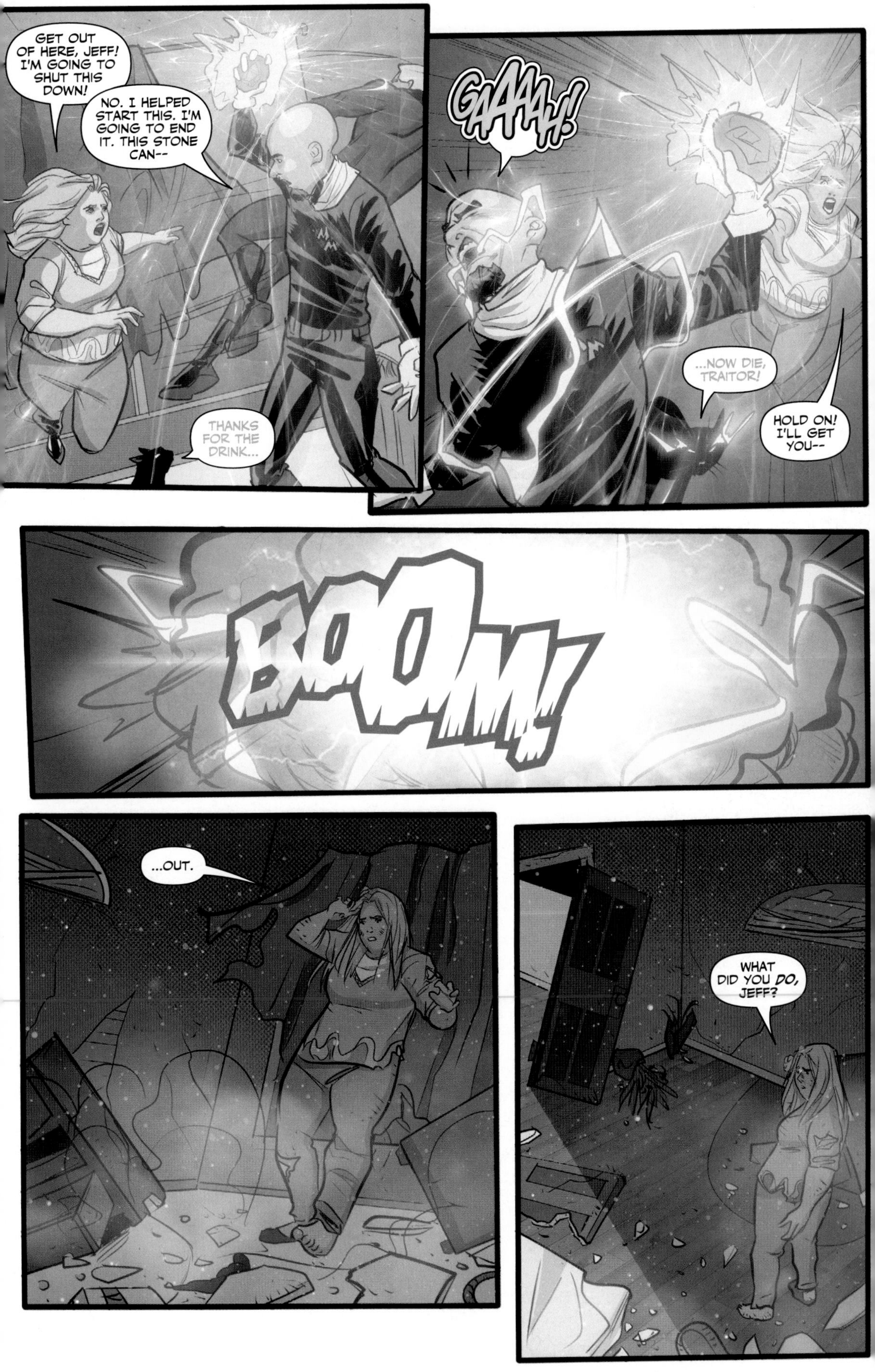
GET OUT OF HERE, JEFF! I'M GOING TO SHUT THIS DOWN!
NO. I HELPED START THIS. I'M GOING TO END IT. THIS STONE CAN--
THANKS FOR THE DRINK...
GAAAAH!
...NOW DIE, TRAITOR!
HOLD ON! I'LL GET YOU--
BOOM!
...OUT.
WHAT DID YOU *DO*, JEFF?

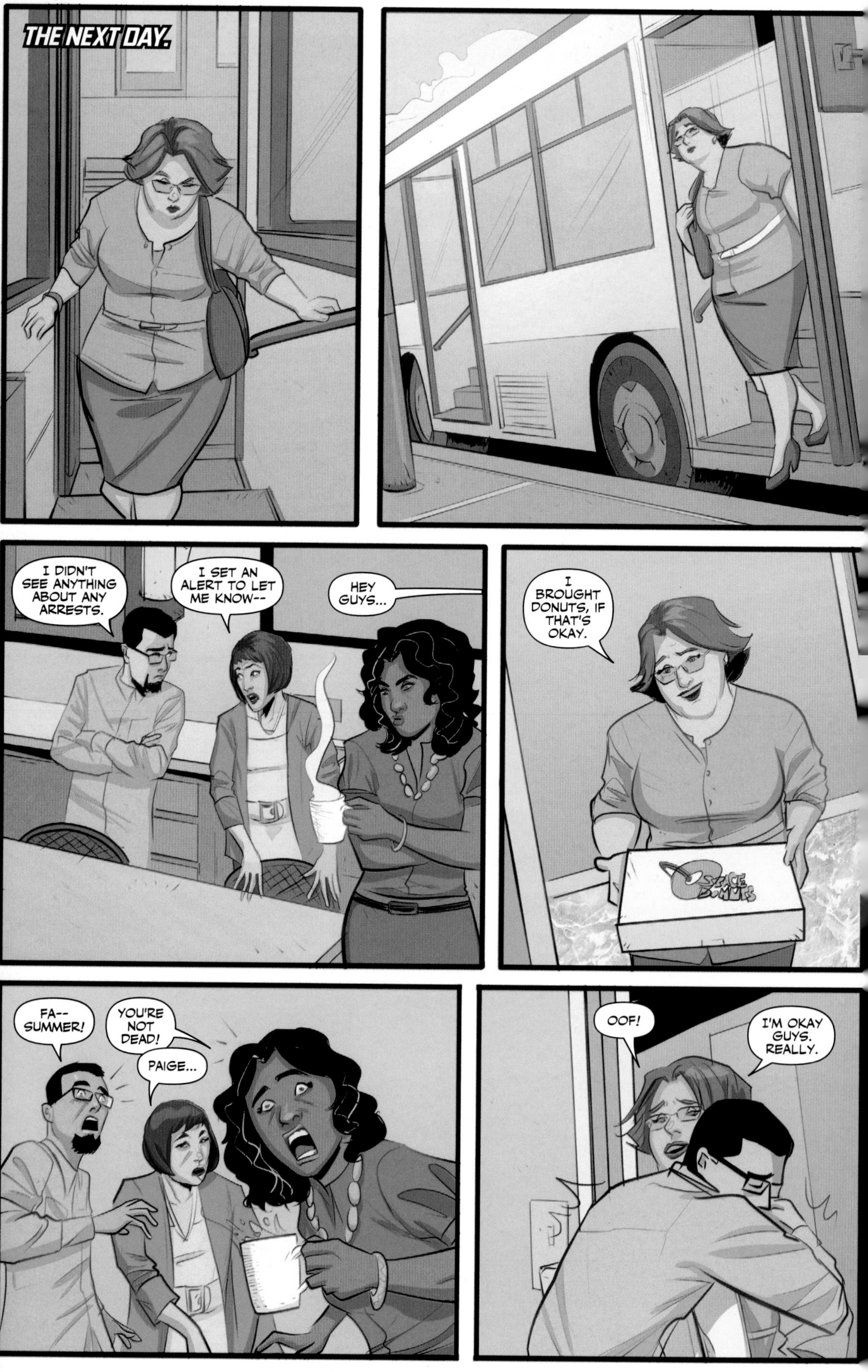
THE NEXT DAY.
I DIDN'T SEE ANYTHING ABOUT ANY ARRESTS.
I SET AN ALERT TO LET ME KNOW--
HEY GUYS...
I BROUGHT DONUTS, IF THAT'S OKAY.
SPACE DONUTS
FA-- SUMMER!
YOU'RE NOT DEAD!
PAIGE...
OOF!
I'M OKAY GUYS. REALLY.

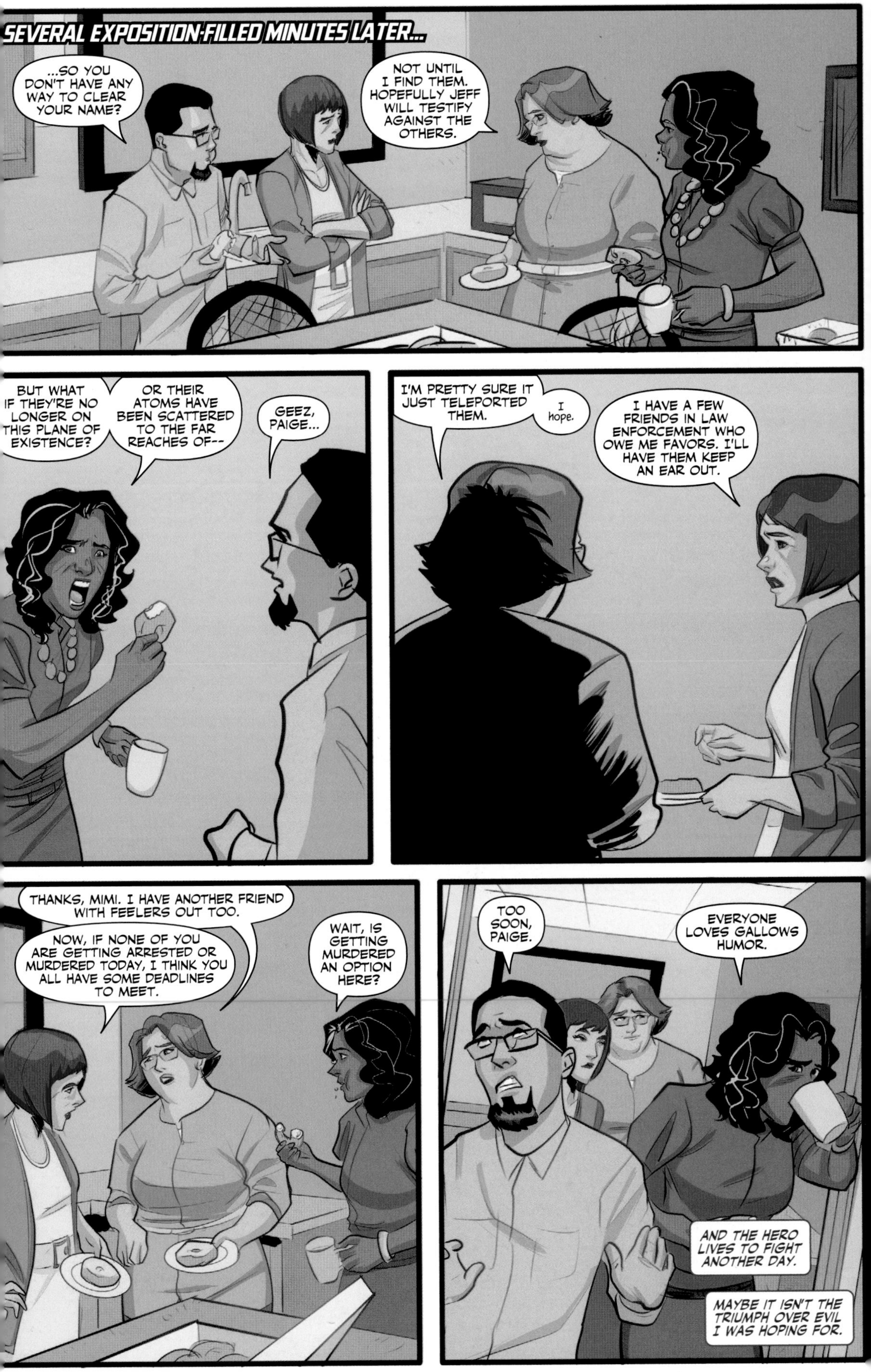
SEVERAL EXPOSITION-FILLED MINUTES LATER...
...SO YOU DON'T HAVE ANY WAY TO CLEAR YOUR NAME?
NOT UNTIL I FIND THEM. HOPEFULLY JEFF WILL TESTIFY AGAINST THE OTHERS.
BUT WHAT IF THEY'RE NO LONGER ON THIS PLANE OF EXISTENCE?
OR THEIR ATOMS HAVE BEEN SCATTERED TO THE FAR REACHES OF--
GEEZ, PAIGE...
I'M PRETTY SURE IT JUST TELEPORTED THEM.
I hope.
I HAVE A FEW FRIENDS IN LAW ENFORCEMENT WHO OWE ME FAVORS. I'LL HAVE THEM KEEP AN EAR OUT.
THANKS, MIMI. I HAVE ANOTHER FRIEND WITH FEELERS OUT TOO.
NOW, IF NONE OF YOU ARE GETTING ARRESTED OR MURDERED TODAY, I THINK YOU ALL HAVE SOME DEADLINES TO MEET.
WAIT, IS GETTING MURDERED AN OPTION HERE?
TOO SOON, PAIGE.
EVERYONE LOVES GALLOWS HUMOR.
AND THE HERO LIVES TO FIGHT ANOTHER DAY.
MAYBE IT ISN'T THE TRIUMPH OVER EVIL I WAS HOPING FOR.

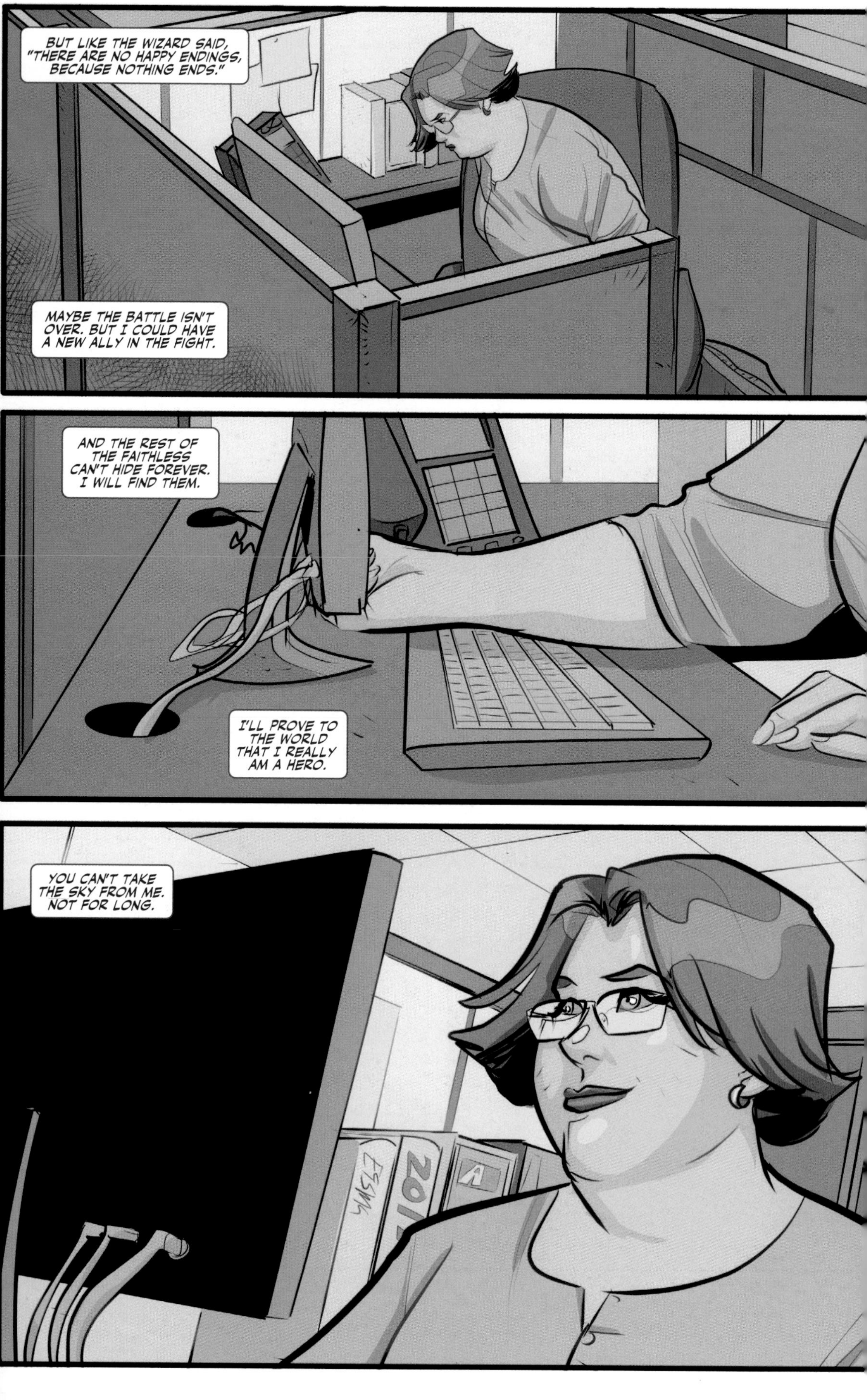
BUT LIKE THE WIZARD SAID, "THERE ARE NO HAPPY ENDINGS, BECAUSE NOTHING ENDS."
MAYBE THE BATTLE ISN'T OVER. BUT I COULD HAVE A NEW ALLY IN THE FIGHT.
AND THE REST OF THE FAITHLESS CAN'T HIDE FOREVER. I WILL FIND THEM.
I'LL PROVE TO THE WORLD THAT I REALLY AM A HERO.
YOU CAN'T TAKE THE SKY FROM ME. NOT FOR LONG.

GALLERY

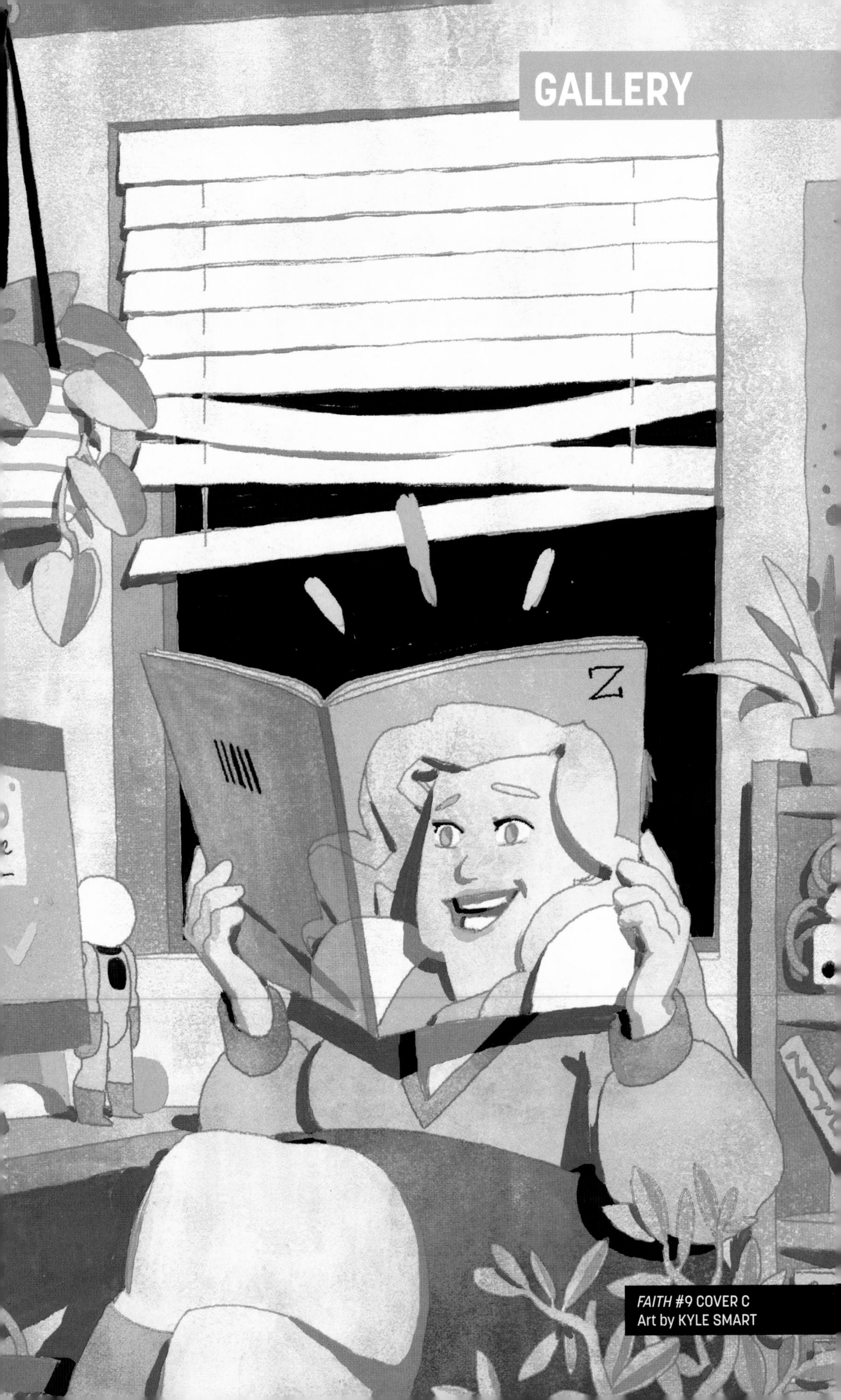

Z

FAITH #9 COVER C
Art by KYLE SMART

FAITH #9 COVER B
Art by SANYA ANWAR

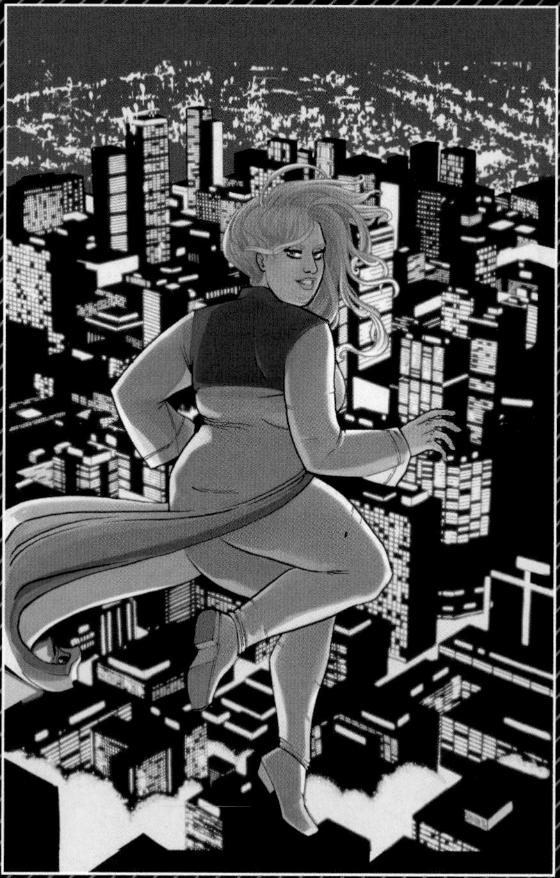

FAITH #11 VARIANT COVER
Art by CRYSSY CHEUNG

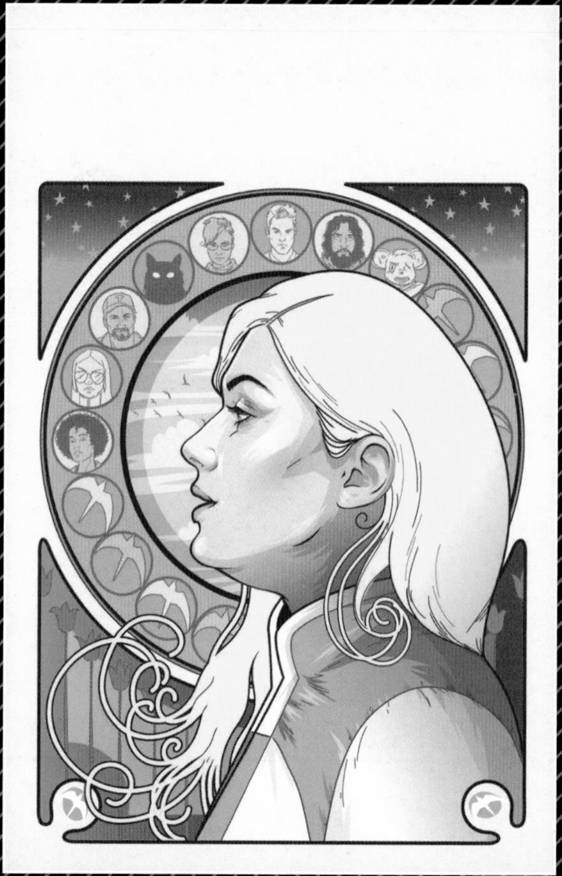

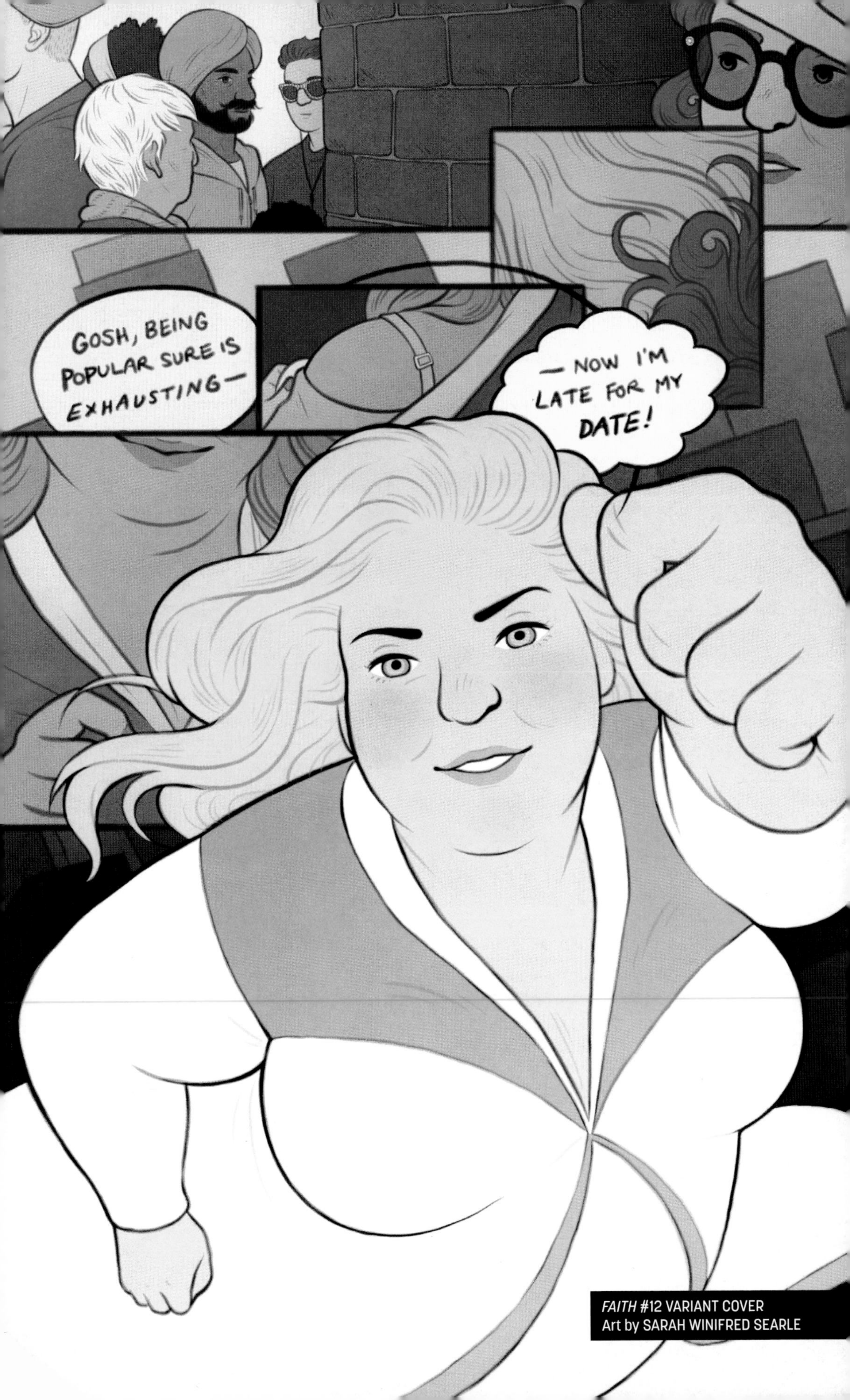
GOSH, BEING POPULAR SURE IS EXHAUSTING—
—NOW I'M LATE FOR MY DATE!

FAITH #12 VARIANT COVER
Art by SARAH WINIFRED SEARLE

FAITH #9, p. 2
Art by KATE NIEMCZYK

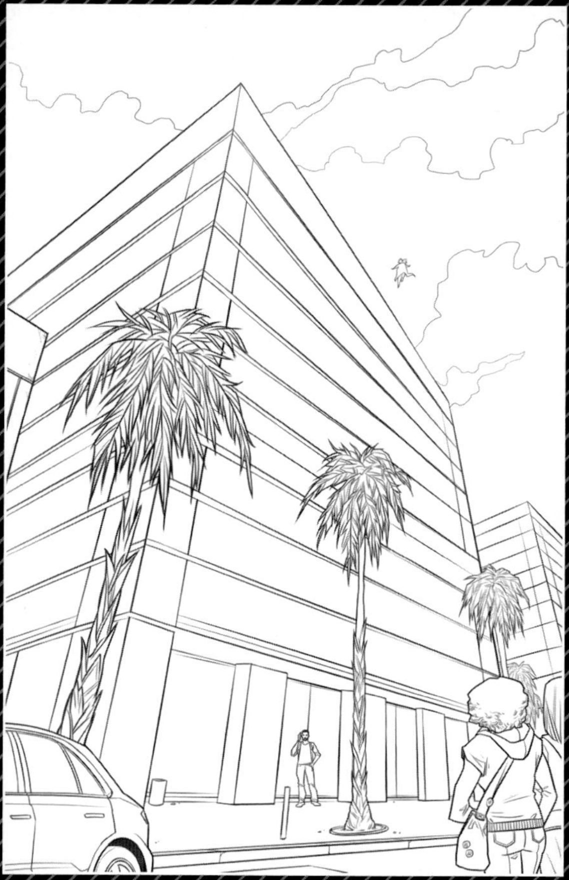

FAITH #9, p. 12
Art by KATE NIEMCZYK

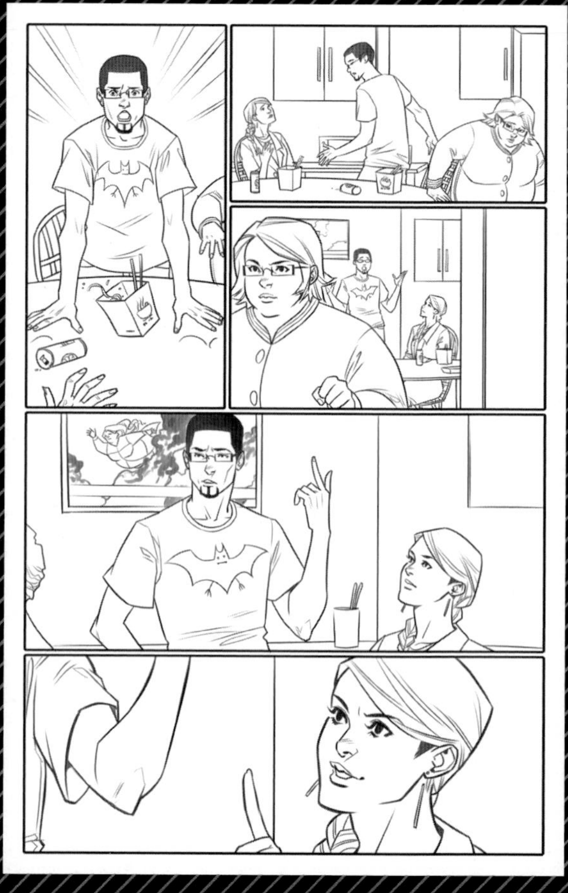

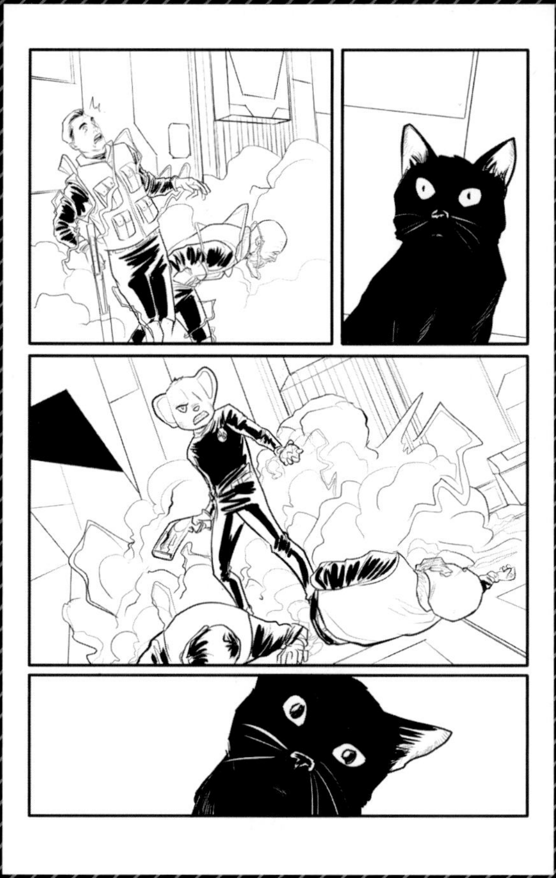

FAITH #10, p. 2
Art by JOE EISMA

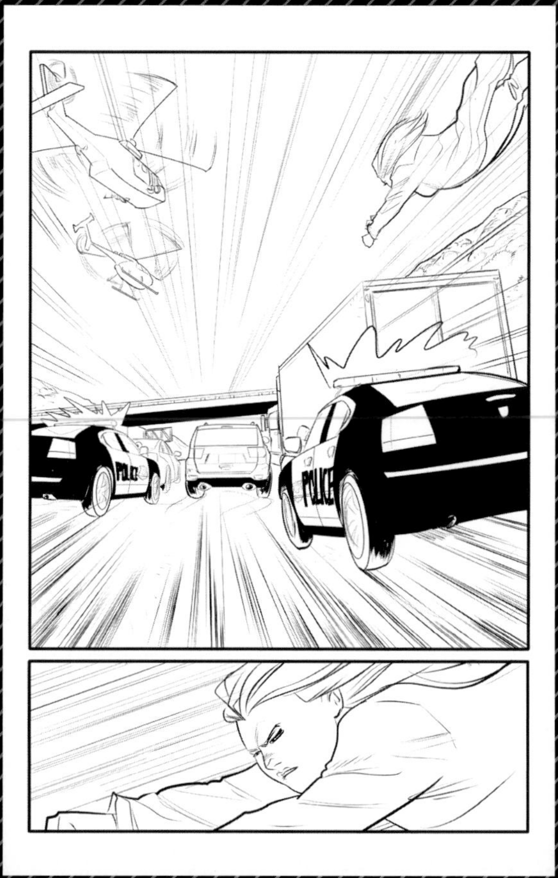
POLICE
POLICE

FAITH #10, p. 3
Art by JOE EISMA

FAITH #11, p. 2
Art by JOE EISMA

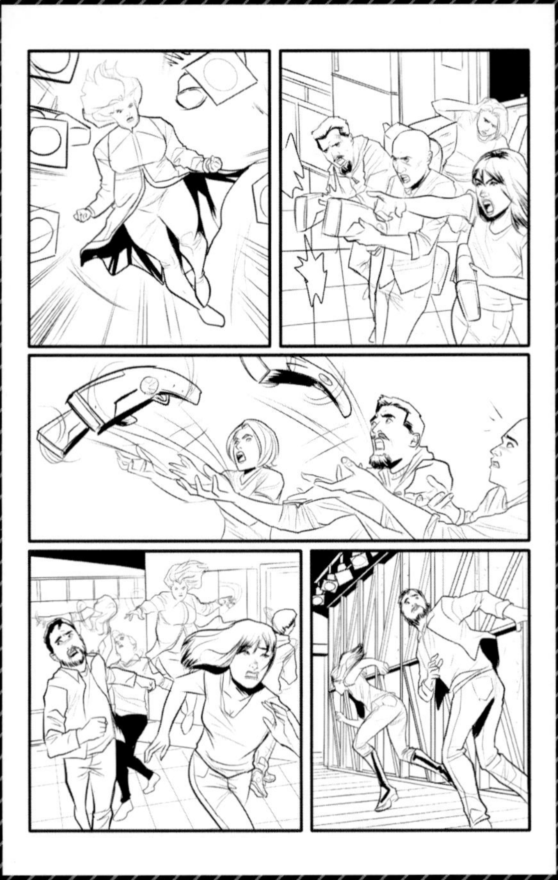

FAITH #11, p. 8
Art by JOE EISMA

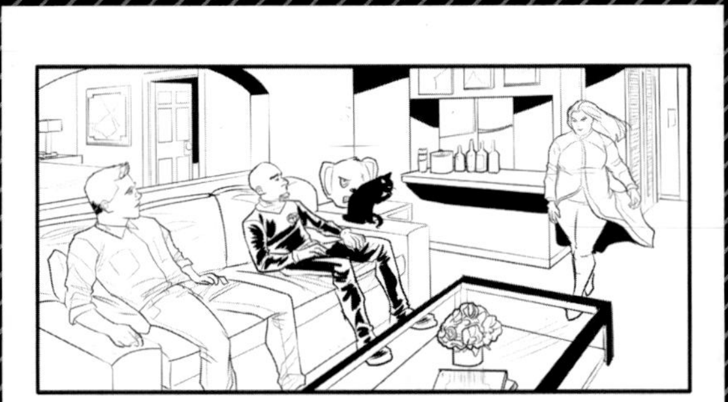

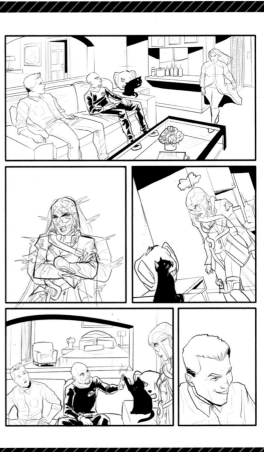

FAITH #12, p. 4
Art by JOE EISMA

FAITH #12, p. 19
Art by JOE EISMA

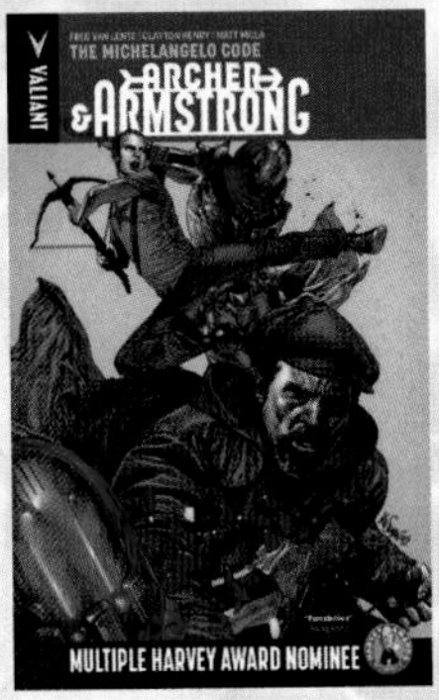
THE MICHELANGELO CODE
ARCHER & ARMSTRONG
VALIANT
MULTIPLE HARVEY AWARD NOMINEE

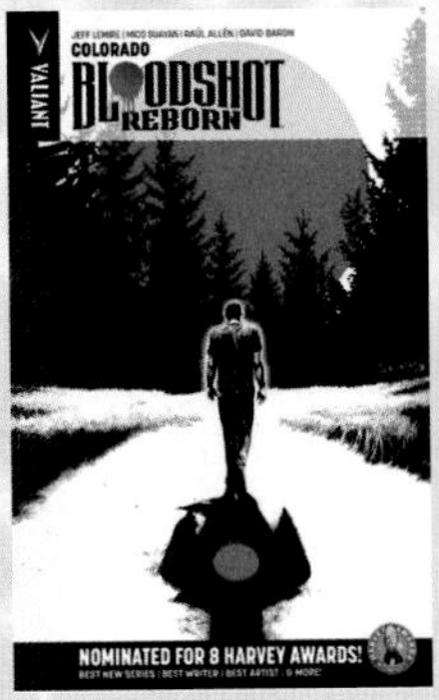
VALIANT
COLORADO
BLOODSHOT REBORN
NOMINATED FOR 8 HARVEY AWARDS!

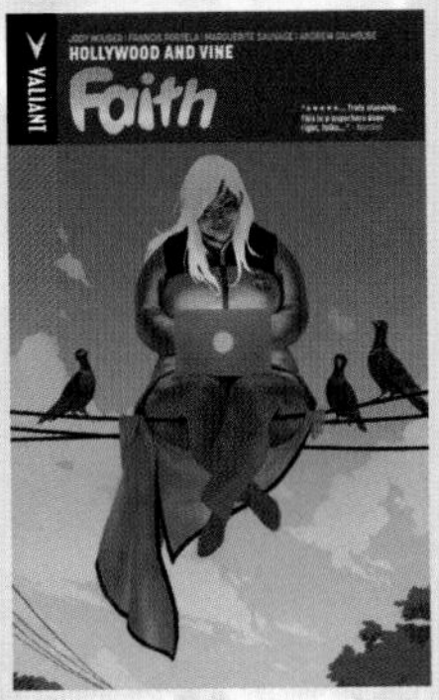
VALIANT
HOLLYWOOD AND VINE
Faith

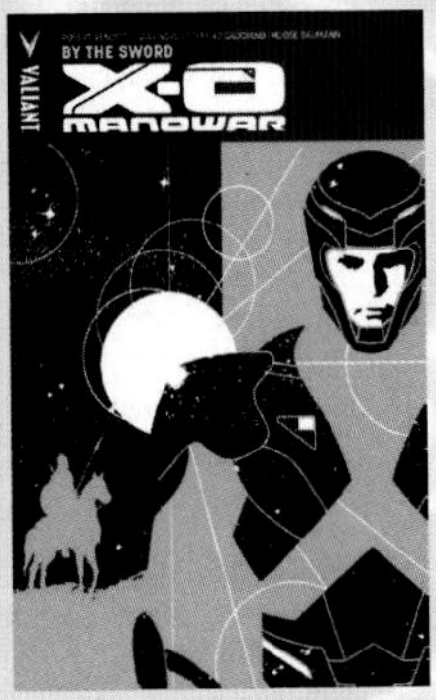
VALIANT
BY THE SWORD
X-O MANOWAR

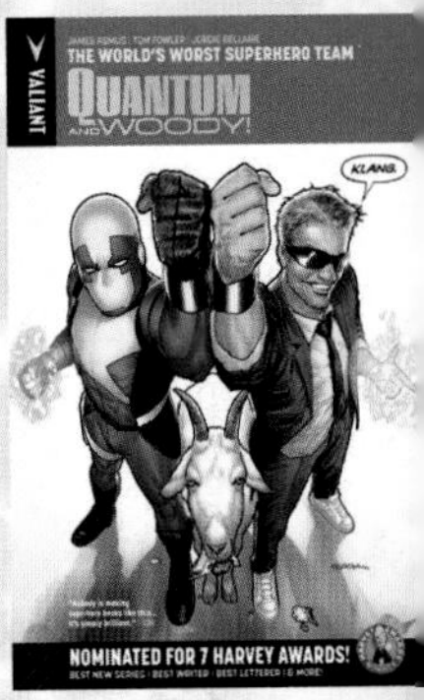
VALIANT
THE WORLD'S WORST SUPERHERO TEAM
QUANTUM AND WOODY!
KLANG
NOMINATED FOR 7 HARVEY AWARDS!

4001 A.D.

4001 A.D.
ISBN: 9781682151433

4001 A.D.: Beyond New Japan
ISBN: 9781682151464

Rai Vol 4: 4001 A.D.
ISBN: 9781682151471

A&A: THE ADVENTURES OF ARCHER AND ARMSTRONG

Volume 1: In the Bag
ISBN: 9781682151495

Volume 2: Romance and Road Trips
ISBN: 9781682151716

ARCHER & ARMSTRONG

Volume 1: The Michelangelo Code
ISBN: 9780979640988

Volume 2: Wrath of the Eternal Warrior
ISBN: 9781939346049

Volume 3: Far Faraway
ISBN: 9781939346148

Volume 4: Sect Civil War
ISBN: 9781939346254

Volume 5: Mission: Improbable
ISBN: 9781939346353

Volume 6: American Wasteland
ISBN: 9781939346421

Volume 7: The One Percent and Other Tales
ISBN: 9781939346537

ARMOR HUNTERS

Armor Hunters
ISBN: 9781939346452

Armor Hunters: Bloodshot
ISBN: 9781939346469

Armor Hunters: Harbinger
ISBN: 9781939346506

Unity Vol. 3: Armor Hunters
ISBN: 9781939346445

X-O Manowar Vol. 7: Armor Hunters
ISBN: 9781939346476

BLOODSHOT

Volume 1: Setting the World on Fire
ISBN: 9780979640964

Volume 2: The Rise and the Fall
ISBN: 9781939346032

Volume 3: Harbinger Wars
ISBN: 9781939346124

Volume 4: H.A.R.D. Corps
ISBN: 9781939346193

Volume 5: Get Some!
ISBN: 9781939346315

Volume 6: The Glitch and Other Tales
ISBN: 9781939346711

BLOODSHOT REBORN

Volume 1: Colorado
ISBN: 9781939346674

Volume 2: The Hunt
ISBN: 9781939346827

Volume 3: The Analog Man
ISBN: 9781682151334

Volume 4: Bloodshot Island
ISBN: 9781682151952

BLOODSHOT U.S.A.

ISBN: 9781682151952

BOOK OF DEATH

Book of Death
ISBN: 9781939346971

Book of Death: The Fall of the Valiant Universe
ISBN: 9781939346988

BRITANNIA

Volume 1
ISBN: 9781682151853

DEAD DROP

ISBN: 9781939346858

THE DEATH-DEFYING DOCTOR MIRAGE

Volume 1
ISBN: 9781939346490

Volume 2: Second Lives
ISBN: 9781682151297

THE DELINQUENTS

ISBN: 9781939346513

DIVINITY

Volume 1
ISBN: 9781939346766

Volume 2
ISBN: 9781682151518

Volume 3
ISBN: 9781682151914

Divinity III: Glorious Heroes of the Stalinverse
ISBN: 9781682152072

ETERNAL WARRIOR

Volume 1: Sword of the Wild
ISBN: 9781939346209

Volume 2: Eternal Emperor
ISBN: 9781939346292

Volume 3: Days of Steel
ISBN: 9781939346742

WRATH OF THE ETERNAL WARRIOR

Volume 1: Risen
ISBN: 9781682151235

Volume 2: Labyrinth
ISBN: 9781682151594

Volume 3: Deal With a Devil
ISBN: 9781682151976

FAITH

Faith Vol 1: Hollywood and Vine
ISBN: 9781682151402

Faith Vol 2: California Scheming
ISBN: 9781682151631

GENERATION ZERO

Volume 1: We Are the Future
ISBN: 9781682151754

HARBINGER

Volume 1: Omega Rising
ISBN: 9780979640957

Volume 2: Renegades
ISBN: 9781939346025

Volume 3: Harbinger Wars
ISBN: 9781939346117

Volume 4: Perfect Day
ISBN: 9781939346155

Volume 5: Death of a Renegade
ISBN: 9781939346339

Volume 6: Omegas
ISBN: 9781939346384

EXPLORE THE VALIANT UNIVERSE

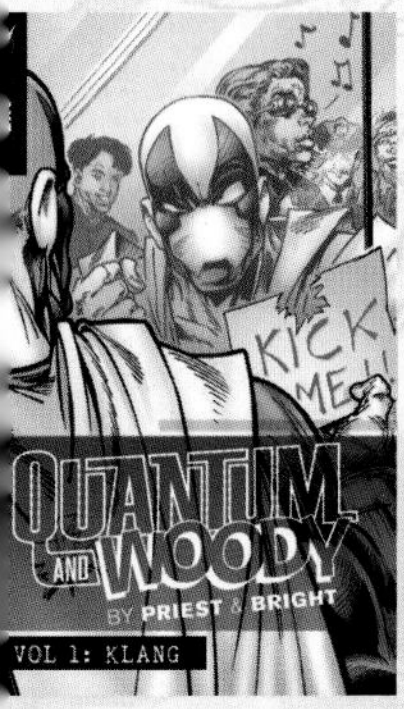
KICK ME
QUANTUM AND WOODY
BY PRIEST & BRIGHT
VOL 1: KLANG

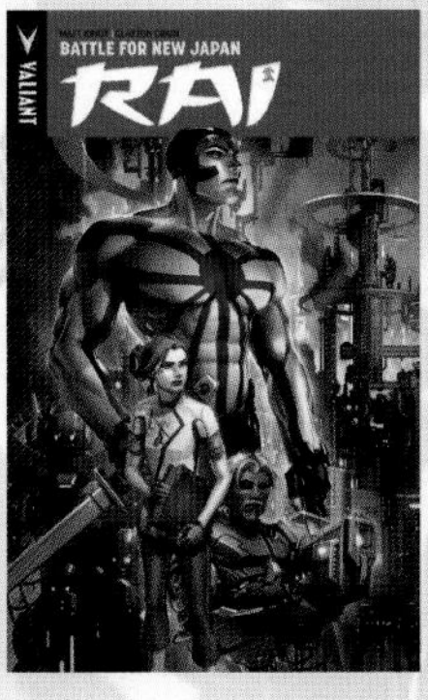
VALIANT
BATTLE FOR NEW JAPAN
RAI

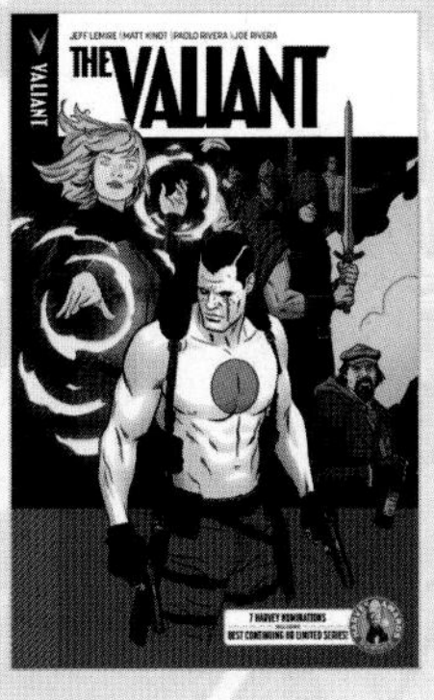
VALIANT
THE VALIANT

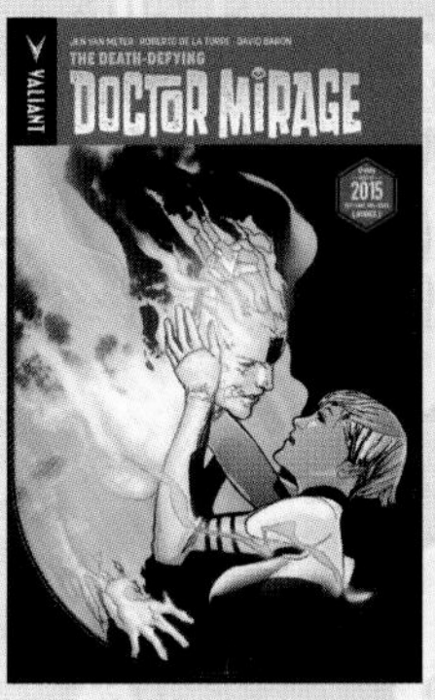
VALIANT
THE DEATH-DEFYING
DOCTOR MIRAGE

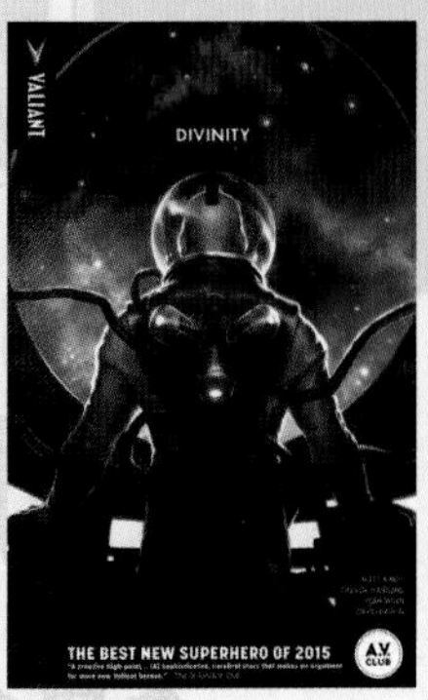
VALIANT
DIVINITY
THE BEST NEW SUPERHERO OF 2015

ARBINGER RENEGADE
lume 1: The Judgment of Solomon
BN: 9781682151693

ARBINGER WARS
arbinger Wars
BN: 9781939346094
oodshot Vol. 3: Harbinger Wars
BN: 9781939346124
arbinger Vol. 3: Harbinger Wars
BN: 9781939346117

MPERIUM
lume 1: Collecting Monsters
BN: 9781939346759
lume 2: Broken Angels
BN: 9781939346896
lume 3: The Vine Imperative
BN: 9781682151112
lume 4: Stormbreak
BN: 9781682151372

INJAK
lume 1: Weaponeer
BN: 9781939346667
lume 2: The Shadow Wars
BN: 9781939346940
lume 3: Operation: Deadside
BN: 9781682151259
lume 4: The Siege of King's Castle
BN: 9781682151617
lume 5: The Fist & The Steel
BN: 9781682151792

UANTUM AND WOODY
lume 1: The World's Worst Superhero Team
BN: 9781939346186
lume 2: In Security
BN: 9781939346230
lume 3: Crooked Pasts, Present Tense
BN: 9781939346391
lume 4: Quantum and Woody Must Die!
BN: 9781939346629

UANTUM AND WOODY Y PRIEST & BRIGHT
lume 1: Klang
BN: 9781939346780
lume 2: Switch
BN: 9781939346803

Volume 3: And So...
ISBN: 9781939346865
Volume 4: Q2 - The Return
ISBN: 9781682151099

RAI
Volume 1: Welcome to New Japan
ISBN: 9781939346414
Volume 2: Battle for New Japan
ISBN: 9781939346612
Volume 3: The Orphan
ISBN: 9781939346841
Rai Vol 4: 4001 A.D.
ISBN: 9781682151471

SHADOWMAN
Volume 1: Birth Rites
ISBN: 9781939346001
Volume 2: Darque Reckoning
ISBN: 9781939346056
Volume 3: Deadside Blues
ISBN: 9781939346162
Volume 4: Fear, Blood, And Shadows
ISBN: 9781939346278
Volume 5: End Times
ISBN: 9781939346377

SHADOWMAN BY ENNIS & WOOD
ISBN: 9781682151358

IVAR, TIMEWALKER
Volume 1: Making History
ISBN: 9781939346636
Volume 2: Breaking History
ISBN: 9781939346834
Volume 3: Ending History
ISBN: 9781939346995

UNITY
Volume 1: To Kill a King
ISBN: 9781939346261
Volume 2: Trapped by Webnet
ISBN: 9781939346346
Volume 3: Armor Hunters
ISBN: 9781939346445
Volume 4: The United
ISBN: 9781939346544
Volume 5: Homefront
ISBN: 9781939346797
Volume 6: The War-Monger
ISBN: 9781939346902

Volume 7: Revenge of the Armor Hunters
ISBN: 9781682151136

THE VALIANT
ISBN: 9781939346605

VALIANT ZEROES AND ORIGINS
ISBN: 9781939346582

X-O MANOWAR
Volume 1: By the Sword
ISBN: 9780979640940
Volume 2: Enter Ninjak
ISBN: 9780979640995
Volume 3: Planet Death
ISBN: 9781939346087
Volume 4: Homecoming
ISBN: 9781939346179
Volume 5: At War With Unity
ISBN: 9781939346247
Volume 6: Prelude to Armor Hunters
ISBN: 9781939346407
Volume 7: Armor Hunters
ISBN: 9781939346476
Volume 8: Enter: Armorines
ISBN: 9781939346551
Volume 9: Dead Hand
ISBN: 9781939346650
Volume 10: Exodus
ISBN: 9781939346933
Volume 11: The Kill List
ISBN: 9781682151273
Volume 12: Long Live the King
ISBN: 9781682151655
Volume 13: Succession and Other Tales
ISBN: 9781682151754

X-O MANOWAR (2017)
Volume 1: Soldier
ISBN: 9781682152058

EXPLORE THE VALIANT UNIVERSE

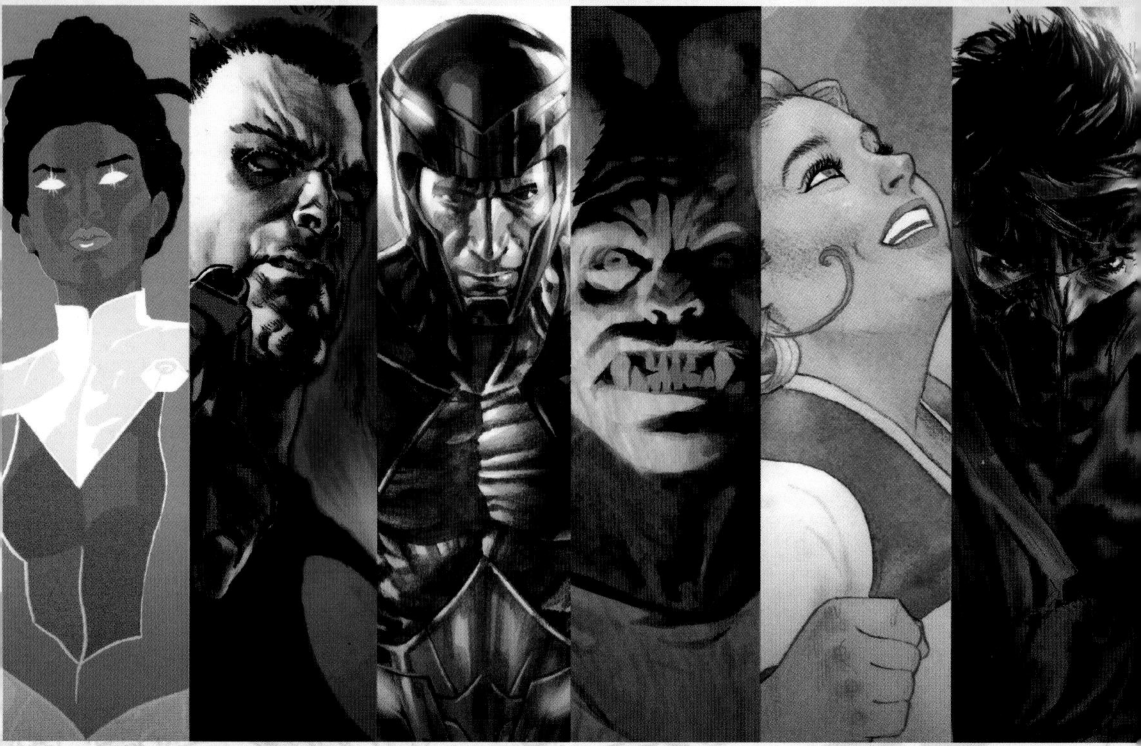

4001 A.D. DELUXE EDITION
ISBN: 978-1-68215-193-8

ARCHER & ARMSTRONG DELUXE EDITIONS
Book 1: ISBN: 978-1-939346-22-3
Book 2: ISBN: 978-1-939346-95-7

ARMOR HUNTERS DELUXE EDITION
ISBN: 978-1-939346-72-8

BLOODSHOT DELUXE EDITIONS
Book 1: ISBN: 978-1-939346-21-6
Book 2: ISBN: 978-1-939346-81-0

BLOODSHOT REBORN DELUXE EDITIONS
Book 1: ISBN: 978-1-68215-155-6
Book 2: ISBN: 978-1-68215-227-0

BOOK OF DEATH DELUXE EDITION
ISBN: 978-1-68215-115-0

THE DEATH-DEFYING DOCTOR MIRAGE DELUXE EDITION
ISBN: 978-1-68215-153-2

DIVINITY DELUXE EDITION
ISBN: 978-1-939346-92-6

FAITH: HOLLYWOOD & VINE DELUXE EDITION
ISBN: 978-1-68215-201-0

HARBINGER DELUXE EDITIONS
Book 1: ISBN: 978-1-939346-13-1
Book 2: ISBN: 978-1-939346-77-3

HARBINGER WARS DELUXE EDITION
ISBN: 978-1-939346-32-2

IVAR, TIMEWALKER DELUXE EDITION
Book 1: ISBN: 978-1-68215-119-8

NINJAK DELUXE EDITION
Book 1: ISBN: 978-1-68215-157-0

QUANTUM AND WOODY DELUXE EDITION
Book 1: ISBN: 978-1-939346-68-1

RAI DELUXE EDITION
Book 1: ISBN: 978-1-68215-117-4

SHADOWMAN DELUXE EDITION
Book 1: ISBN: 978-1-939346-43-8

UNITY DELUXE EDITION
Book 1: 978-1-939346-57-5

THE VALIANT DELUXE EDITION
ISBN: 978-1-939346-91-9

X-O MANOWAR DELUXE EDITIONS
Book 1: ISBN: 978-1-939346-10-0
Book 2: ISBN: 978-1-939346-52-0
Book 3 : ISBN: 978-1-68215-131-0
Book 4: ISBN: 978-1-68215-183-9
Book 5: ISBN: 978-1-68215-215-7

VALIANT CLASSIC

ARCHER & ARMSTRONG: THE COMPLETE CLASSIC OMNIBUS
ISBN: 978-1-939346-87-2

QUANTUM AND WOODY: THE COMPLETE CLASSIC OMNIBUS
ISBN: 978-1-939346-36-0

Q2: THE RETURN OF QUANTUM AND WOODY DELUXE EDITION
ISBN: 978-1-939346-56-8

VALIANT MASTERS: BLOODSHOT VOL. 1 - BLOOD OF THE MACHINE
ISBN: 978-0-9796409-3-3

VALIANT MASTERS: HARBINGER VOL. 1 - CHILDREN OF THE EIGHTH DAY
ISBN: 978-1-939346-48-3

VALIANT MASTERS: H.A.R.D. CORPS VOL. 1 - SEARCH AND DESTROY
ISBN: 978-1-939346-28-5

VALIANT MASTERS: NINJAK VOL. 1 - BLACK WATER
ISBN: 978-0-9796409-7-1

VALIANT MASTERS: RAI VOL. 1 - FROM HONOR TO STRENGTH
ISBN: 978-1-939346-07-0

VALIANT MASTERS: SHADOWMAN VOL. 1 - SPIRITS WITHIN
ISBN: 978-1-939346-01-8

X-O MANOWAR CLASSIC OMNIBUS
Vol. 1: ISBN: 978-1-939346-30-8

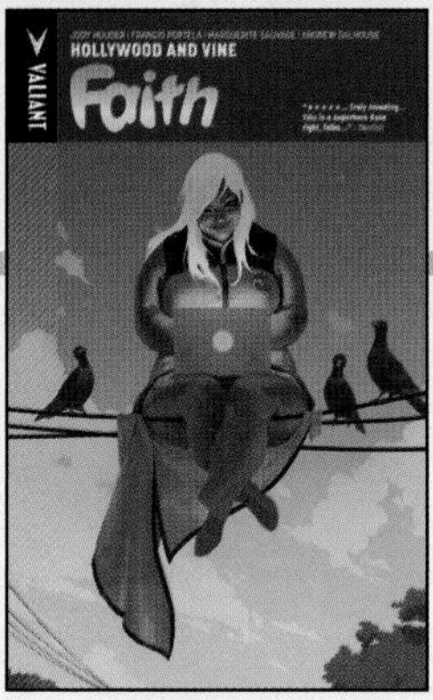
VALIANT
HOLLYWOOD AND VINE
Faith

Faith Vol. 1:
Hollywood and Vine

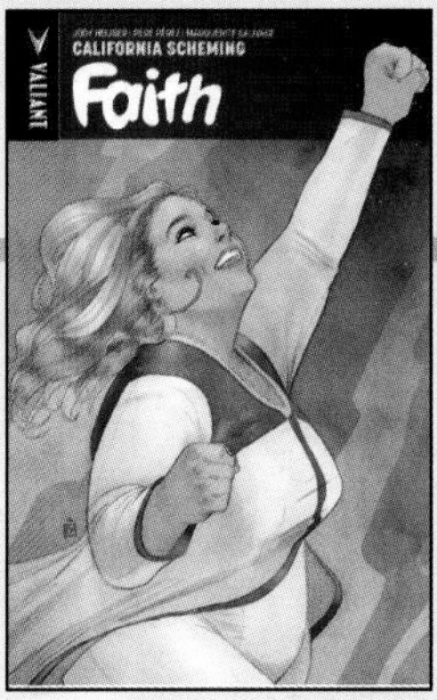
VALIANT
CALIFORNIA SCHEMING
Faith

Faith Vol. 2:
California Scheming

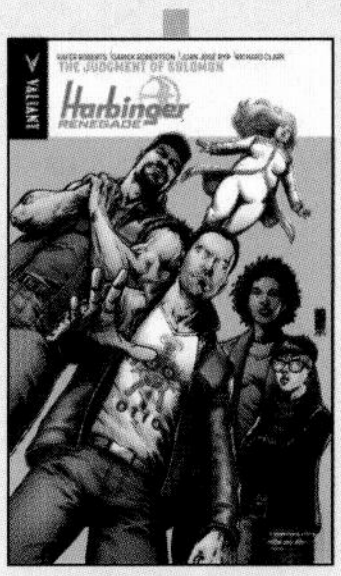
VALIANT
THE JUDGMENT OF SOLOMON
Harbinger
RENEGADE

Harbinger Renegade Vol. 1:
Judgment of Solomon
(OPTIONAL)

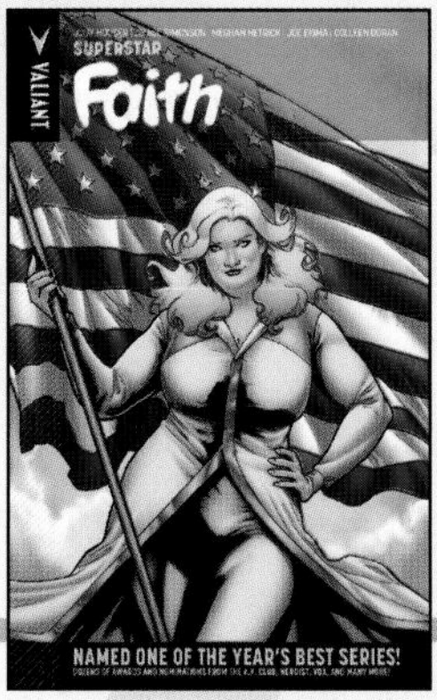
VALIANT
SUPERSTAR
Faith
NAMED ONE OF THE YEAR'S BEST SERIES!

Faith Vol. 3:
Superstar

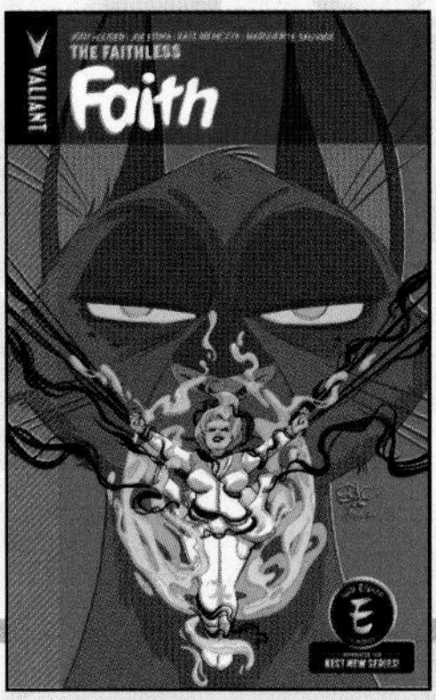
VALIANT
THE FAITHLESS
Faith
BEST NEW SERIES!

Faith Vol. 4:
The Faithless

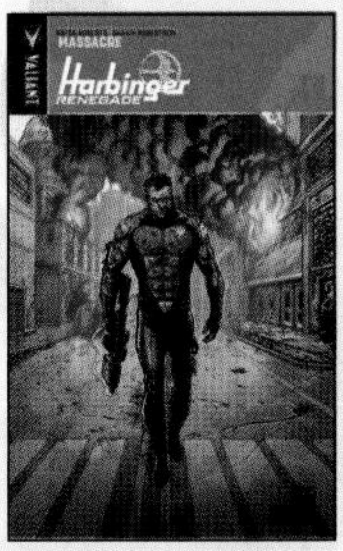
VALIANT
MASSACRE
Harbinger
RENEGADE

Harbinger Renegade
Vol. 2: Massacre
(OPTIONAL)

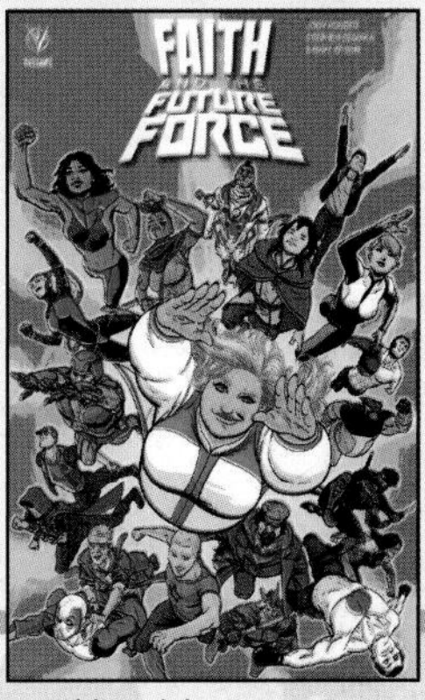
VALIANT
FAITH
FUTURE
FORCE

Faith and the Future Force

Read the origin and earliest adventures of the sky-soaring Zephyr!

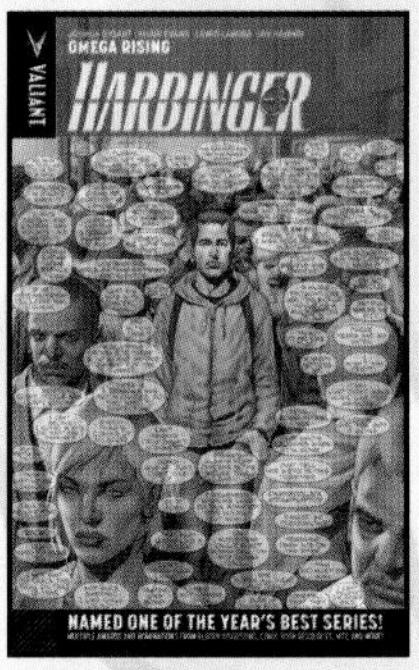
VALIANT
OMEGA RISING
HARBINGER
NAMED ONE OF THE YEAR'S BEST SERIES!

Harbinger Vol. 1:
Omega Rising

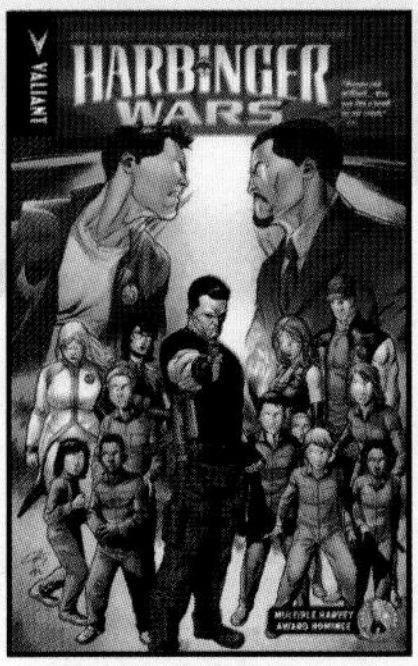
VALIANT
HARBINGER
WARS

Harbinger Wars

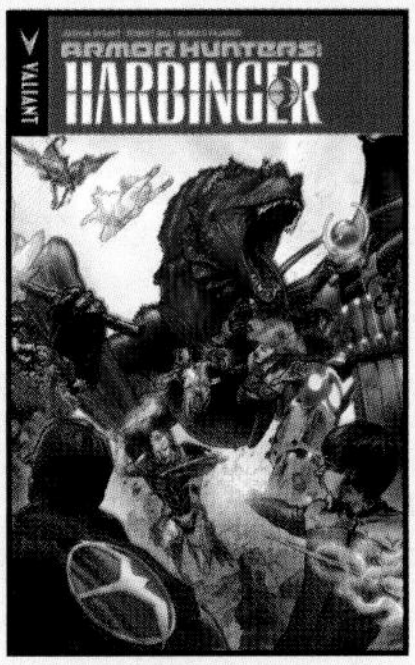
VALIANT
ARMOR HUNTERS:
HARBINGER

Armor Hunters:
Harbinger

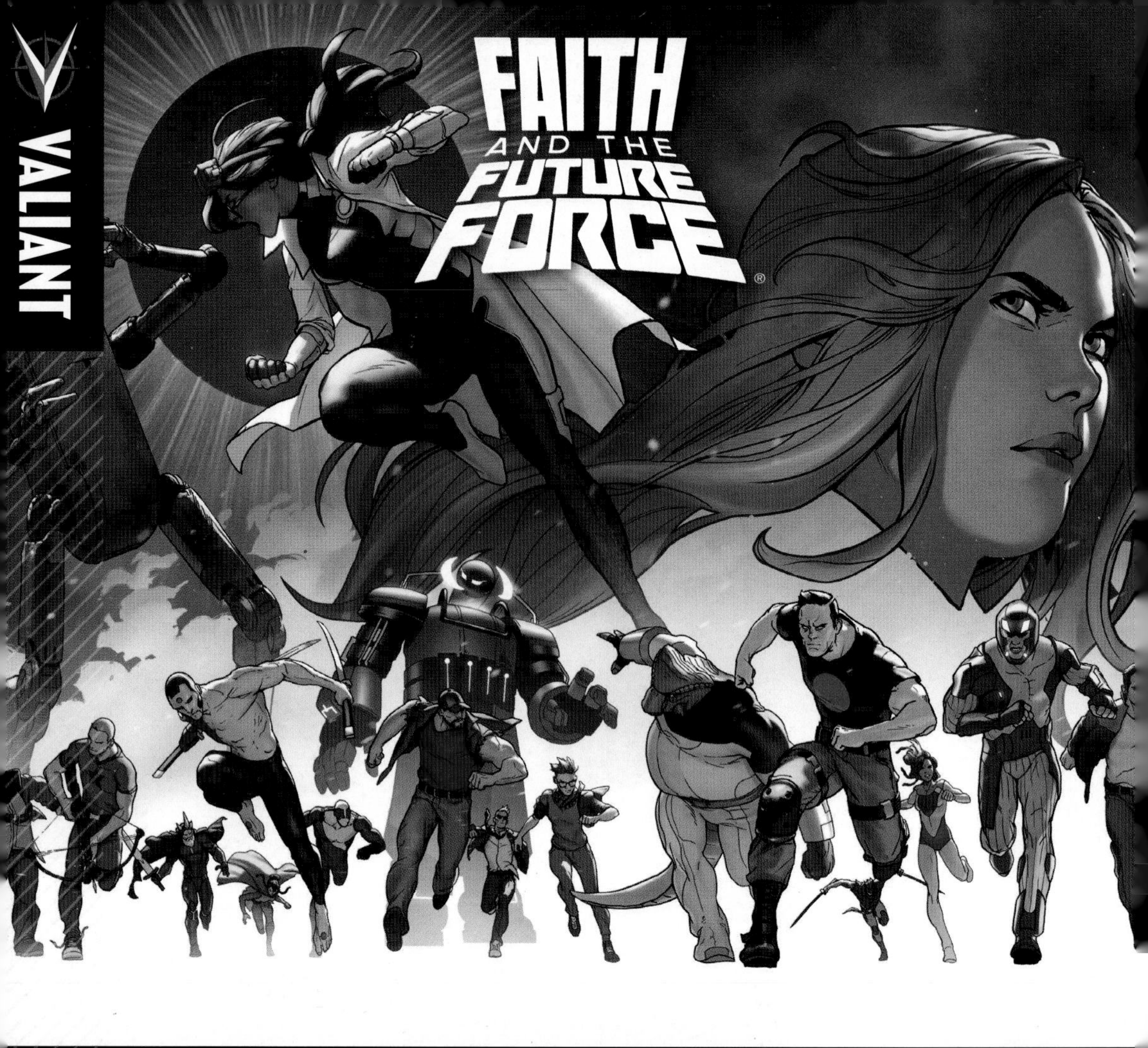
VALIANT
FAITH AND THE FUTURE FORCE®

EVERY SECOND WILL COUNT WHEN ACCLAIMED WRITER JODY HOUSER (*MOTHER PANIC*, *STAR WARS: ROGUE ONE*), EXPLOSIVE ARTIST STEPHEN SEGOVIA (NINJAK, *ACTION COMICS*), COMICS LEGEND BARRY KITSON (*FANTASTIC FOUR*), AND SPECIAL SURPRISE GUESTS PUSH FAITH INTO A CENTURIES-SPANNING FIGHT FOR EXISTENCE ALONGSIDE THE GREATEST HEROES OF THE VALIANT UNIVERSE...PAST, PRESENT, AND FUTURE!

Faith "Zephyr" Herbert - former member of Unity, current Harbinger Renegade, and Los Angeles' #1 super-hero - is the universe's last, best chance at survival! Centuries from today, a devious artificial intelligence has unleashed a blistering attack on the very foundations of time...one that is the unwriting history from beginning to end! Now, with her options exhausted, Neela Sethi, Timewalker - the self-appointed protector of what is and will be - has returned to the 21st century to recruit Earth's greatest champions of today and tomorrow to oppose this existential threat...and she needs Faith to lead them! But why Faith? And why now?

Fly to the farthest edges of the future right here in a death-defying race to save time itself as Faith leads the charge alongside Valiant's greatest heroes...and becomes a new legend for the ages!

Collecting FAITH AND THE FUTURE FORCE #1-4.

TRADE PAPERBACK

ISBN: 978-1-68215-233-1

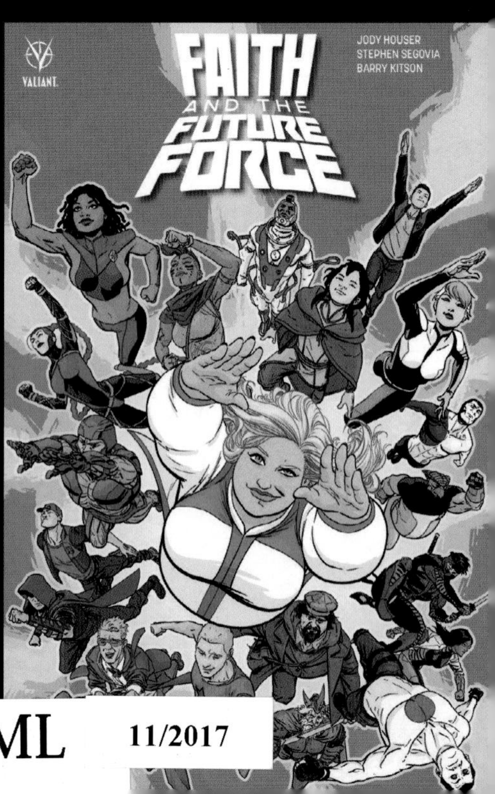
VALIANT
JODY HOUSER
STEPHEN SEGOVIA
BARRY KITSON
FAITH AND THE FUTURE FORCE